25.

14⁹⁵

EUROPEAN FOLK ART

EUROPEAN FOLK ART
in Europe and the Americas

General editor H. J. Hansen

Introduction by Robert Wildhaber

With contributions by Peter Anker, Tancred Banateanu, Alf Böe,
Luis Cortés Vázquez, René Creux, Bernward Deneke, Gerd Dörner,
Pierre-Louis Duchartre, Kristján Eldjárn, Albert Eskeröd, Edit Fél,
Alexander Fenton, Richard S. Field, Margaret Fuller,
Fernando Barbedo Galhano, Tjaard W. R. de Haan, Valentin Jaquet,
Toini-Inkeri Kaukonen, Marcel B. Keezer, Ludvík Kunz, A. T. Lucas,
Zagorka Marković, Ksawery Piwocki, Leopold Schmidt, Sigurd Schoubye,
Georg R. Schroubek, Paolo Toschi, Christo Vakarelski and Popi Zoras

109 colour plates, 350 monochrome plates, 100 line illustrations

McGRAW-HILL BOOK COMPANY
NEW YORK · TORONTO

Translated from the German
Europas Volkskunst
by Mary Whittall

This edition © 1968 Thames and Hudson Ltd, London

© 1967 Gerhard Stalling Verlag, Oldenburg and Hamburg

Library of Congress Catalog Card Number: 68–16683,
26052

Printed in West Germany

Contents

Wrought iron griddle, Netherlands, seventeenth century

THE WIDE RANGE and variety of the essays in this book is a reflection of the many facets of the term 'folk art'. Let us, for convenience, accept the definition implied, rightly or wrongly, in the majority of instances of its use: articles decorated in traditional styles, associated with specific communities.

There exist already an impressive number of books on folklore and folk art, some popular and entertaining, others painstaking and scientific, and whole series of publications which cover single geographical or ethnic regions of Europe. But we have not yet seen a work of comparable authority treating Europe as a whole. So far as I know it was only once attempted; under the auspices of the League of Nations, a 'Congrès international des arts populaires' was held in Prague in October 1928. The very disparity of the papers read at that congress betrays uncertainty as to what folk art is. Attempts were made at the time to arrive at a clear definition, but they foundered in a sea of nebulous theories, and the subsequent national and regional monographs, in spite of some ambitiously comprehensive titles, leave no doubt that the scientific study of folk art was still in its infancy. The position was further complicated in that folk song, folk music, folk dancing and folk drama were all counted as folk art, but folk tales and customs were not. A small report on the congress, with a résumé of the proceedings, was published in Paris in 1928, and some of the papers were published in two imposing volumes, *Art populaire* (Duchartre, Paris 1931), but these are now extremely hard to come by. No similar project has been undertaken since, probably because the decades of war and cold war have not favoured international collaboration.

Now H. J. Hansen has edited the first general outline of European folk art. The fact that a definitive scientific study still remains to be written should not be allowed to detract from the achievement of this book and its contributors; it is not intended for the academic and the specialist but for the interested layman, one who would like to approach a foreign country and its people from a new and highly attractive angle, who has perhaps his own modest collection of the kind of objects under consideration, or who simply takes pleasure in the naive confidence and astonishing beauty of their forms.

What we have here is the first comprehensive survey, written by experts, of the folk art of all the countries of Europe. Unlike other books which have the words Europe or European in their title but select for study those few countries which happen to be known to the authors, this book offers a truly overall view and makes possible far-reaching comparisons. An astonishing similarity of form and decoration between many of the objects immediately becomes apparent, and this raises further points. The first conclusion forced on us by this book is the need for a study of folk art, not as a national phenomenon, but as the expression of a general human love of visual beauty. For it

7

becomes increasingly clear that the concept of folk art as an expression of nationalism is itself a piece of nineteenth-century folklore. More and more scholars reject this theory or at least have reservations about it. We have known for a long time that folk tales are not the property of individual nations, and any study which confined itself to a nationalist view would be hopelessly unscientific; the same must now be recognized as true of the visual arts. Perhaps I can best illustrate this by a few examples, beginning with my own country, Switzerland. Let us be quite clear that there is no Swiss folk art, any more than there is a Swiss culture: there are only folk art and culture in Switzerland. Switzerland is a political entity, and art and culture ignore political boundaries, thank goodness. They are conditioned by geographical situations and ethnic characteristics, and follow great, international stylistic movements. Switzerland's folk art has historic and ethnic connections with all her neighbours. Another example is 'German folk art'. If 'German' is taken to relate to an ethnic group, at the very least the Sorb area (between the Elbe and the Saale) and probably parts of Bavaria as well, would have to be discounted; but the German-speaking regions of Lorraine, Alsace and Switzerland and very nearly the whole of Austria would have to be added. But if 'German' is given a political or geographical sense, then it loses its ethnic sense, because the Slav and Sorb populations must be included with people of Germanic descent. Equally, there is only folk art in Italy, not an Italian folk art; for on the one hand there are Slovenes in the Passo de Resia, Croats in Molise, and Albanians and Greeks in southern Italy and Sicily, all of whom live in Italy as Italians, but have to a large extent retained their ethnic peculiarities; on the other hand the culture of Sardinia and the Val d'Aosta cannot be ascribed ethnically to Italy without some reservations. But if 'Italian' is taken to apply to an ethnic unit, then there are Italians, of Lombard stock, in Switzerland. Even Austria, apparently so close-knit ethnically, has minorities of Slovenes in Carinthia, and of Croats and Hungarians in Burgenland; hence the title of Leopold Schmidt's recent book *Volkskunst in Österreich* ('Folk art in Austria'). These racial mixtures and subdivisions are particularly numerous in Southern and Eastern Europe, but exist to some degree in practically every European country; only Iceland might claim to be an exception. If this book assists the recognition of the difficulties that arise from the political divisions of Europe (the dream of a politically united Europe is likely to remain a dream) then it will have played a part in establishing mutual understanding between nations and between their cultures, which include folk cultures.

Our European culture has been shaped by many influences, which reach across political and geographical boundaries: we speak of a Mediterranean culture, of the Hellenic, Roman and Byzantine worlds and of invasions from Central Asia, by which we understand factors which have contributed, in part at least, to the formation of the nations and the culture of Europe. We must also include movements which affected the whole continent: Christianity in its various forms, chivalry and courtly culture, the organization of cities and towns, the guild system, the travels of craftsmen who married and settled far from their birthplace.

So far we have spoken more of the general, unifying traits of European folk art and folk culture, but that is not to deny that there are also individual characteristics peculiar to single regions. It must be emphasized, however, that they are not determined by

Silhouette, England, 1844

Page 9 Farmhouse, Twente, Netherlands, seventeenth century

8

a

b

c

d

e

f

national boundaries; one of the most absorbing tasks of a scientific study of folk art is to find out just what does constitute their essence. It is a curious fact that there are regions in Europe in which a natural delight in colour and form manifests itself with exceptional force; the Schwalm region of Hesse for instance, Appenzell in Switzerland, or the area in the vicinity of Kurpie in Poland. Why is this? Can it be attributed to ethnic substrata, survivals of a vanished, aboriginal population, or to the peculiarities of a unique social structure, or simply to the forcefulness of individual artists? Sometimes the availability of specific raw materials causes, or at least facilitates, the evolution of certain art forms. Incised designs in ivory occur only where walrus tusks are to be found; only where there are old salt mines have the miners produced sculpture in salt. Mountain regions, and others where forests are near, are distinguished for their woodwork; but why do some areas specialize in chip carving, others in incised technique and yet others in burning the decoration in the wood? These are all questions which can only be answered by a comparative study of European folk art as a whole.

The question of the origin of decorative motifs, the meaning and significance of symbols, must also be studied in the context of Europe as a whole, in order to avoid interpretations based on national preconceptions. This particular field calls for the greatest scepticism and there are times when the layman would do well to be more critical than the so-called specialist.

Let us hope that this beautiful book about European folk art will not only give aesthetic pleasure but also stimulate thought and further study.

Basle, August 1967 ROBERT WILDHABER

Page 10 Peasants' houses: *a* Hodonin, Moravia, Czechoslovakia; *b* Öszed, Hungary; *c* Island of Amrum, Germany; *d* Fetlar, Shetland Islands; *e* South-western Finland; *f* Glaumbaer, Iceland

Wrought iron grave monument, Sweden, late eighteenth century

General Editor's Foreword

WE HAVE LONG BEEN accustomed to the increasing use of popular, colloquial speech in modern literature as well as, or in place of, a literary language which is spoken in real life only by the educated. A comparable trend is taking place in the world of the visual arts, where there is a growing interest in simpler, cruder, naive – in a word, popular – forms. As yet, however, unlike the exegetes and pundits of modern literature, the historians and theorists of the fine arts have made hardly any response to this development. Pierre-Louis Duchartre has pointed out that the general histories of art, with the significant exception of René Huyghe's *L'Art et l'Homme* (1967), completely ignore folk art. It must be that the art historians have neglected the important contribution to art of the vulgar, popular element, because they have been used to leaving it to the ethnographers.

This book is intended as a practical introduction that will stimulate proper study and evaluation of this wide and important field of western art. The most satisfactory way of achieving this end is to offer a comprehensive survey of the entire field in question by means of copious, well reproduced illustrations of typical works of folk art from all significant areas of European culture, described by the leading experts in the individual countries. The reason why the text is sub-divided by countries is that most of the finest and most characteristic pieces are to be found today in national museums of folk art and are there available for scientific study, and it therefore seemed appropriate to enlist the collaboration of the directors of such museums, as the people with the best knowledge of the subject, both with regard to national specialities and to the state of current research. Almost without exception they agreed to co-operate, and we are most grateful for their contributions which mean that this work is in line with the most recent work in the field. Within the sections on separate countries, and in the arrangement of the illustrations, the following order is generally observed: houses, furniture, utensils, ceramics, glass, textiles and costumes, painting and sculpture. The presentation of facts seemed to us to be more appropriate to our purpose and of greater value than abstract interpretation. The reader, whether layman, collector or specialist, will be able to form his own conclusions.

In addition to the European and American publishers whose undertaking to publish the work has made its production feasible, the editor wishes to thank the following for suggestions and information imparted in personal conversation while he was preparing this book: Torsten Gebhard in Munich, Ernst Schlee in Schleswig, Sigurd Schoubye in Copenhagen, Bernward Deneke in Nuremberg, Andrew Jewell in Reading, Paolo Toschi in Rome, Leopold Schmidt in Vienna, Pierre-Louis Duchartre in Paris and, above all, Robert Wildhaber in Basle, whose own research and field work have surely made him the leading authority on folk art in Europe and America. We subscribe fully to the views he has expressed in his introduction, not least to his avoidance of a hard and fast definition of folk art.

Iron door-mounting, Sweden

Every contributor has been allowed to interpret the concept of 'folk art' in his own way, whether this means approaching the word 'folk' from an ethnic viewpoint, or sociologically, from the point of view of roles within the broad mass of the population. The reader may look on this book as being a collection of contributions to social anthropology as well as examples of art. I can only emphasize that as such they represent an important chapter in the history of art. It is as hard to find a satisfactory definition for the word 'folk' as it is for those well-worn terms 'folk art', 'art' or even '*kitsch*'; it is hard enough to fix the boundaries between them, even without regard to the fact that they are constantly shifting, according to the taste of the times. At the beginning of the present century people with a knowledge and understanding of art would not have hesitated to class many products of folk art, such as paintings on glass, chip boxes, painted clocks from the Black Forest, trays decorated with panoramic views of towns or the countryside, Staffordshire figures and other types of garish pottery, as *kitsch*. Nowadays, however, since the expressionists have made the lurid colours of popular paintings on glass socially acceptable, and since 'electric' and 'jungle' colours, which put the most violent mauve of Nailsea rolling pins in the shade, have become universally fashionable, the products of folk art are among the most treasured possessions of serious collectors and museums. But far be it from me to assert, as a cynic might, that folk art is entirely and exclusively the popular *kitsch* of the day before yesterday, or, as an extreme 'convert' might, that there is no such thing as folk art. Art itself is hard to define, but it certainly exists.

This book sets out to furnish a general survey of the almost limitless variety of the products of folk art in the western world. These products are distinguished as often by creative originality as by primitive, grotesque simplification of fine art forms; they also embody a naive delight in artistic creation on the part of the maker, and in artistic appreciation on the part of the consumer, neither of whom has ever devoted a moment's thought to the question 'What is Art?' All kinds of amateur art are similar in their origins. A similar artistic insouciance is the source of some of the aspects of modern Pop Art, in which the '*kitsch* of the day before yesterday' plays its iconographic part: used with irony, mockingly and yet not without affection. Perhaps this is a sign that the bruised spirit of modern man is seeking and finding in Pop Art compensation for something that is missing in our age. We should approach the products of folk art or popular art in the same way, reflecting the gaiety and human warmth that radiates from them.

Island of Amrum, August 1967   HANS JÜRGEN HANSEN

14

foliage, can often be most effective. The highest standard of *rosemaling*, as a style and in individual achievements, was reached in eastern Norway, in Telemark and the Hallingdal. Stylistic comparisons, confirmed by oral tradition, establish the existence of a number of individual artists of real distinction.

Rosemaling ended, as it began, as the result of changes in fashion. Around 1850 the peasants began to decorate their living-rooms with colours imitating the mahogany of the Empire style, and the gay floral painting disappeared. The tradition lingered on until the end of the century only in the roses painted on dower chests.

Who were the folk artists and where did they come from? In 1800 there were barely twenty towns in Norway, and very few of them numbered more than two thousand inhabitants. Nine-tenths of the population lived on the land, for the most part not in villages, as in Central Europe, but on isolated farms. Such circumstances favoured individuality, in art and in other respects. It is worth noticing that such artists as are known to us by name were not often landowning yeoman farmers. The rose-painters and the woodcarvers were specialists, recruited, like other craftsmen, from the class of small tenant farmers. Their artistry was an extra source of income, a virtue arising out of necessity. The old idea of rural folk art as something practised by everybody, comparable perhaps to the principle of subsistence economy, has long been discredited. The essential distinction between the rural and urban craftsmen was that the former lacked any kind of systematic training or apprenticeship; they were self-taught and guarded their technical secrets jealously. This explains the freedom with which they adopted, mixed and misunderstood European stylistic motifs but nevertheless created a synthesis in which the different elements are organically fused. This is particularly true of eastern Norway. In the west, where there was a greater tendency to form village communities and there were fewer social distinctions among the peasants, the folk art is more collective in character, and is more of a domestic industry.

Left and above:Wrought iron grave monuments, Sweden, *c.* 1800

SWEDISH farm architecture shows distinct regional variations. In the pine forests of the north, people built log houses. In central Sweden, log houses still occurred, but dwellings were also made of planks, lying between vertical corner posts. In the southern part of the country, the walls were made of clay or brick, again between vertical posts. As a general rule farm buildings were arranged in enclosed squares, though a more open layout was preferred in some districts. Following a tradition which had persisted since Viking times, the farmyard consisted of a number of separate buildings, which served different purposes. The enclosed yards were a later development, and it was only under the influence of the landowning classes, and particularly in the south, that farmers once more came to dispose their buildings apart from each other.

It was an old custom, probably dating from the very earliest times, to build furniture into the walls. In some regions, built-in benches and beds could be found even at the end of the nineteenth century. Benches, beds, tables and stools were home-made with axe and knife. Mediaeval techniques, Romanesque and Gothic ornamentation, were still employed in remote areas as late as the eighteenth century, though changes in the forms and types of peasant furnishings used had begun with the Renaissance. The traditional chest was replaced by the cupboard. During the baroque period, cupboards were

36

usually richly decorated, and rococo influences carried the painting of furniture and domestic utensils to extremes of ornateness. The various regions are distinguished by individual styles. Dalarna, in particular, developed an original, very attractive style in the painting of cupboards and clock cases. The Empire style was most influential on the shape of chairs and sofas, which rural carpenters continued to imitate until the end of the nineteenth century, particularly in the northern forest regions. Clothes presses were larger and more richly decorated than the chests which held household equipment. Chests for personal possessions often bore the owner's initials, an inscription and a date, and were a popular betrothal present. Many of these chests used an ancient technique of wickerwork. Long thin strips of wood, cut along the grain, were fixed to a base and drawn tightly round it. The ends were hammered in and birch roots were knotted in to form decorative patterns. The chests were oval or round and usually had an ingenious spring lock. The woods most commonly used were birch, oak, beech, pine and fir.

56h
57d

Although other materials were available, wood was the one most used in earlier times. Plump bowls were hollowed out of tree roots, and natural growths turned to decorative ends. Every domestic utensil was decorated, though not so as to interfere with its proper functioning. Geometrical patterns were the most prevalent, but other motifs, often of prehistoric origin – dragons, eagles, lions, horses and birds – were also common.

There were numerous wooden vessels, made of staves fixed round a wooden base and held together with wooden hoops. Very simple containers, hollowed out of a piece of wood, had been in use for centuries; the type made in the manner of a barrel was known to the Vikings and was perhaps even older. The art of chip carving was also very old. A knife was used to cut a pattern, most often geometrical, into which soot or lamp-black was rubbed. Later pointed or V-shaped tools allowed the carving of reliefs and more varied ornaments, which were repeated all round the object. Carving, as a method of ornamentation, was used much earlier than painting or burning. In this latter method, metal branding-irons, with a pointed or ring-shaped end, burned lines or repetitive patterns, made up of straight lines, circles, curves or hoops, into the wood. Some of these patterns had been handed down from the very earliest times; the geometrical ones were probably the oldest. Others evolved during the Renaissance, in particular those arranging long lines of animals between continuous enlaced ribbons and symbolic motifs. There are also human figures to be found in Swedish folk art, originating in the Middle Ages or earlier. Towards the end of the eighteenth century rococo influences made themselves felt, ornamentation began to include painted naturalistic flower patterns.

58a, 90a, c, g

Metalwork in Sweden has an unbroken tradition reaching back to prehistory. Smiths in rural areas produced a large variety of work of a high artistic standard: fire irons, candlesticks, crosses and mountings for doors and windows. While the fashioning of candlesticks was a traditional art dating from the Middle Ages, and originated in southern Sweden, the practice of planting iron crosses on graves only began in the eighteenth century, in western Sweden. Typical examples of Swedish wrought ironwork are the small ornamental pendants which take the form of horseshoes in Skåne and of leaves elsewhere. These leaves have been known in Sweden since prehistoric times.

13–17

Page 19 a Granary, Serbia, Yugoslavia; *b* Farmhouse, log construction, north-east Bohemia, Czechoslovakia; *c* Farmyard building, Cîmpeni, Rumania; *d* Farmhouse, Emmental, Switzerland

Swedish peasants continued to use wooden utensils from the very earliest times until the middle of the nineteenth century; pottery did not come into use until about 1650,

a

b

c

d

and then it was reserved for storing provisions and for particularly decorative tableware. Wood was preferred because the peasants could work it themselves, while earthenware had to be bought from the potters in the villages and towns. When a household did possess any earthenware – and the same applied to tin and silver plate – this was a sign of wealth and a source of pride to the mistress of the house, who would put it on show along the wall where the master sat. The oldest pottery is brown in colour, with yellow and green ornamentation. Later the basic colour was usually a pale yellow, decorated with green, reddish brown, deep purple and sometimes even white. The painting of ceramics varied little from one part of the country to another. The most common patterns were broken or wavy lines, stylized tulips, roses, birds and other representational motifs. Ceramic art in Sweden was closely related to that of Central Europe.

Textiles served all manner of functions in Sweden: woven or embroidered wall-hangings, blankets, seat-covers, rugs for use in sledges and carriages, tablecloths, bedspreads and the peasants' best clothes. The old custom of hanging tapestries on the walls began to die out in the fifteenth century, when it became fashionable to paint the whole room; only in the south-western part of Sweden did the older tradition live on. There were various different techniques of weaving, some very old, some, like the so-called Flemish weaving, picked up in the eighteenth century from the upper classes. Embroidery also preserved certain elements that dated from the Middle Ages; in this art and in lacemaking every region had its special characteristics. As well as techniques the patterns and motifs are of the greatest importance for the historical study of the survival of traditions in textiles, within the study of folk art itself. Many of the figurative motifs are from the world of fable and saga. Others have a sacred origin, like the monograms A and M which occur in decorative hangings. These devices, as well as AVE MARIA, are found in the so-called *rölakan* tapestries, woven by generations of women who had no idea of their meaning. Newer motifs, such as parrots, swans and fruits, found their way into folk art from Flemish tapestries.

Like so many other things in traditional culture, peasant costumes show the influence of bygone eras. Sometimes very different costumes were worn in one parish for different occasions. In the parish of Vingäker, for instance, the everyday dress in the late nineteenth century was basically what had been fashionable in the late eighteenth and early nineteenth centuries, but the festive dress showed clear traces of the Middle Ages and the seventeenth century. Peasant women usually owned a dress for everyday wear, another for Sundays and holidays, and a third for special occasions: feasts, weddings and burials. In some areas costume played so important a part in village society that there were rules governing dress according to the seasons of the church year. There was a very important distinction, strictly observed, between the costume of married and unmarried women. There were also marked differences between summer and winter clothing, and the change from one to the other was made on specified dates. In northern Sweden winter clothes were usually made of leather.

The ornaments the peasants wore, though made by urban silversmiths, must also be counted as folk art, since the professional craftsmen made what their customers wanted, and where clothing and ornaments were concerned country people were always very much bound by traditions. Necklaces, for example, were made according to a very

133b

178a

174a

old tradition. The old Germanic bracteate survived Sweden's conversion to Christianity with new symbols; the round and +-shaped medallions were decorated with sacred ciphers, IHS and AM, and with crucifixes. Otherwise they kept their traditional forms. Peasants wore other pieces to adorn their dress: rings, buckles, eyelet rings, clasps and buttons. Two items in particular deserve mention: the bridal belt and the bridal crown. The belt has been part of women's dress since prehistoric times and the bridal belt is part of this tradition, given to the bride by the groom. The bridal crown, in Christian iconography an attribute of the Virgin Mary, became a symbol of virginity.

Above and right: Patterns from reversible fabrics, west Finland

The most significant form of folk painting is that done on wall-hangings. This form of decoration, which is unknown outside Sweden, flourished particularly from the mid-eighteenth century to the end of the nineteenth. There was also another, older form of wall-painting of which a few examples have survived. The wall-hangings usually depicted biblical themes, but scenes of daily life and pictures of important people and events are also found. When the home of a newly-married couple was being decorated, the Marriage at Cana was a popular subject, sometimes giving a faithful picture of local wedding customs. Woven hangings are mentioned in the Icelandic sagas. During the eighteenth and nineteenth centuries this particular form of folk art was most prevalent, in the south, in Småland, Halland, Blekinge and Västergötland and, in the north, in Dalarna, Hälsingland and Gästrikland. It is worth noting that this form of mural decoration was known at an earlier date in some areas, but only in the residences of the upper classes and the clergy. It did not become a fully developed folk art, with abundant decorative motifs, until the second half of the eighteenth century. There are a number of distinct differences between the north and the south. In the south the peasants painted on material and later on paper; in the north they often painted directly on the walls and sometimes on the ceiling also. Another characteristic difference is that in the south the hangings were put up in the living-rooms only for special occasions, such as weddings or Christmas, while in the north the usual custom was to decorate only those rooms which were reserved for special occasions. Even in biblical scenes, the painters dressed their figures in the clothes of their own time, with the exception of Christ, his family and his disciples. Their choice of colours was very free and idiosyncratic. Swedish peasants painted blue horses almost two hundred years before Franz Marc. A further typical difference between the mural decorations in the two halves of the country consists in the choice of motifs and the composition. In southern Sweden the artists liked to portray huge human figures, surrounded by a few relatively unimportant ornaments, whereas in the north, particularly in Dalarna, the human figures played a subordinate role in large scenes dominated by fantastic cities and houses and enormous stylized flowers.

In the nineteenth century, when paper became available in suitable formats, these murals came to be painted almost exclusively on paper.

FINLAND's traditional popular art is characterized by the cultural differences between the western and the eastern halves of the country. These have their roots in the history and geography of Finland as much as in the ethnic developments of the last few centuries. The western provinces were always more prosperous, and their folk art was also richer and more varied, particularly in the furniture and decoration of houses.

233

46a

22

Many of the products of Finnish folk art were connected with betrothal and marriage. Marriageable daughters prepared linen and clothing for their dowry; young men made household utensils for their betrothed, which they carved as skilfully as they knew how. A bride's dowry always included a capacious linen-press and a few decorated chairs.

Other impressive buildings include the fine barns and the great log farmhouses, with their spacious living-rooms, which were often ten yards square. The remarkable two-storey barns, with a roofed balcony projecting from the upper storey, are the glory of those few farms where they are still found today. There are also lovely smaller barns, with only a single chamber; the projecting gables are often decorated in relief.

The customary furniture of the peasants in the coastal areas, which can still be found today in places, was influenced to a certain extent by the furniture of the upper classes, and thus indirectly by that of Western Europe, but these extraneous influences do not obscure a distinctly individual character. The long tables found in peasants' living-rooms preserve the Gothic style in varying degrees. Chairs did not become common in peasant houses until the eighteenth century, but the traditional log stools and bench chests probably go back to the Middle Ages. Renaissance styles in tables, seats and cupboards remained popular in western Finland until the nineteenth century; the baroque and rococo styles had little influence on peasant furniture, except in some decorative touches such as the beading on top of wall cupboards and corner cupboards and the curving sides of rococo clock cases. Classical forms were obviously better liked. A kind of couch-bed with straight or curved back boards became popular and was also found in eastern Finland. Among particular kinds of furniture typical of individual regions, the most notable is the corner cupboard of East Bothnia, in three parts and incorporating a clock.

The oldest surviving wooden utensils are not painted. The use of paint, in one colour only, began in the fifteenth and sixteenth centuries, though it was not very extensive; really decorative painting, which typically incorporates flower motifs, did not become popular until towards the end of the eighteenth century. It was then used on furniture, sledges, harness and tools, but was still largely restricted to the coastal areas of western Finland. Further inland, in the nineteenth century, there were the painted boxes carried to church by the women of the northern part of Häme, in central Finland, playfully decorated in pale blue, red and yellow.

The production of glass and ceramics in Finland was negligible; the simple earthenware vessels used in the house were usually made in the towns by professional potters. The Finnish glass industry did not really begin until after 1740. Far older are the objects in horn and bone with an incised decoration of circles, zigzags, hatched lozenges and other geometrical patterns. Crossbows and snuff horns are among the objects which we can still admire today. The usual materials for domestic utensils in Finland, as elsewhere in the mixed forest regions of Northern Europe, were wood and birch-bark. One of the oldest decorative motifs in the carving of wood, horn and bone is a pattern of braiding; in Finland it continued to be used on certain traditional articles until comparatively modern times: on skis, on Lapp sledges, on the long bow, on the handles of scythes, on distaffs, and on mangle boards. This is not the only mediaeval motif to have persisted; others are the pentagram and the swastika. A particular kind of linear ornament, called 'dark drawing' is found on the unpainted chip boxes, made by bending a thin board of aspen wood until the ends met. Chip carving occurs frequently, in luxuriant rosette patterns. The earlier geometrical patterns were followed by naturalistic plant motifs, rococo bows, and horses' and lions' heads in relief. The magnificent carved goblets made in Finland proper were in demand overseas, even in the Middle Ages.

Examples of Finnish metalwork include the copper keyrings produced in eastern and northern parts of the country, which housewives hung on their belts. In Karelia women wore broad silver clasps, decorated with leaf patterns. These clasps, like other components of the traditional folk costumes of southern Karelia, are prehistoric in origin. In some parts of south-west Finland brides wore metal crowns. The costume worn by men on festive occasions in southern East Bothnia included magnificent buckled belts made of copper and white metal, with numerous long pendants attached. Other examples of metalwork are the iron candlesticks and the ornate iron clasps customarily found on clothes presses in the Loimijoki valley in south-west Finland; their form reflects the survival of a Renaissance tradition.

The finest achievements of Finnish folk art are reached in textiles. In western Finland, multicoloured blankets were made by a variety of techniques, but the most famous, by virtue of their high artistic standard, are the *ryiji*. These knotted tapestries, woven by peasant women in original patterns and colours, are among the most interesting folk products in the whole of Scandinavia. Known in Finland since the earliest times, the *ryiji* were traditionally used as blankets, but could also serve as carpets at weddings, or as wall coverings on festive occasions. The earliest mediaeval *ryiji* were plain or checked and had a long pile. The idea of making patterned *ryiji* eventually filtered down from the upper classes to the peasants; the best period for their manufacture was the end of the eighteenth century and the whole of the nineteenth. The *ryiji* reflect the influences of changes in style, and thanks to the conservatism which prevails in the manufacture of textiles, baroque characteristics can be traced in the trees, tulips, hearts, vases, lions and similar motifs until the end of the eighteenth century. Rococo and neoclassical influences can also be traced, but the naive, childlike imagination of the makers transmuted the various styles into original compositions, and this naivety is to a great extent the secret of the charm of the *ryiji*. Every imaginable colour was used in them without resort to garish tones.

195a, 200c

To this day, the inhabitants of the coastal areas of western Finland use home-made woollen blankets, woven in stripes of agreeable natural dyes or in gay light checks. Southern Karelia, most of which is now part of the Soviet Union, preserved the art of folk embroidery until the end of the nineteenth century, for as long as the traditional costumes were worn there. In this respect eastern Finland was generally more backward. The patterns, usually made in Holbein stitch, hem stitch and cross stitch, were strictly geometrical and extremely varied; the colours were brilliant, mostly red, green and blue. Embroidery was used on women's stomachers, collars and aprons, on the caps of women belonging to the Eastern Orthodox faith, and on handkerchiefs. In these geometrical patterns the Karelians preserved a primeval, international tradition. But in the borderlands of eastern Karelia, Russian influences produced Oriental motifs of birds, horses and plants. It has been claimed that the folk textiles of southern Karelia show traces of the Iron Age culture of pre-Christian Finland.

198c

Page 25 Farmhouse, Altes Land, Germany
Pages 26–7 Storstuen, Genner, Denmark, 1637

24

a

b

c

d

e

f

ICELAND, the large island in the north Atlantic which lies just south of the Arctic Circle, was discovered and colonized by Norwegians and other Viking peoples in about the year AD 900. The people of Iceland are therefore Scandinavian in race and language, and their culture is a part of northern Germanic culture, though it has a distinctive character of its own, conditioned by the particular nature of the island and the circumstances of life on it. Settlements were always widely scattered and until the latter part of the nineteenth century the population never rose above something between fifty and seventy thousand. Until well into the nineteenth century the Icelanders were all farmers, chiefly occupied in breeding sheep, cattle and horses; the climate does not favour crop farming. As well as the raising of livestock there was also, from the very earliest times, a certain amount of fishing.

Iceland is poor in the raw materials which might have formed the basis of native crafts. The only stone present in any quantity is basalt, which is hard to work and is not even very suitable for building. Since Iceland is, geologically, a young country, there are no mineral ores. Iron was at one time obtained from bog ore, but this was exhausted around 1500. The only woods are stunted birch coppices, although this particular shortage is alleviated to some extent by the large quantities of driftwood washed up by the sea. The small amount of clay is also impossible to use, so that pottery is unknown on the island; the same applies to glass-making. On the other hand there is a plentiful supply of good quality wool for the manufacture of textiles, as well as horsehair, skins, horn and bone. Imports from other countries have always helped to make up for the paucity of natural resources, but it has left its mark on Icelandic folk art, just as the barren, grudging land they have farmed for generations has affected the imagination of the people.

10f

The Icelandic farm has a remarkable history of development which can be traced from the Viking period into the nineteenth and twentieth centuries. The two factors permanently affecting this development have been the inhospitable climate and the scarcity of native building materials. Walls were made of turf and uncut stone, upright supports and roof beams of wood, either imported or gathered from the shore. The roof was always made of turf. With their overgrown walls and roofs, these buildings must have looked as if they had grown up out of the ground. In the past the Icelanders liked to give every building an imposing gable end and erected the various farm buildings, three, five or more, in a row. The protruding ends of the gables were often carved. The chief building within the farmyard itself was of a striking appearance; originally a single room for sleeping in, it later developed into a room for both living and sleeping, called a *badstofa* (lit. 'bathroom'). Every aspect of its construction derived from this dual function. It was long and low, the ceiling being supported by pillars, while the beds stood in a row parallel to the long walls. The room itself was usually quite plain, but some features – pillars, doors, the ends of the beds – were decorated by carving. Surviving remains of buildings of this kind show that the Viking settlers, and the mediaeval Icelanders, were concerned to decorate their homes in an artistic manner.

The peculiarities of the dwelling house meant that very little furniture was needed: a few simple tables, chairs and benches were all. Objects of everyday use included, first of all, the tools for work out of doors, for tilling the soil, and fishing. Their design was so simple that they offered little or no opportunity for artistic embellishment. Indoors,

Page 28 Colonial American houses: *a* Boston, Mass., seventeenth century; *b* Boston, Mass., eighteenth century; *c* Living-room, Kershner house, Pennsylvania, *c.* 1755; *d* Living-room, Pennsylvania, late eighteenth century; *e* Pennsylvania, eighteenth century; *f* Farmer's house, Pennsylvania, late eighteenth century

268a, b

29

however, there were large numbers of wooden containers for milk, *skyr* (a kind of yoghurt) and other food stuffs, many of these containers took the form of casks, ranging from the *askur*, a barrel-shaped bowl, out of which people ate, to the vast tuns in which winter provisions were stored. These wooden casks were often well proportioned; but, apart from the eating bowls, which always had a decorated lid, they were not usually carved. Clothes were kept in presses, and in the living-room were various pieces of equipment for making woollen cloth: looms, distaffs, spindles and combs. There were also a large number of wooden mangles for pressing linen and silk, and chests and boxes of all sorts and sizes, smaller ones for personal possessions, round ones for jewellery and precious cloths. Finally we must not forget the bed-panels, elaborately carved planks a yard or more in length placed at the side of the bed to protect the covers. The Romanesque style of decoration reached Iceland by about 1100, and it was then that Icelandic artists got to know the Romanesque vine ornament which remained the dominant motif in their carving until the art died out in the nineteenth century. There are of course traces of baroque and rococo influences but they never went very deep. It is the Romanesque vine which occurs again and again in new designs in Icelandic carving. No less important is a calligraphic decoration based on a special alphabet known as *höfdaletur* ('head letters'); it consists of the 'minuscule' letters of the Gothic alphabet, adapted to the art of woodcarving. Icelandic woodcarving is restricted to the decoration of functional objects; it has much in common stylistically with the carving of horn and bone. There are particularly lovely spoons of cow horn, tobacco boxes of whalebone or horn, and, not least, drinking-horns and powderhorns made from strong cattle horns, often decorated with fine carving in the style of decorative woodcarving.

59h, 276e

The Icelanders were also proficient in metalwork. They used copper to cast lamps, numerous rings, stirrups and other pieces of harness. The horse was their only means of transport and they set great store by well-made, beautifully decorated harness, above all saddles and bridles. There was great scope for the craftsman in metal. Saddles were often decorated with thin plates of brass bearing ornate designs resembling those made on wood, while cruppers and bridles had metal discs fixed to them, with ornamental engraving that shows affinities to Iceland's superlative silverware. Women's costumes were richly adorned with silver ornaments – belts, buttons, buckles and pins. Some of these pieces were made by casting, but more often they are filigree work, the speciality of Icelandic silversmiths. These craftsmen were mostly simple farmers, with no special training in their art; they worked with traditional patterns, which were basically somewhat simplified forms of late Gothic decorative art.

185b

In every Icelandic house there was a loom on which was woven every garment worn by the members of the household. But the same loom was used to produce weaving of a more artistic kind, not tapestry but so-called 'cross' weaving, brocades, multi-coloured cloth and blankets. They took particular care in the weaving of multi-coloured blankets which served as bedspreads, and of the typical saddle-cloth which was spread over the saddle before a woman mounted her horse. They also wove plush, using smaller looms known as plush-boxes, to make trimmings for various garments, particularly women's dresses. An art found all over the island was the weaving of braids, using board looms. Decorated with ornamental patterns, letters and dates, these braids were used as belts,

195d

Above and left: Wrought-iron candlesticks, Valkeala, Finland

garters and braces, and the women of Iceland achieved a high degree of skill in making them. All these textiles were made of sheep's wool; horsehair was used for plaiting such things as saddle girths, an occupation reserved for the men.

The Icelanders practised a great variety of embroidery techniques, using coloured wool threads on linen or woollen cloth. In the Middle Ages it was customary to embroider altar cloths in the old broad stitch, of which the best known example is probably the Bayeux Tapestry; this particular technique continued to be used in Iceland later than in other countries, and some interesting examples, depicting, for instance, legends of the saints, have survived to the present day. Later on they used other techniques such as cross stitch, brocade stitch and *broderie anglaise*, which was used on the great bedspreads, and the so-called 'flower stitch' and 'contour stitch' which were used in particular to embroider national costumes which were often further enriched by gold and silver embroidery and lace. It is thus no exaggeration to say that Icelandic wool, quite apart from providing the population with their everyday woven garments for centuries, was of great significance in Iceland's native art.

It cannot be claimed that painting has ever flourished as an independent art form on the island; but since the early Middle Ages the Icelanders have been eager producers of books, which gave graphic artists their opportunities. The great mediaeval illuminated parchment manuscripts of the sagas are famous, and the Icelandic artists continued to cultivate the illustration of books when they came to be written on paper instead of parchment. Libraries still contain a substantial number of these manuscripts with their miniatures and their inventive, intricately decorated initials.

Delight in artistic creation and the wish to enrich and embellish the bleak surroundings in which they lived have left traces of remarkable variety in Icelandic folk art. But this ceased to exist as a living tradition in the general change in customs and the way of life that took place as the nineteenth century drew to a close.

DENMARK consists of the Jutland peninsula, the two large islands of Fyn and Zealand, a dozen other sizeable islands, and several hundred very small islands. So far as folk art is concerned, the Fyn archipelago is often closely allied to the mainland. The fact that the capital city, Copenhagen, is on Zealand, has meant that the cultural traditions of eastern Denmark tend to dominate, particularly in the field of professional art. There were important centres of folk art in the area immediately surrounding Copenhagen, because the agricultural and small town communities there had close connections with the capital. This was particularly the case on the island of Amager, where there was a Dutch colony, in the town of Magleby, from about 1520 onwards. Through horticulture and overseas trade, the inhabitants of Amager attained the prosperity which is the prerequisite of good living. Then there was the Hedebo area, lying within the triangle Copenhagen–Roskilde–Køge, which was remarkable not only for its joinery and painting but principally for the style of linen embroidery, known after the area as *hedebosyning*, which can only be compared to that of south Jutland and Slesvig. A similar embroidery is also found on Amager and on Falster. Linen was used both for the cloth and the thread.

The southern part of Fyn and its surrounding archipelago, particularly the smaller islands, was very rich, and folk painting flourished there. The northern part of Jutland seems to have been influenced by Norway, but otherwise on the peninsula the movement of styles is clearly and consistently from south to north. Notable among the crafts restricted to the north are the production of carved furniture, which centred on Aarhus and the Djursland peninsula, and the making of painted wooden furniture at Lemvig.

The most significant area in Danish folk art lies in southern Jutland and the neighbouring duchy of Slesvig, where Danish and German (i.e. Lower Saxon and Frisian) culture met with the most fruitful results from the time of the Renaissance onwards, particularly in Angeln (Anglia, the region to the east of Flensburg), on Als and the Lojt peninsula in the east, and in Eiderstedt, Ostenfeld, North Frisia and Ribe in the west. The Frisian influence, emanating from southern Slesvig, is noticeable all over Jutland and even in Norway, but far less so on the islands to the east of Jutland.

Living-rooms as an architectural complex are a relatively recent invention. In the Middle Ages there was only one living-room in the house, with an open fireplace, and it was not until around 1600 or later that a second room, warmed by a stove, was added. Thereafter houses were invariably built with two kinds of living room, the *storstuen* ('large room'), which was intended for summer use and originally lacked any means of heating, called a *Pesel* in German-speaking Slesvig, and the *dagligstuen* ('everyday room'), called *Döns* in Slesvig and in Lower Saxony. The earliest of such rooms to have survived intact are kept today in the museum in Flensburg. There is a *dagligstuen* from Nieblum on Föhr (1637) and a *storstuen* from Genner near Aabenraa (1638). The wooden panelling on the walls is in imitation of middle- and upper-class houses of the sixteenth century and remained customary until the nineteenth. It appears that in north Frisia and the rest of western Slesvig specific forms were laid down by the larger joiners and painters, for the rooms are surprisingly similar in structure, for instance in the so-called 'commander houses' on Rømø, built for whaler captains. The best example of this type is in the open-air museum at Lyngby. The rooms in the Flensburg museum are unpainted, in accordance with tradition. The material then used was oak, and the oldest chests and cupboards were also of oak. The change to painted walls took place around 1650. It was then that the open fireplace was finally banished from living-rooms, so that the smoke could no longer spoil the paint. One of the main reasons why the painting of wood became customary was the increasing scarcity of oak, which was replaced by pine and ash. The panelling of the Nieblum *dagligstuen* is in the pure Renaissance style which was most prevalent in Frisia, although baroque influences are the strongest on the folk art of the rest of Denmark. A list of the ornamental motifs — scale, diamond-shaped boss, denticle and stars — sounds like a description of a church. The division of the walls into rectangular areas and the arched doorways are also features of the later, painted rooms. The tiles, which occurred in particular in the northern part of western Slesvig and on the west coast of Jutland instead of panels, were usually of Dutch origin, or else came from Kellinghusen, near Itzehoe.

There was no comparable wealth on the Danish islands. When it did occur it was only after 1750, and in the areas, already mentioned, near Copenhagen: Magleby and Taarnby on Amager, Avedøre, Grimstrup and Røsnaes on Zealand, Ibsker on Bornholm, Sønder Ho on Fanø, Byrum on Læsø. The Danish living-room was generally very plain, and any kind of wall covering or decoration was extremely unusual. A bench ran the length of

26–7

Page 33 a Kitchen interior, showing dresser and chair, Aberdeenshire, Scotland; b Cupboard, Aabenraa, Denmark, 1792; c Corner cupboard, Alsace, 1830; d Chest of drawers, Denmark, eighteenth century

Page 34 Farmhouse interiors: a Pettneu, Arlberg, Austria, 1700; b West Frisia, eighteenth century; c Norway, eighteenth century; d Grenjadarstadur, Iceland

Page 35 Farmhouse interiors: a Satakunta, Finland; b Dragus, Rumania; c Grimstrup, Denmark; d Bourgen-Bresse, France, early nineteenth century

Page 36 Corner cupboard, Skåne, Sweden, 1845

32

a

b

c

d

a

b

c

d

a

b

c

d

a

b

c

d

a

b

c

d

a

b

the room, beneath the windows, with the table running parallel to it. At the end of the table stood the chair of the master of the house, the panels of which might be richly decorated. The grandest piece of furniture was usually behind this chair: either a cupboard whose corner posts were extended to raise it off the floor, or a hanging cupboard. The stove usually stood at the opposite end of the room. Another bench stood along the other long side of the table. Chairs did not become common until after 1700, except in Slesvig, for the master of the house. The beds lay along the other long wall, opposite the windows. Fully panelled rooms with alcoves occurred mostly in Slesvig and Jutland, and four-poster beds principally in Jutland.

46d, g

The first large pieces of movable furniture were chests. The earliest models, from Slesvig, are the work of carpenters rather than cabinet makers, but chests in the same Gothic style, with feet formed by the extension of the corner posts, and tall, gabled lids, often decorated with quatrefoils as in the Middle Ages, were still being made in the eighteenth century. As early as the mid-sixteenth century a flourishing industry in the region between Rike and Tønder was producing chests in a Renaissance style. The front was always in four panels, each carved with the same leaf ornament, and often with a scroll of text running across it: Set til Gvd alene din lid og tro så fanger dv løcke og

53c

øvig roo ('Trust in God alone, thus you will win joy and eternal rest'). Several of these west Jutland woodworkers are known to us by name. But the large workrooms of the Flensburg joiner Heinrich Ringerinck turned out innumerable dower chests, carved even more richly, which were copied, on a less lavish scale, in the country around Flensburg and Sundeved and in Angeln. This kind of carved oak chest was found all over Jutland and Fyn, but was rarer on Zealand, where as a rule chests were painted with iron clasps and arched lids, and with the owner's initials surrounded by various ornamental devices. This kind of decoration is also found on the fronts of cupboards.

Like the benches and beds, cupboards were originally built into the wall, and had one or more doors; it was again in west Slesvig that they were first made as separate pieces of furniture. These were treasure cupboards with as many as five doors, decorated with fan tracery, vines and chip carving, produced like the chests, between 1560 and 1630. Dressers, made in a similar fashion, occurred even earlier; these have a flap in the middle, which can be pulled out. Developing from the mediaeval cupboards which used to be decorated with fan tracery, they spread over the whole of Jutland from the fifteenth century onwards. They had an open rack for dishes and a shelf for pitchers. The treasure cupboards were similar to the type most frequently found on Zealand, made in the mediaeval fashion, with the corner posts extended to form feet. They performed exactly the same function as the Slesvig corner cupboards (hjørneskab, German Hörnschapp), which were made to stand on the floor, because this region was the first to replace built-in furniture with separate pieces. Those who could not afford free-standing cupboards of this type used to have wall cupboards, sometimes built-in, sometimes hanging, where they kept their money and valuables. A more elegant rococo version, with glass fronts, was found most frequently in Slesvig. Strong boxes, which originated in towns at the same period, also spread into country districts in Slesvig. The strong box and the chest of drawers eventually took the place of the treasure cupboard and the wall cupboard, particularly on Als, on the Lojt peninsula and in central Jutland.

Page 37 Cupboard, Upper Bavaria, 1845

Page 38 Cupboards: *a* Spain, seventeenth century; *b* Castile, Spain; *c* Upper Bavaria, 1729; *d* Hem, Skive, Denmark, 1813

Page 39 Cupboards: *a* Zillertal, Austria, 1770; *b* South Tyrol, seventeenth century; *c* Gaerup, Denmark, c. 1770; *d* Upper Bavaria, 1800

Page 40 Small painted chests: *a* Upper Franconia, c. 1770; *b* Olinalá, Guerrero, Mexico

41

Wardrobes did not come into general use until around 1700 and they never completely replaced chests for storing clothes, at least not on the islands. The earliest wardrobes are made in imitation of the great baroque cupboards of Holland and northern Germany, but in simpler materials and decorated by painting. An abundance of widely differing types emerged, each with regional characteristics. There were first those with ponderous cornices in the style of the Hamburg baroque, then the lighter *Régence* cupboards with broken segment cornices; later there were the rococo shapes with lattice work, and later still those based on neoclassical models, with urns, fluted panelling, bows and wreaths. These cupboards normally had two doors, the larger panels of which gave the painters scope to achieve new heights in folk painting, particularly a style of floral painting which was surpassed only in Norway. The areas where this was most common were Fyn, Jutland and, again, Slesvig.

39c
33b

The chair really deserves a chapter to itself. Even the very earliest cylindrical log stools, made from sections of tree trunks, are decorated. Amid the manifold variety of types of chairs, where features derived from the newest fashion and the oldest tradition are often found simultaneously, the most interesting, in respect of folk art, are the armchairs reserved for the master and mistress of a house. The wooden backs of such chairs were covered with the most elaborate carving: foliage, vases of flowers, figures, proverbs, the owner's initials and dates. After 1800 the seats produced in carpenters' workshops became very common, with particular regional types emerging, such as the three-legged stools made on Fyn, which had backrests carved elaborately like mangle boards, the chairs made in Jersie on Zealand which were decorated with scrolls bearing proverbial inscriptions, and those found on the west coast of Slesvig, where the posts supporting back and arms were beautifully turned to resemble small pillars. Chairs without armrests are rather rare in folk art: in the only region where they were common, in Slesvig, they vary only very slightly from the pieces made by professional craftsmen for the upper classes; like the Ballum chairs for example, these hardly count as folk art at all.

57a

Decorated wooden boarding played an important role in fittings, from the Middle Ages onwards. Carved with proverbs and such Renaissance ornamental devices as denticle and egg-moulding, they served a purely decorative purpose at the top of alcoves. They could be used to make handy small square or three-sided tables. On Zealand, the smarter glass-fronted cupboards or strong boxes, for the display of faience, porcelain

and silver, were rare, and shelves, usually decorated in a baroque style, performed the same function.

Wood was also the material for countless tools and utensils which come within the category of folk art if only because many of them were the work of non-professional craftsmen. Even so, there were still many things, including mangle boards, clothes-beaters, weavers' reeds, ell measures, clock cases, footwarmers, jugs, rolling-pins, boxes and spectacle cases that were made by professional craftsmen. It is true to speak of many of these objects as love gifts, but they were very seldom the work of amateurs. The seafaring men of the Danish islands produced many proofs of their dexterity, but without the help of the village carpenters or the woodcarvers working in the churches there would be very little of 'art' in, for instance, the richly inventive mangle boards.

The smaller utensils conform to the same topographical patterns as the other forms of folk art. The same groups of motifs are repeated with astonishing consistency from the Skaw to Tønder, from Ribe to Bornholm: chip carving of rosettes, stars, scale ornament, bosses, hearts, tulips, vases, lions, horses, unidentifiable birds, cherubs, the Crucifixion, the Fall of Man, but always with variants stemming from the practice of the local workshops, which means from the imagination of individual master craftsmen. And then as now, makers knew what customers wanted better than the customers themselves.

The manufacture of metal articles is a complicated process that must generally be left to professionals. And yet metal, iron at least, is essential to every household. For this reason, the village smith was always an important member of every community. As well as agricultural tools, which if made of wood — like the hames on a horse's collar, yokes, flails and spare parts for wagons — were seldom decorated, the smith made all kinds of household utensils, particularly those which had anything to do with fire, using not only iron but also brass and copper, and occasionally even tin. He made various kinds of candlesticks, lanterns, curfews, footwarmers, braziers, kettle hooks, gridirons, cake tins, smoothing irons, and so on, and village smiths even produced quite skilful clocks and navigational instruments on occasion.

Some examples of goldsmith's work must also be included in this account of folk art, since the goldsmiths produced some things specifically for their rural customers which were essentially the same as what was made for city dwellers, but with different ornamentation. In Slesvig, spoons, sugar tongs, prayer-book clasps, scent boxes

60d, 84a, 90i, j, 101b, d, 114c

280d

68a

Left and right: Patterns from reversible fabrics; northern Slesvig, late eighteenth century

and so on were set in vitreous paste for the peasants. The goldsmiths of Copenhagen made special kinds of scent boxes for the people of Amager. They had the usual heart shape, supported by two lions, and with a plaque on the lid for inscribing initials, between the club-carrying savages who normally support the Danish royal coat of arms. In addition the heart was enclosed in a network of gilt filigree. The traditional costume worn on Amager included a particular kind of brooch, which was also specially made in Copenhagen or on Læsø off the coast of Jutland. The fact that in Slesvig there were a number of village goldsmiths, specializing in the silver ornaments native to the region, particularly on Föhr, is yet another instance of the creative vigour of that part of Denmark.

Pottery developed as a domestic industry in the poorest regions of Jutland at a relatively late date, and the so-called *jydepotter* were soon well known beyond Denmark. These pots, made for the most part by women, are easily recognizable by their colour, black, and by their primitive style of decoration using scrolls, zigzags and wavy lines; their shape alone gives them a special charm. Pedlars sold them throughout Germany and Holland. The best examples come from the Varde district of south-west Jutland. The workshops there produced pots, cans, jugs, plates, funnels, apparatus for distilling brandy, butter-crocks, strainers, cheese forms, rings for baking apple cakes, lamps, foot-warmers, flower-pots, beehives, toys, even tiled ovens for those who could not afford iron ranges.

The Jutland *jydepotter* were not, of course, the only pottery produced at the cottage industry level; the craft flourished throughout the land. The Silkeborg district was famous for it, as was the Himmerland in northern Jutland, where the potters were particularly imaginative. A special variety which enjoyed great popularity everywhere consisted of spherical pots for soup or gruel, like those from Holbæk on Zealand. Another popular form was the double dish used for serving fish, which was often inscribed. There is a large number of different forms, for once again these were the work of the professional craftsmen. After the establishment of faience factories in the eighteenth century, which, particularly the Kellinghusen workshop near Itzehoe which held the royal patent, sold genuine folk pottery, the potters tried to copy the more complicated forms: flower-pots, tea-caddies, inkwells, lamps and human figures.

134, 3rd row l., 146b, c, i, 147b

Slesvig led, again, in the popular production of textiles. The linen embroidery of Amager and Jutland has already been mentioned. Rugs and cushions, some woven and knotted, some embroidered, had a prominent position in the living rooms of Slesvig. There are two main kinds of knotting, one where the pile is clipped and the weft hidden, and one where the pile is not cut and the pattern appears in tufts. Large numbers of cushion covers in many colours were made in this second manner. The reversible materials used as wall-hangings and curtains were much grander. They were also found on Amager and Bornholm, with the Danish name of *rylagen*. They correspond to the tapestries of nobles' houses, and were made by professional weavers, probably after Dutch models. The patterns include plants and human figures, the plants being found mostly in the eastern part of Slesvig, Angeln, Als and the Lojt district, and the human figures in north Frisia. The subjects fall in a narrow range: besides biblical scenes like the Entry into Jerusalem, the Samaritan Woman at the Well and the Prodigal Son, the themes of Pyramus and Thisbe and the four quarters of the world recur constantly.

176c, e, 27, 42, 43

Page 45 a Hanging corner cupboard, closed and the inner sides of the doors, England, *c.* 1800; *b* Chest, Zillertal, Austria, 1774

Page 46 Chests: *a* East Bothnia, Finland, 1804; *b* South Tyrol, seventeenth century; *c* Suceava, Rumania; *d* Tønder, Denmark, sixteenth century; *e* Lancaster, Pa., 1788; *f* Tisza valley, Hungary; *g* Sommersted, Denmark; *h* England

44

a

b

a

b

c

d

e

f

g

h

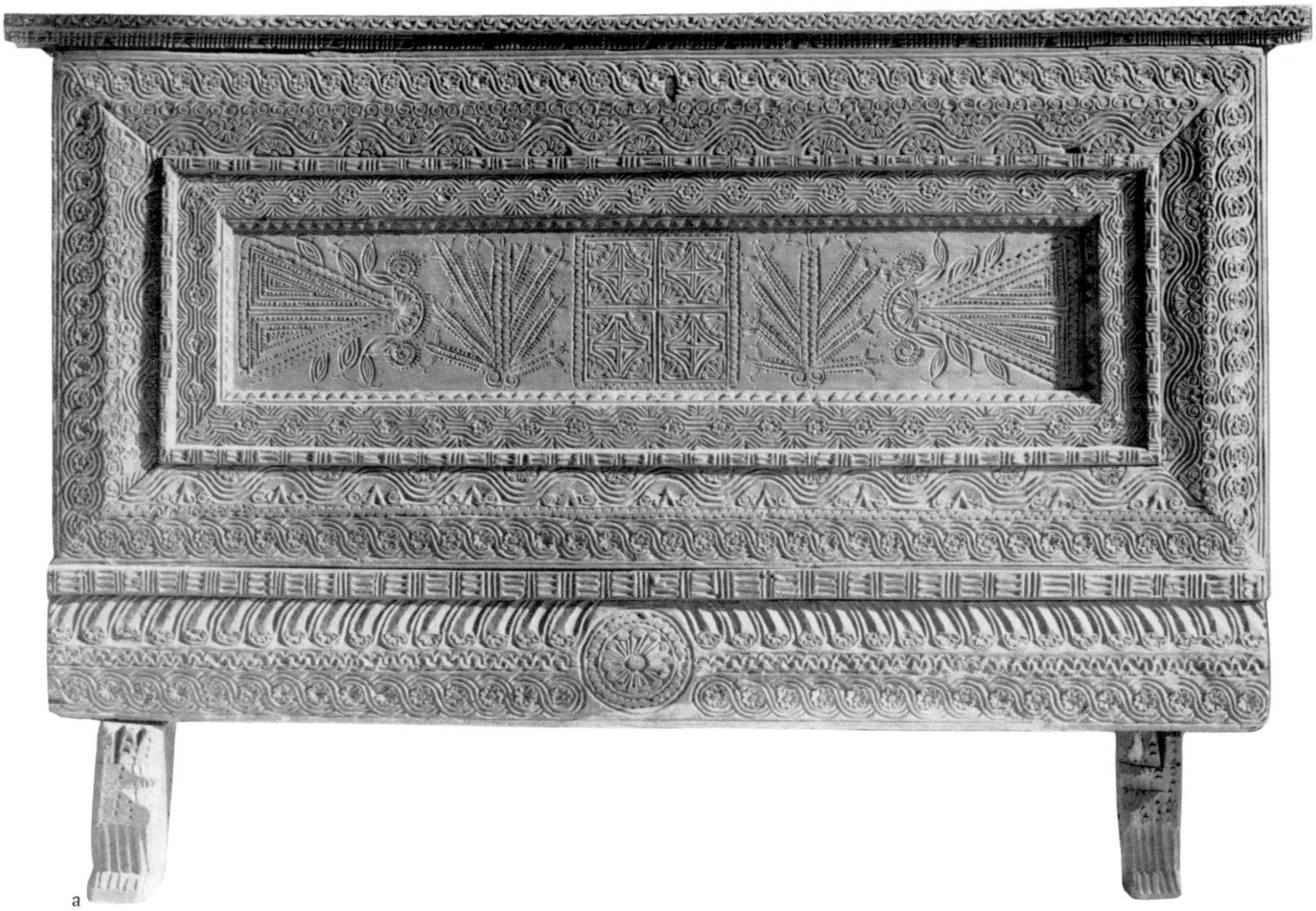

a

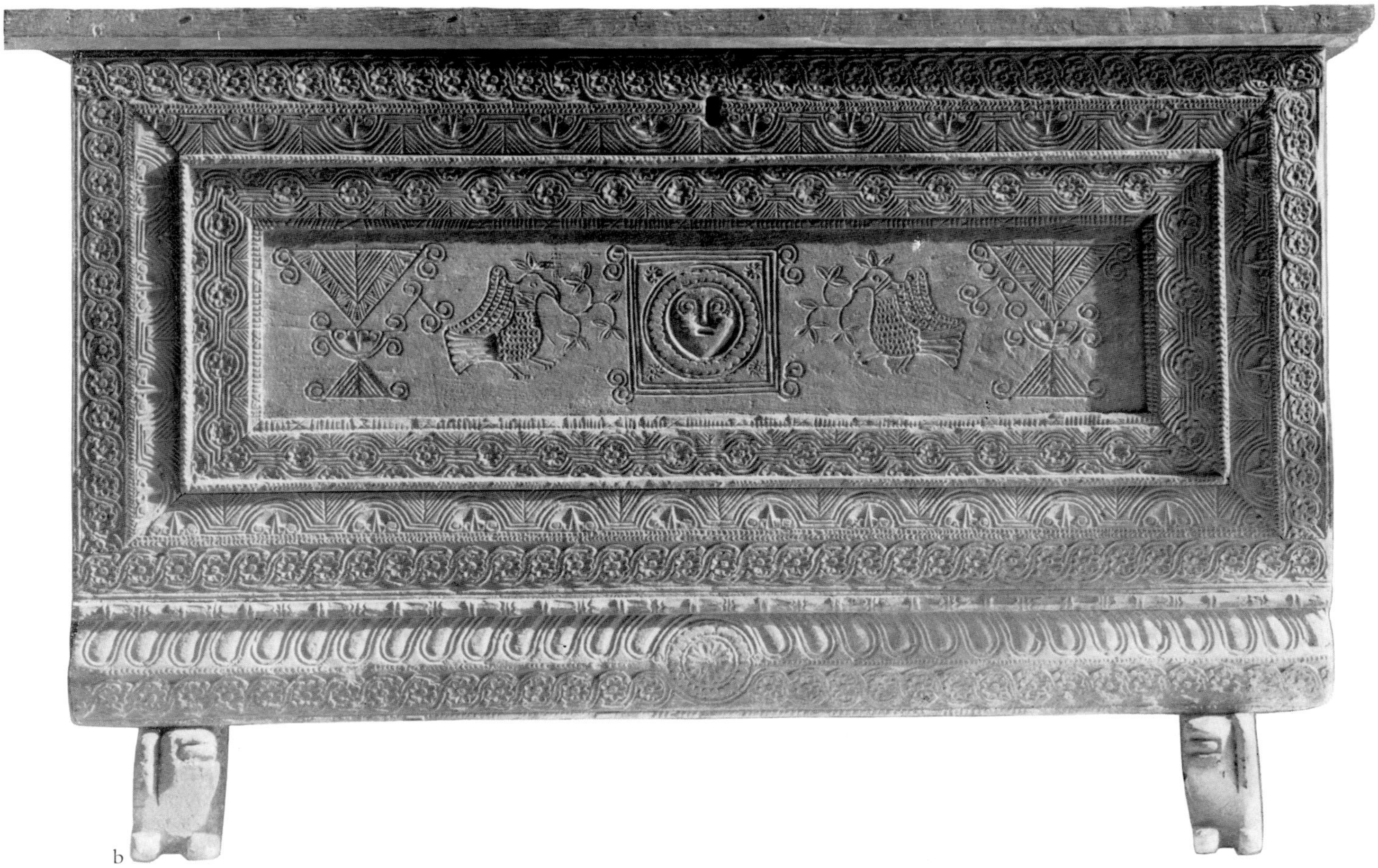

b

a

b

The British Isles

Scotland · England · Ireland

SCOTLAND had lost nearly all its native timber resources by the late seventeenth century, with the result that the building of timber-framed houses virtually died out. For the last two centuries, in the towns, in the villages that started to develop in the late eighteenth century, and in the countryside, the characteristic building material for houses of any size has been stone.

Rural housing, however, has a number of regional features. There are clay walled houses on the east coast and in the south-west, built of clay mixed with chopped straw or heather, or small pebbles, puddled thoroughly together and laid in courses about thirty inches high by twenty inches wide, each course being allowed to dry before the next went on. The bottom course was often of stone, to prevent damp from spoiling the base of the wall.

Clay was also used with straw, bent grass, reeds, or heather, in thatching the roofs of houses in an area extending on the east coast from Inverness to Fife. Overlapping bunches of straw, pressed into position by a two-pronged instrument called a stob, were bedded in clay applied with a trowel, and the whole roof finally washed down with a watery mixture of clay. When dry, the clay bound the straw firmly, and no ropes were needed to keep the thatch down.

10d In Shetland and the Outer Hebrides, the older 'black-houses' had double walls with a packing of peat mould or turf between. The thatch came down to the centre of the wall so that rainwater percolated through the earthy core. When thatching the roof, it was possible to walk right round on top of the outer section of the wall. On such roofs, the thatch was roped and anchored by stones. Where walls were of single thickness, the ropes could also be attached to pegs in the walls.

Other forms of roofing are the flagstones of Orkney, resembling enormous slates, and the red pantiles of central and southern Scotland, which make the little fishing towns along the Fife coast so attractive. Pantiles and slates began to be used extensively at most social levels in the late eighteenth and early nineteenth centuries.

One feature from the days when native timber was more plentiful is the cruck frame, where the roof is borne on couples whose feet come down to, or close to, ground level, and the walls serve merely as infilling, playing no part in supporting the roof. Crucks have been thought to derive from Scandinavia. This theory no longer holds good, and their absence in Shetland and Orkney and the Outer Hebrides, former areas of Norse settlement, is significant. Otherwise, they were found throughout most of Scotland, and many still survive.

An open hearth is always the focal point of a living-room, and this is especially true of the central hearth, around which the daily activities of the household were carried on.

Page 47 a, b Sardinian chests
Page 48 a Painted clock faces (Alsace, Lorraine or Black Forest); *b* Oxyoke, Ovar, Beira Litoral, Portugal

49

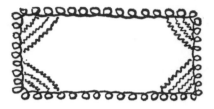

Even yet it is possible to visit houses in Lewis where the haze of peat smoke is kept just above the level of a seated person's head by the rising warmth of the central fire. One such hearth at Calbost consists of the top stone of a disused horizontal water mill. More advanced in type, though still of Neolithic parentage, is the central hearth with a back stone, which might later develop into an internal gable. Gable fireplaces, with wooden canopy-like chimneys pinned against the wall, terminating in a large square wooden opening around which broom or heather was bound with straw ropes, were ultimately replaced by hearths having chimneys in the thickness of the gable.

Where flagstones were used for hearths, doorsteps, and the floors of kitchens and milkhouses, a delightful custom of decorating them with geometrical and floral designs was in vogue in central and southern Scotland until recent years. Housewives vied with each other in making these designs and in keeping them fresh, and thought, rightly or wrongly, that they were a defence against ill luck. A hearth at floor level required specially adapted cooking equipment, like the upright toasting stones against which bannocks (oatcakes) were leaned to toast in front of the open fire. Some are finely carved, and may also have initials, perhaps those of a married couple. These were replaced by iron toasters that hooked on to the bars of the grate. There are some fine specimens of these, showing the art and skill of local blacksmiths. When bannocks were baked on flat iron gridirons or griddles above the fire, bannock spades of metal or of wood shod with iron, usually heart shaped and with cut-out designs of hearts, diamonds, etc., were used to turn them.

Furniture, like architecture, reflects the scarcity of local timber. Scotland has nothing to compare with the magnificently ornate painted furniture made in more favoured parts of Europe. Until a generation or two ago, the furniture in most rural dwellings was exclusively functional and utilitarian in character. Commonly, there was a hard wooden bench about six feet long, with arms at each end, sometimes open below and sometimes boxed in to provide storage space. A folding table could be hinged to the back.

In areas like Orkney, a good deal of straw was used in the construction of stools and chairs. The wood-framed, straw-backed chair now popularly known as an 'Orkney chair' is essentially a development of the 1870s. Earlier, the base too was of straw, arranged in thick coils like an upturned basket, and the only wood was a couple of struts as a frame to support the back. Some had a rounded hood added at the top to protect the sitter more completely from draughts. Occasionally there is a wooden drawer under the seat, allegedly to hold the family Bible, but in fact a repository for odds and ends of all kinds. They are still made by the firm of Eunson in Kirkwall, Orkney. Caithness had a localized type of wooden armchair with a strongly sloping back, in which the husband could stretch himself before the fire whilst his wife sat on a low, straight chair which had no arms to get in the way as she carded wool or turned the spinning wheel. Brown paint was applied to these all over, as it was to most other furniture in country households.

The largest piece of furniture was the box bed, with hinged or sliding doors, often acting as a partition between rooms. The sliding doors could be embellished with hearts, clover leaves, or diamonds, cut out to serve as finger holds. The mattresses could be stuffed with straw or chaff, or a species of seaweed, *Zostera marina*, said to be proof

56e

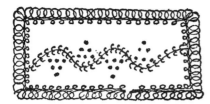

33a

against fleas. Box beds became prevalent among all classes in the eighteenth century, though they have a much longer ancestry in the rest of Europe.

Crockery and containers for food and liquid sat on a dresser with a high, shelved back. This had a set of large and sometimes of small drawers, and the lower part could be boxed in to make cupboards or could be open, with room for buckets, baskets and large bowls on the wooden crossbars. The shelved back held the more decorative plates, saucers, and cups for ornament and formal use. Smaller houses had a separate plate rack, dooked into the wall with wooden pegs or hung on a nail, and low dressers without shelves.

Crockery for display and use had a variety of origins, but most houses had some Scottish pieces from one or other of the potteries that began to proliferate in the eighteenth century in and around Glasgow and Edinburgh, in Fife, and elsewhere. It must be confessed that their products owed a lot to influences from outside Scotland. For example, the attractive Wemyss ware has designs of roses and other flowers by Karel Nekola, a native of Bohemia who came to Fife to work in Robert Heron's pottery in 1883. The ubiquitous plates and ashets (dishes) from the pottery of J. & M. P. Bell of Glasgow (after 1842) include the willow pattern, and have Oriental or classical scenes like the popular Triumphal Car design, with a charioteer drawn by horses or leopards, driving past an urn on a pedestal and buildings with Grecian lines, or Oriental palaces and temples, in blues, whites, and blue-greys. The designs were sometimes made by Chinese artists, and though these, like the Paisley shawl pattern that originated in Kashmir, are scarcely indigenous Scottish folk art, yet they have been accepted and adopted at most social levels and in the popular imagination are regarded as traditional. The potteries also produced figures representing fishwives, characters taken from literature, especially the poems of Robert Burns, and animals of various kinds, the cow milk-jug being very popular. Particularly interesting is the representation in pottery (e. g. by the North British Pottery, Glasgow), and even in glass, of older types of wooden containers such as the one-handled 'luggie', of which various sizes were made, ranging from drinking-cups to milking-pails. Wooden luggies continued to be made well into the nineteenth century, but were, like their pottery and glass imitations, intended as ornaments and souvenirs. In the district of Barvas in Lewis, hand-made pottery, not wheel-turned, was being made into this century, and baked in hot peat ash. It could be dipped in milk while hot to give it an elementary glaze. Latterly, it attempted to imitate the designs of fine china in the Derby style, but the results can scarcely be said to have artistic merit.

For textile production, an essential part of the household equipment was a wheel for spinning wool and flax. Over sixty makers of wheels have been recorded, and though it is not certainly known when spinning-wheels like the 'muckle' or great wheel, or types with flyers, first came to Scotland, they were well established by the mid-seventeenth century when the descriptions in contemporary writings imply six or seven varieties and sizes. The spindle and whorl, and distaff, continued as the main equipment for twisting wool and flax into threads until well into the nineteenth century in the remoter areas, though government stimulation of the flax industry extended the use of wheels in the late eighteenth century. There are many good examples of wheels that appear as more than objects of strictly utilitarian use through the skill and craftsmanship

127b

101a, e
166a

Left and above: Patterns on floor tiles, Scotland

of the joiners who made them, and these are being increasingly sought by collectors. A method of knitting, now almost obsolete, was to fix the end of one needle into a sheath or stick held in the apron band, so leaving one hand free. From the Borders come several examples of finely-carved knitting sticks, matching those in the north of England and elsewhere, with hearts, diamonds, leaves and flowers, one with an inset piece of mirror glass, and some with a cut-out section in which a little metal ball is retained. Further north, sticks were uncommon, and instead there were sheaths in the form of tapered cylinders of straw or feathers bound with twine or red and blue wool. A Shetland example is of goose quills, bound with brass wire into which are plaited strips of red and blue leather, with a tassel at the foot. Knitting belts, with leather pads stuffed with horse hair, are still used.

As regards dress, apart from the Highland garb that has become synonymous with the romantic image of Scotland, there is little to compare in quantity or quality with the Continental material. Fishwives in the main fishing villages, and female farm servants in the south of Scotland, wore characteristic clothes of mainly eighteenth century ancestry. Women outworkers in the south still wear a type of hat with a hood over the face and a flap at the back of the neck, ungallantly known as an 'ugly' or 'crazy'. Men's dress was undistinguished, though the style of the garment known as the 'slope', of blue and white striped cloth, is descended from the eighteenth-century type of shirt with a ruffle.

The vexed question of the origins of tartan and the kilt is likely to be a matter of discussion for some time to come. In broad terms, it appears that the adoption of particular tartans by particular clans did not precede the second half of the eighteenth century. The word 'tartan' goes back at least to the sixteenth century, and seems to refer to an arrangement of coloured checks and stripes, with the soft tones of natural dyes. The kilt itself probably evolved from the ubiquitous plaid, common to the Highlands and the Lowlands alike, capable of serving as a dress by day and a blanket at night. When held in position by a belt round the waist, the lower portion could hang like a kilt, and the separation of the top and bottom halves to avoid a mass of folds under the belt is a reasonable hypothesis. The later development of the kilt owes a great deal to the Scottish regiments that adopted it as part of their uniform in the eighteenth century. One may speculate that the popularity of tartan derives from the Scottish fondness for infinite repetition of a basic pattern with slight changes in detail, also evident in the decoration of brooches and in dance and bagpipe music.

One of the most attractive pieces of Scottish jewellery is the heart brooch. The heart shape has had a religious meaning (as elsewhere in Europe) from mediaeval times, and appears as a symbol of love and marriage in Scotland from the seventeenth century onwards, on stone marriage lintels above doors, on chair backs, on sewn samplers, on bannock spades, and on brooches. Heart brooches are usually of silver, and were frequently given as love tokens, with inscriptions like 'My heart ye have, and thine I crave'. They were also worn as charms, often under the petticoat since part of the virtue of the charm lay in keeping it hidden; they were used both by mothers anxious to prevent witches from taking away their milk, and by children of both sexes to avert witchcraft and the evil eye. Formerly, they might be made by tinker craftsmen, as were the flat,

Page 53 Chests: *a* Salamanca, Spain, eighteenth century; *b* Holstein, 1797; *c* Emmerlev, west Slesvig, *c.* 1750

Pages 54-5 a Cupboard, Arles, France, early nineteenth century; *b* Four-poster bed, Ellede, Kalundborg, Denmark, 1623; *c* Armchair, Telemark, Norway, *c.* 1300 (?); *d* Chair ('*kubbestol*'), Vestfold, Norway, eighteenth century; *e* Shelf with pictures on glass and jugs, Podhale, Poland, nineteenth century; *f* Wall rack, Sweden, eighteenth century; *g* Spoonrack, Netherlands, 1848

Page 56 Chairs: *a* Alsace; *b* Burgenland, 1815; *c* Alsace (?); *d* Gloucestershire; *e* Orkney Islands; *f* Shropshire; *g* Windsor rocking chair, eighteenth century; *h* Armchair, Hällstad, Skåne, Sweden, 1831; *i* Trentino, seventeenth century

a

b

c

a

b

c

d

a

b

c

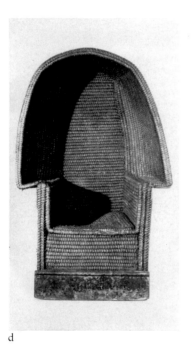

d

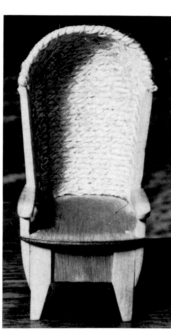

e

f

g

h

i

a

b

c

d

a

b

c

d

e

f

a   b   c

d   e   f

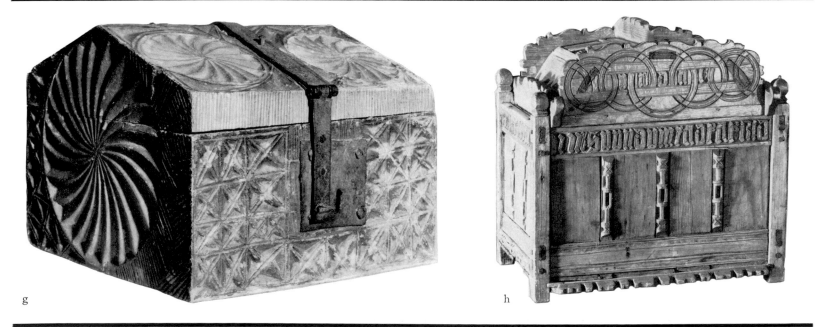

g   h

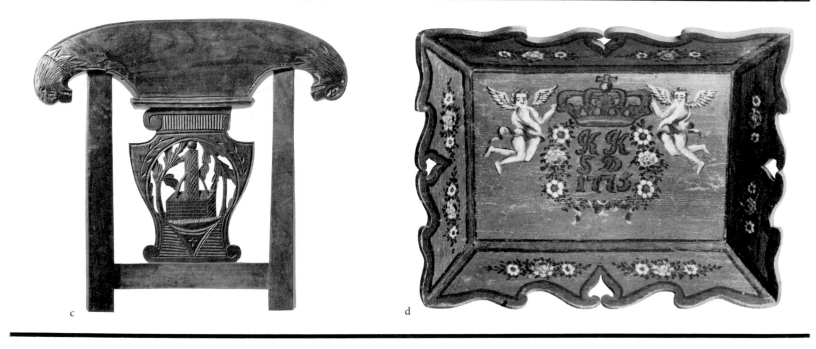

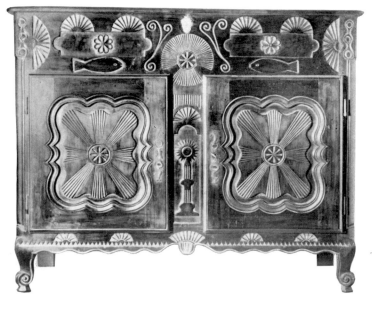

a

b

c

d

e

f

Jugs, bowls, baking dishes, salt jars or 'kits', mugs, egg stands, cream piggins, cups, money boxes and model cradles were among the simply-made slipware objects. Brown earthenware with white slip decoration was common, but colours included buff, umber and cream. Decoration was sometimes a pictorial symbol or simply a series of flicks or parallel lines dragged across at regular intervals with a feather to produce an undulating pattern of lively texture. Ralph, Thomas and James Toft are known for their great trellis bordered dishes bearing naive royal portraits such as King Charles II hiding in the oak, or the Royal Arms.

136a

The *sgraffito* technique, drawing scratched in the slip to reveal the clay body beneath, characterized lead-glazed pottery made at Donyatt and Crock Street in Somerset from the mid-sixteenth century until the nineteenth. It was also employed notably on the large harvest jugs made at Fremington, Bideford and Barnstaple. A mariner's compass and other nautical pictures, such as mermaids, ships and waves, with a convivial verse, comprised the typical ornament. One Bideford jug, for example, made in the 1770s, is inscribed:

Above and left: Brass badges, probably Bristol, *c.* 1800

> Work on Brave Boys and never fear,
> you shall have Ale, Cyder and Beer.
> Beef, pork and pudding as I thinke
> is Rear good eating with strong Drink.

Tableware with decoration of trailed slip and the addition of star-shaped indentations filled with clay in a contrasting colour was made in three areas of Sussex: at Rye, Brede and Hastings; at Dicker and Hellingly; and farther west at Chailey, Keymer and Clayton. The high iron content of the Wealden clays in Sussex made the body a deep red.

Among the objects made for entertainment, as well as use, there was the Sussex pig, whose head is detachable for use as a drinking-cup while the body can be used as a flask. The better known bear jugs, made in Staffordshire of white stoneware and in Nottingham of brown earthenware, incorporate a similar function. These bears were made sitting upright, usually hugging a small dog in reference to the popular sport of bear-baiting; but a more topical point is made by the Russian bear which hugs a small Napoleon with the nickname 'Boney' impressed on his plumed hat. The Nottingham bear jugs were often endowed with shredded-clay fur. In Staffordshire, owl jugs were also made with detachable heads, the details of face and plumage picked out in brown often giving them very amusing expressions.

Of all the small and lively figures sold around the country by the itinerant image-seller, the chimney-piece ornaments modelled by John Astbury (1688–1743) and Thomas Whieldon (1719–95), and the so-called 'pew groups', are now the most prized for their character and beauty. Although they were once the unconsidered ornaments of farmhouses, cottages and taverns, they are now rare. The Astbury and Whieldon figures, on a smaller scale than the pew groups, comprise a wide range of tiny musicians, cobblers, cavalrymen, street sellers, actors, topers, dancers and other everyday figures whose merit lies in the deft manipulation of the clay to form an appealingly naive and witty statement. The smallest of these figures is about six inches high, basically white with touches of only two or three colours such as blue, green, chocolate brown and ochre yellow. Whieldon added glazed colour by staining or splashing the figures with copper, manganese or cobalt.

The salt-glazed or lead-glazed pew groups, modelled from cylinders, rolls and balls of clay, appear to be the product of a group of no more than five or six modellers. The style of all the figures is very consistent. In spite of the term 'pew group', the figures are, apart from one of Adam and Eve, secular. The basis of the group was a solid high-backed settle (the 'pew') seating a man and woman. Love and music are the most frequent themes. In three typical examples, the settle arms have black and white twisted rope decoration. In one group of a woman sitting with a small dog on her lap and a piper playing his instrument by her, the woman wears an elaborate skirt of alternating strips of black and white clay, a pleated cap and long white apron, while the man has boldly curled clay ringlets, ribbed white stockings and buckled black shoes with a skirted coat over buttoned waistcoat and striped breeches. Pew groups date from the middle of the eighteenth century.

148a

The first Toby jugs are attributed to Ralph Wood (1716–72) of Burslem. It is hard to understand the long-standing popularity of this form of jug, subsequently made in numerous versions by many hands up to the present day. Although a number of different people were portrayed in this form, it traditionally depicts a short, corpulent, grinning man with long hair under a tricorn hat, wearing a deep-pocketed coat with large buttons and wide cuffs. Sitting on a low seat, mostly obscured by the skirts of his coat, he usually balances a jug on his left knee and raises his tankard with his right hand. A mezzotint print of Henry Elwes, nicknamed Toby Fillpot, made at the time of his death in 1761, has led to the belief that the Toby jug depicts this hard-drinking Yorkshireman.

Transfer printing on cast pottery was an important development which brought decorative blue and white tableware into use in the country kitchen in the 1830s alongside the much older plain wooden trenchers and simple pewter. The willow pattern plate, the best known of the many landscape designs, is said to have been originated in 1780 by Thomas Turner at the Caughley Pottery Works in Shropshire.

By means of under-glaze transfer printing (engravings printed from copper plates on to paper and thence transferred to pottery), the English commemorative, seafaring and farmers' mugs and jugs were created in prolific variety and quantity, often coloured with patches of bright over-glaze colour and splashes and bands of pink copper lustre.

127e

The frog mug, another potter's joke, was made between about 1750 and 1880. Innocently decorated like many other transfer-printed mugs of the period, they contained a model toad or frog, sometimes hollow so that it croaked as the last drops of liquid were drained by the unwary drinker. The nautical mementos from Sunderland depicting the 'Sailor's Farewell' were typical and often included a verse on the reverse side such as:

> Thou noble bark of brightest fame,
> That bear'st proud England's honoured name.
> Right welcome home once more!
> In England's name I bid thee hail!
> And welcome to her shore.

Page 65 a–f Weather-vanes, Castille
Page 66 Wooden house in colonial style, Boston, Mass., 1800

a

b

c

d

e

f

northern counties of Northumberland, Cumberland, Durham and Westmorland. Quilts were very common in farmhouses, where there were often several quilts to a bed. Women field workers in Northumberland and fishermen's wives on the north-east coast wore quilted petticoats. A great deal of quilting was done in the household, but there were also professional quilters who worked at home, as well as itinerant quilters who travelled from place to place, staying where they worked. Some people specialized in marking patterns for others to sew. The layers of material were stretched in a large frame while the quilter worked over it, one hand above the work and one underneath, the needle passing between them. Pattern elements, square diamonds, circles and segments of circles, were very simple, but the ways in which these were arranged, linked, and overlapped could be complex.

198b Patchwork, although it was sometimes quilted, was an art in its own right. The idea of combining a mosaic of cloth fragments arises from the demands of economy, but the rich rhythms of plain coloured or printed calico hexagons, triangles, diamonds and stars, sometimes combined with appliqué details, give no hint of this. Special patchwork coverlets, as well as quilts, were designed and made as marriage gifts.

The banners of country friendly societies were a fertile but little-known ground on which the art of appliqué patchwork could be employed. Some good examples of these banners, notably two from Midsomer Norton dated 1850 and one from Stratton-on-the-Fosse dated 1830, survive in Somerset. One of those from Midsomer Norton portrays one-armed Nelson with the inscription, 'This day England expects every man to do his duty'; the second banner from the same source depicts King Charles II in the oak tree. Both subjects were popular and frequently-recurrent themes in many branches of English folk art through two and a half centuries.

228c The composition of pictures from pieces of silk, felt, satin and coloured paper was a widespread activity, but one which yielded few recognizable traditional art forms. The tinsel picture did however have a character of its own, influenced, it has been said, by the vogue for romantic, unrealistic acting of the barnstorming type. This kind of portraiture was at its best between 1830 and 1850 when theatrical prints of actors were published together with packs of stamped-out tinsel ornaments, including not only metallic stars and dots but also shiny helmets, breastplates and swords.

215a–d So-called glass pictures, also based on engravings, became popular in the early eighteen-hundreds. Although they were usually religious or historical scenes in a bold and colourful style, the technique by which they were produced had been used earlier for more sophisticated portraits, after Kneller for example, and hunting scenes. These pictures were made by attaching a black and white mezzotint face downwards to a sheet of glass; the paper was then carefully removed, leaving little more than the ink behind, and coloured pigments were applied to the back of the engraving. The best examples are characterized by deep rich blacks, reds and blues with a luminous quality, a feeling of static drama, and boldly defined shapes; they are slightly reminiscent of stained glass.

The increasing popularity of seaside resorts led to the making of shell pictures and other articles, such as boxes and pin-cushions, for souvenirs. The pictures comprised a circular arrangement of rows of matching shells glued round a central seascape or seaweed group. A convex glass over the centre gave an impression of three dimensions.

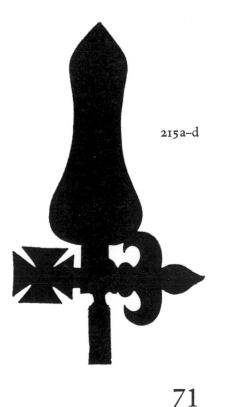

Prize cattle were the subjects of a considerable number of animal portraits from the 1790s until about 1845, and many of these paintings were, in turn, the subjects of widely-sold engravings. The usual hallmarks of the pictures were a formal side view of the animal with close attention to its massive outline shape, a sense of pattern evident in the careful placing of its markings on the canvas, and isolation of the animal in an insignificant landscape with low horizon line.

The desire for cheap family portraits was met by the itinerant painter of miniatures who is said to have made a practice of painting costumed shoulders and backgrounds in readiness for the next household on his journey. There, the most appropriate picture could be selected and the face rapidly painted in.

45a

Painted floral decoration, so often found on European peasant furniture, is not a traditional feature of English country furniture; but it is found in splendid but strangely isolated profusion in the narrow boats of the Midland canals. The boats are shallow-bottomed, with a large cargo capacity of thirty to thirty-five tons and a dwelling cabin, only about seven feet wide by ten feet long, for the family to live in. The boats usually worked in pairs and were hauled by horses on the towpaths.

All these narrow boats share a particular style of bright, shiny, rapidly executed paint-work, usually predominantly green, with white, scarlet, black and yellow roses and daisies. A bold geometrical pattern of diamonds and circles is another element in the decoration; idiosyncratic castles, with crenellated turrets and onion-shaped domes, are depicted by a river with a bridge in a hilly landscape. There are traditional positions for all these details. A castle occupies the centre of the underside of the hinged wooden flap table, and reappears in the centre of a wooden stool and sometimes on the inside of the cabin entrance doors, often bordered by exotic roses. The metal drinking-water can bears groups of roses, rows of daisies and a striped band along the lower edge. The dipper, for washing-water scooped from the canal, has bunches of roses and daisies on its sides. The teapot and tea-caddy sport groups of four roses. All the flowers are accompanied by rounded light green leaves, with small flicks of white paint accurately placed to fill empty spaces. Any area in the cabin's interior which is not entirely covered with decoration of this kind is painted with brown imitation wood-graining over lemon yellow. The decorators have exact methods of applying the paint: first the background, which is allowed to dry, then the basic petal and leaf shapes, in single bold brushstrokes made with a different brush for each colour and a generous use of turpentine, and finally the small details.

The boat's exterior is well but less exuberantly painted, the name of the owner, accompanied by several sprays of roses, on the sides of the cabin and the boat's name round the stern in bold shaded letters. The rudder post is ornamented with white rope work and, perhaps, a white horse's tail for luck. The tiller bar is banded with bright paint.

Speculation about the origin of this style of painting, unique in England and only matched for boldness and vigour by gipsy caravan and fairground painting, has not led to any conclusive theory.

The best examples of woodcarving as a folk art now survive in the fourteenth- and fifteenth-century misericords of English mediaeval churches and cathedrals. Misericords, curved wooden ledges on the underside of tip-up seats, were provided for the priests to

Page 73 a Mirror-back with wax intarsia, Somogy, Hungary; *b, c* Lids of chip boxes: *b* Rogaland, Norway, 1827, *c* Berchtesgaden, Germany, *c.* 1780

a

b

c

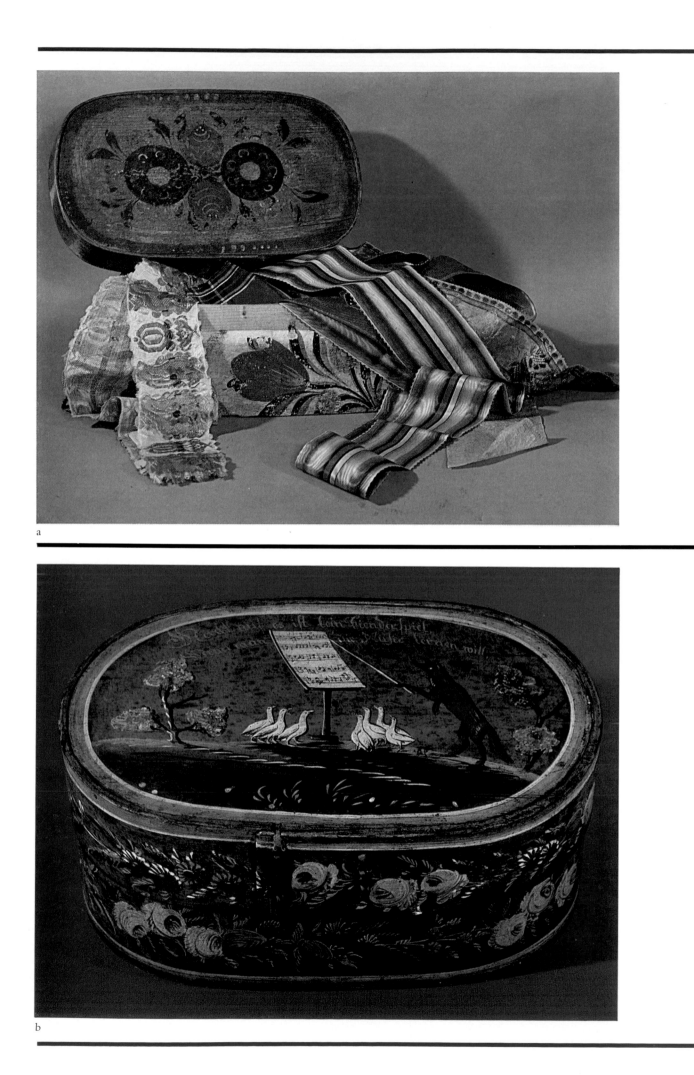

a

b

enable them to combine the comfort of sitting with the appearance of standing during long services. Many homely subjects were vividly portrayed; work, domestic life, sport, romantic tales and curiosities were all represented, often with little regard for their religious context. A domestic brawl at Westminster, a tapster at Ludlow, footballers at Gloucester and hare coursing at Ely are a few instances of the secular range.

Relatively few old carved wooden trade signs have survived to the present day but there is ample evidence that they were a very flourishing branch of folk art. According to a description published in 1808, they were 'very large, very fine and very absurd, golden periwigs, saws, axes, lancets, razors, trees, knives, salmon, cheeses, blacks' heads, halfmoons, sugarloaves and Westphalian hams,' repeated, it was said 'without mercy from the Borough to Clerkenwell'. Many were carved in the round, and all were heavily and brightly painted or gilded.

As with the still-recognized barber's striped pole and the pawnbroker's golden balls, the figures originally indicated the trade of the shopkeeper below, the grocer's three sugarloaves, the glovemaker's golden hand, the hatter's three hats, for example. But confusion arose when owners changed trades and shops changed hands. As symbols, many signs lost their significance although they were still incorporated in addresses, resulting in humourous contradictions to which Addison referred when he advised, 'A cook should not live at the *Boot* nor a shoe-maker at the *Roasted Pig* ... I have seen a *Goat* set up before a perfumer and the *King's Head* before a sword-cutler's.'

Some signs were puns, or had technical significance not always clear to us now. Common tobacconist's signs, a few of which still survive in use, were the Moor or Oriental and the Highlander. The former indicated that 'Black Jack' tobacco was sold and the latter referred to Scotch snuff. A finely-uniformed midshipman meant a nautical instrument maker, and two eighteenth-century schoolboys in the dress of their day indicated a school.

Ships' figureheads formed another group of effigies, carved in greater size (as much as fifteen feet high). These were invariably human figures. Because of their size, and the fact that people felt more romantic attachment to the sea than to trade, more good figureheads than trade signs have survived the destruction of their former sites.

267b

The development of increasingly grand fairground carving was contemporary with the decline in ships' carving during the nineteenth century. Of the many figures, including clowns, which filled the nineteenth century fairground, and are still to be seen occasionally, the galloping merry-go-round horses are the most notable, with their flowing wooden manes, tossed heads, carved and painted rococo harness, and extravagant names. 'Anderson, Carver, Decorator, Bristol' was one craftsman who was responsible for a particularly fine set of horses.

Stay busks (stiffeners inserted into the bodice of women's dress) were often chip carved with delicate geometrical patterns incorporating hearts, pairs of initials and dates, indicating their presentation as love tokens. Knitting-sheaths, which were tucked into the belt or apron-strings to take the weight of knitting, were similarly decorated as gifts.

Page 74 a Chip box with ribbons, Alsace, *c.* 1800; *b* Chip box, Germany

The majority of decorated stay busks date from the eighteenth century, especially the latter half, after which the style of dress requiring them went out of fashion.

The earliest dated knitting-sheath is inscribed '1686' and is known to have come from Wimborne in Dorset, one of the important knitting centres in the seventeenth century.

This and eighteenth-century specimens are usually straight and rectangular in section or only slightly tapered, with finely detailed chip carving and incised lines. A different shape, the 'goose wing', was made late in the eighteenth century and during the nineteenth, and was widely used in the North of England.

Gingerbread biscuits, formed into thin and imaginative shapes, must have been enjoyed by many generations of children during the three-hundred-year span of their sale at fairs, bakers' shops and village stores. The moulds were rectangular blocks of wood, about an inch thick, with a shallow intaglio carving in the centre. Two of the most interesting subjects were the Biddenden maids (an almost legendary pair of Siamese twins also portrayed on pottery) and the horn book (the alphabet on a small plaque with a handle).

Butter-pats, commonly made of sycamore, had a more limited range of subjects. Cows, swans, thistles, squirrels, strawberries and flowers were usual and there were some purely geometrical patterns. A heart motif was used on the round pounds of butter sent to market from Ormskirk, and a rose motif on rectangular pounds identified butter from Preston.

The brass poleheads of West Country friendly societies constitute an unusual group of vernacular objects whose design and purpose have only recently been fully investigated. Although many thousands of friendly societies of various kinds existed throughout the country during the eighteenth and nineteenth centuries, the use of brass poleheads was limited to Somerset and the surrounding counties. Each 'ordinary' club member had a brass, officers usually had a larger version, and there was sometimes an even larger one for the top of the flagpole. There are two main groups of designs, flat and three-dimensional. The majority of shapes in the flat group show interplay between the spear and the fleur-de-lis; besides the spear shapes, there is a range of figurative emblems, representing crowns, hearts, ships and anchors, animals, birds and stars. Many of these were adopted in reference to the sign of the public house where the club had its headquarters. Thus, the emblem of the 'Friendly Society of all Trades held at the House of Samuel Emmett known by the sign of the Salutation' depicted two men in top hats shaking hands. The three-dimensional friendly-society brasses were knobs of various kinds, often resembling the urn-shaped finials used on clocks and other household furniture. The turned column-shaped knobs, especially those with a cast eagle at the top, are reminiscent of English church lecterns.

Another range of brass ornaments, quite unrelated to club brasses except for their material and method of manufacture, was used on horse harness. Horse brasses were consistently designed within a circle about three inches in diameter, with a projecting loop at the top for suspension from a leather strap. They were made and used extensively by farmers and tradesmen during the nineteenth century. The horse wore a 'facepiece', a single brass, on its forehead and, above, a 'fly terret' or 'swinger'. This consisted of a brass, sometimes with a loose hanging centre, which stood upright. The 'martingale', running from the collar over the chest to the belly band, usually bore three or four brasses but could carry up to ten. Additional brasses hung on each side of the runners at the shoulders or loins. Narrow parts of the harness, the necklace and the leading rein had a row of small studs in the shape of hearts or diamonds. A 'flyer', a red or red-white-and-

and technique, and it is only in the very latest examples that degeneration of workmanship sets in.

Some simple children's toys and many items connected with popular customs and festival observances were made of straw and rushes. The toys include openwork rush rattles, ornamental whips and swords; the festival objects include straw and rush 'crosses' made for the feast of St Brigid. Only a minority of these latter objects are, in fact, cross-shaped, the commonest designs being the swastika, triskele and lozenge. The most attractive of the ceremonial items are the harvest knots which were made and worn during the corn harvest, particularly in the north of the country and in the extreme south. The straws were braided and bent into concentric loops or trefoils, the ears of the corn being incorporated in the knots worn by the women but cut off in those worn by the men.

The most considerable body of representational Irish folk art is to be found on a series of tombstones carved in the eighteenth century and the opening decades of the nineteenth. These are particularly numerous in the south-eastern quarter of the country, where many examples are to be seen in rural graveyards, but they are by no means restricted to that area. A number are signed with the sculptors' names, but the majority are the work of unknown local craftsmen. The tombstones are tall and rectangular, with rounded, cusped or triangular tops. The figure sculpture is confined to a relatively small panel filling the upper part of the stone in front. The scene depicted is, almost invariably, the Crucifixion, the cross occupying a central position in the panel. The remainder of the space is devoted to the symbols of Christ's Passion and to the Virgin, centurion, lance-bearer and other personages attendant on the Crucifixion. On many of the stones these figures are shown wearing the contemporary costume of the sculptor's day. While their arrangement differs from stone to stone, such symbols as the ladder, hammer, pincers and spear do not lend themselves to variety of treatment. Exceptions to this are the sun and moon, on the presentation of which many of the sculptors seem to have lavished all their powers of invention, the symbols being often partly anthropomorphized. In addition to the Passion symbols, doves, floral patterns, vases and urns of classical lineage, and churches appear on certain of the stones. The churches are sometimes rendered as elaborate confections of spires, cupolas, gables and other conspicuous architectural features and sometimes reduced to a mere symbolic dome or elementary Gothic façade. In view of the conspicuous axial position occupied by the cross, both figures and symbols tend to be arranged symmetrically about it, but in many of the better compositions any feeling of rigidity is successfully avoided. A lively note is frequently introduced by an attempt to portray the figures in action, their movements frequently taking the form of naively flamboyant gestures.

From this brief review it will be seen that Ireland presents an interesting case-history in the matter of folk art. It is evident that the political history of the country, which ultimately shaped its economic history and profoundly influenced its cultural history, was, to a considerable extent, responsible for the relatively rudimentary development of visual art. The extraordinary level of mental sophistication to be found among the people in general may to some extent be interpreted as a compensatory reaction to this visual deprivation; but no one at all familiar with the older native literature can doubt

Gable ornament, Geervliet, Netherlands

that a very substantial fraction of this intellectual creativity must be regarded as an old inherited tradition. Since, therefore, the national psychology ordained that so much of the time and energy of the population was to be spent in the aesthetic appreciation of non-material subjects, it is probable that, no matter how favourable conditions of life might have been, Ireland would still have lagged behind the average of European self-expression in folk art.

'*Stiepel*' ornament, Rikmans farm, Albergen, Netherlands

Gable ornament, Raatsink farm, Vasse, Netherlands

THE LOW COUNTRIES, stretching across the coastal plain from Dunkirk to Delfzijl, have been divided by centuries of political manoeuvre. For all their linguistic and cultural kinship, the people form a number of distinct and varied groups. There are more than eighteen million 'Netherlanders' in Europe, living in three separate political states: the north-western corner of France, more than half of Belgium (the two provinces which together make up Flanders) and the Netherlands proper, commonly known both abroad and, unofficially, at home, by the name of their most important province, Holland. North Germany too, where the North Sea plain continues up to the Baltic coast and along the lower Rhine, has many traits which are characteristic of the Low Countries. This is due not only to the close racial ties but also to the strong cultural influence which the Low Countries have exercised in the region over the last two centuries. Low German *(Nieder-deutsch, Nederduits,* 'Low Dutch'), a term which historically covers a range of dialects spoken from Dunkirk to the Baltic, has been a literary language since the twelfth century; it has always been a language of the people, just as nearly all the culture of the Low Countries is a popular culture. Dutch has always been able to accommodate neologisms and urban slang with greater ease than the High German language which sounds pedantic to the Dutch, and with immeasurably greater ease than polished, educated French, which has been so restricted in the last three centuries by the iron hand of the Académie Française. And what is true of the language is true of the people, of their culture and their art. Nowhere has 'high art', the art of the élite, been more 'popular' than in the Netherlands and nowhere, probably, does folk art cover such wide areas. They say that every nation has the régime it deserves; and the princes of the House of Orange were for centuries merely 'Servants of the State'; they did not exchange the title of *Stadhouder* for that of king until 1813. Holland and Flanders were governed by the representatives of the middle and lower classes, and their art has always had its roots in the life of ordinary people; painters like the Brueghels and Jan Steen have as much to say to the student of folk lore as to the art historian. Monumental art developed late, imported from the south for reasons of prestige. Its most imposing product is Amsterdam's massive Town Hall, followed by the sumptuous Stijlkamer in the Rijksmuseum. The Town Hall, faced in Bentheim stone, looks almost foreign and makes an effective contrast to the many gabled house fronts of Amsterdam, with their delightful alternation of red brick and sandstone, which are surely themselves typical products of Dutch folk art. Inscriptions and decorations on the gables bear witness to the occupants' love of art and of life, and no less cheerful are the hanging signs and the brightly, even garishly painted figures beside or over shop doors. Tobacconists used to display a pipe-smoking Red Indian, or West Indian Negro, and chemists the so-called *Gaper,* a yawning man; a number of examples of this particular figure have been preserved in the old apothecary's shop Van der Pigge in Haarlem. A German traveller in the nineteenth century tells how he came across a similar 'gaper' in the German town of Cleves and realized he must be near the Dutch border.

The popular, regional culture is still very strong in Frisia, the north-western part of the Netherlands, which has its own customs and way of life, its own language and its own literature. The traditional Frisian farmhouses of the type called *Kop-Hals-Romp* ('head-neck-trunk'), or with pyramidal roofs and gables decorated with swans, are still predominant in the green, fenlike country. The women still wear their elegant traditional costume on festive occasions. The traditional furniture of Hindeloopen, usually painted red, is still made today, and so are the standing clocks made in Joure in Frisia and the blue, hand-painted Frisian tiles, the manufacture of which has been in the hands of one family in Makkum for centuries.

The eastern provinces of the Netherlands – Drente, Overijssel and east Gelderland – are the least influenced by urban culture. The Twente farmhouse preserved an early Germanic layout until recent times, with its one extraordinary, unpartitioned room to house men and beasts alike. This diluvial region has centuries-old links with the neighbouring part of Lower Saxony, along the river Ems, and its houses are very closely related to the Lower Saxon farmhouse found throughout north Germany. The huge double barn doors are characteristic. Above them is a carved oak beam with an inscription, usually a biblical text, and the year of the building's construction. The central doorpost, called a *stiepel*, is removable, and often carved. There is a *stiepel* in the Rijksmuseum, Twente, dated 1637, which has at the top a clearly delineated Calvary and below it a six-pointed star, probably an elementary archaic year symbol. Its two triangles give it an unmistakable resemblance to the hour-glass, a common symbol of passing time, particularly in cemeteries. The *stiepel* protected the house and thus played an important role in folk customs. The traditional Easter dance performed by

Left: Pilgrimage banner, Flanders, eighteenth century

Page 83 a, b Painted lids of lacquer boxes, Russia, nineteenth century

a

b

a

b

c

d

e

f

g

the entire population of the village of Ootmarsum, led the men, singing Easter songs, round the *stiepels* of several farmhouses, which backed on to the street as is usual in eastern Holland. In folk myth, the *stiepel* is the protective boundary of the farmhouse. Anyone who fled behind the *stiepel* in time was safe from pursuing witches and evil spirits. The *stiepel* of the Venrink farm in Hengelo has an hour-glass carved on it, painted white

80

and dark green, with above it a yellow six-pointed star in an oval frame. The *stiepel* of the Rikmans farm in Albergen, on the other hand, has a solar disc divided into six parts, in chip carving. The *stiepel* is painted white and the doors green, the usual colours for exterior paintwork in the Netherlands. Symbols relating to popular myths are also

81

carved on the gables, frequently stylized horses' heads, like those on the Raatsink farm in Vasse. The owl-hole at the peak of the gable is also typical, an opening for owls to fly through at dusk.

In the neighbouring, Protestant region of Vriezenveen, the decoration of the gables is strictly ornamental and allows hardly any symbolic interpretation. This is probably due to the influence of the 'chalet' style, which was once very popular for summer houses, verandas and the like. The gable ornament of cross and crescent moon on the Ter Braak farm in Geesteren appears to have sprung from the same influence. The Ensink farm in Volthe displays true peasant, Catholic piety in the ornament on its gable: the three crosses of Golgotha above a six-pointed star. There are *stiepels* with other symbols in other

79

provinces, for example, arrows, as in Geervliet near Rotterdam, but nowhere are they so fine or so pronounced as in Twente, which before industrialization had one of the largest stocks of traditional lore in the Netherlands. The only ornaments analogous to the *stiepels* outside these three provinces are the gables found in Frisia.

It is amazing to see how local and regional popular culture has remained alive, even near the big cities of the west. Within the administrative boundaries of The Hague, for instance, lies Scheveningen, where the older women remain faithful to their traditional costume with its delicate, pale shawl. In the immediate vicinity of Amsterdam are the village of Volendam and the former island of Marken. Volendam is a Catholic community, and although the men have almost all abandoned the ancient ways, the women's charming costume alters slightly with the seasons, proof that the tradition is still a live

102a

one. Protestant Marken, for its part, has preserved seventeenth-century garments which the people wear at Whitsuntide, for the *Baslopen*. Their dress is so bound by traditions, so conservative, that it even escaped the general tendency of costumes in other regions to become more sober and restrained during the nineteenth century: the women of

168b

Marken present a blaze of brilliant colour like an Oriental carpet. They and the women of Volendam are still to be met with in the middle of bustling Amsterdam, doing their shopping. The finest examples of the art of the people who lived on the shores of what

Page 84 a Casket, Denmark; *b* Casket, Briançon, Hautes-Alpes; *c* Horn salt cellar, Somogy, Hungary, 1869; *d* Casket, Hame, Finland; *e* Spoonbox, Scotland; *f* Cork casket, Alentejo, Portugal; *g* Hanging box, Austria, 1697

was once the Zuiderzee are in the Zuiderzee-Museum in Enkhuizen. As well as in Volendam and Marken there are still many remnants of the traditions of the old fishing communities, including fine costumes, in Bunschoten-Stakenburg in the province of Utrecht. On the former island of Urk the men's costume is preserved from extinction by local glee-clubs. Another museum of folk art, one which is still building up its collection, is the Zaanse-Schans, not far from Zaandam. Immediately opposite the Dutch Mill

Museum where 101 windmills are ranged impressively along the busy river Zaan, this museum is preserving the popular domestic culture of the region. By far the most important collection of Dutch folk culture, however, is in the large open-air museum in Arnhem, the Nederlands Openluchtmuseum.

Among the many forms in Dutch folk art not found in other countries are the characteristic wall tiles (in so far as their subject and quality do not mark them out as made for the urban or courtly élite by professional artists). From the seventeenth to the nineteenth century these typified the appearance of living-rooms all along the North Sea coast from France to Jutland, particularly where the walls and stove-surrounds were not panelled with wood. They depicted ships, sea monsters, proverbs, children's games, animals, flowers and any number of biblical subjects. They were all painted by hand from stencils and present perhaps the most interesting and original picture of the life of ordinary Dutch people, and certainly the best known, thanks in no small measure to the enthusiasm of many modern collectors. A fine example of their use is a room fitted with tiles in 1767 in the old farmhouse at Noord-Akendam. As well as a whole gallery of biblical scenes, a kind of ceramic *biblia pauperum*, which may have stimulated the imagination of storytellers in a bygone age, there are bouquets of flowers in the luxuriant, popular baroque style, painted bird cages and something rather rare: four naive drawings of *commedia dell'arte* figures, which presumably reflect a love of the theatre on the part of the former owner. One of the harlequins, in a costume of bright checks, carries a *billet-doux* addressed 'To my darling, 1767' which establishes the date of the wall. The second is dancing and swinging a club, while the third, in a striped costume, is carrying a basket full of round-headed kittens, which he is apparently going to drown. The fourth wants to play the violin but cannot find his bow – a tragicomic routine which is still in the repertoire of the modern circus clown.

The province of Zeeland has a remarkable stock of magnificent costumes which vary from one village to the next, according to whether the population is Protestant or Catholic. Another art which is still practised in this province is the carving of knife handles. In the heart of the Low Countries, where the broad, stately rivers make their way to the sea, the richly decorated carts of the peasants used to roll along the narrow winding dikes. These carts are hardly less impressive than the festive carts of Sicily, though quite different. Some idea of their past glory can be gained in the museum in the small town of Buren in Gelderland.

The folk art peculiar to the province of North Brabant includes the large, top-heavy caps, called *poffers*, worn by the women, and the grotesque walking-sticks, carved by shepherds. Most of these come from the marshy region called De Peel, on the border of Limburg. The most interesting centre of folk art in this province is the pottery at Tegelen, near Venlo. This flourished during the mid-nineteenth century and has been revived recently as a rural industry.

266a–d

A feature of the Catholic provinces of North Brabant and Limburg is the number of works of religious folk art – crucifixes, pictures of St Rock, field chapels, wayside crosses, and images of saints and martyrs – which stand at cross-roads and waysides and have become an inseparable part of the landscape.

The region known as Flanders, too, the Belgian provinces of Limburg, Antwerp, Brabant, East and West Flanders, the corner of France about Dunkirk and French-speaking

Wallonia, has its own characteristic forms of folk art. Where the soil is sandy the farmhouses are very simple, with all the windows and door on one side only. In loess regions farms are built on the square plan, which is certainly autochthonous and not derived from the Roman villa, found across Europe from the Atlantic to Slovakia. Wallonia is noted for its imaginative glass animals, for copper and tin ware and for the famous puppets which have made Liège the capital of European puppetry. This region also produces interesting pilgrimage banners. Last but not least, we must mention the famous Flanders lace which, among other uses, is one of the main materials on the traditional headdresses worn in the Netherlands.

Belgium too has its public collections of folk art and lore; there are folk museums in Bruges, Ghent, Antwerp and Liège, and there is an open-air museum in the wooded park of Bokrijk in Belgian Limburg. Here in barren, sandy Kempenland there is a whole village of which the centre consists of the simple, old-fashioned buildings, living rooms and stables typical of the region, with an additional part in the style of a west Flemish village. The peasants' day-to-day existence, their past way of life, is here reconstructed in a manner that conforms closely to the known facts.

GERMANY offers as great a variety in native types of houses as it does in landscape. The exteriors bear witness to the activities of folk artists: horses' heads or other animal figures, which crown the gables of farmhouses in northern Germany, the half-timbered *Fachwerk* houses, particularly in Hesse and Franconia, are richly carved; the same is true of gates and doors everywhere. In Hesse the surfaces between the individual timbers are skilfully decorated with patterns scratched in the plaster. The simplicity of this art is in sharp contrast to the elaborate painted façades of houses in the south, a style which originated in the cities of Innsbruck and Augsburg, and was influenced by the painting on church ceilings. Inside houses, the main living-room, the *Stube*, is the one most demanding attention, all over Germany, from the south, through the farms of central Germany, where the various buildings group themselves round a courtyard, accessible from the road by a tall gate, to the north. Here, since the late Middle Ages, the *Stube* has formed a part of the long main building of the farm, a simple rectangular structure with a gabled roof. It is open at one end so that the wagons can drive right in and the corn can be stored under the roof. The cattle stalls and stables are on either side of this broad entrance hall *(Diele)*, while at the inner end is the kitchen area *(Flett)*, which often occupies the whole width of the building and has an open fireplace. Other rooms for living and sleeping were added on the far side of the wall behind the fireplace, rooms which were warmed but remained free of smoke. In southern Germany the *Stube* resembles the living-rooms of Switzerland and Austria. The walls are often panelled, and sometimes even painted, like the furniture, as in Bavaria, Swabia and Baden. The stove may be tiled, or made of cast iron plates, as it is in Baden and Swabia. In one of the corners across the room from it hangs a crucifix, surrounded by holy pictures; this is the 'Lord's corner' *(Herrgottswinkel)*. The table stands below it, with benches running along the two walls.

In northern Germany, where walls are either panelled or tiled in the Dutch manner, box beds, known as *Butzen* or *Durks*, are concealed behind the panels or tiles. In the south, beds are rarely found in the living-room. The rooms are heated by cast iron stoves,

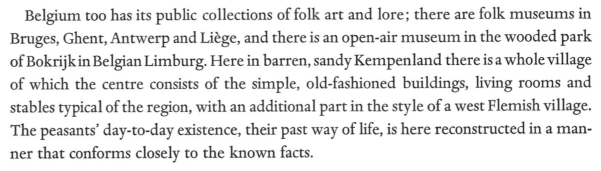

82

86, 87

25

Above and left: Lace, Bruges

20, 34a

87

decorated in this part of the country, as elsewhere, with biblical scenes or other representational motifs. Painted walls were once common, as for example in the 'summer rooms' of the Wilstermarsch region. These rooms had no fireplace, like the *Pesel* of eastern and northern Frisia and other parts of Slesvig (Schleswig) and Holstein. They were intended for formal entertaining, while the *Döns*, which could be heated, was the real living-room.

The principal articles of furniture in peasant houses were benches, wooden settles, chairs and stools, beds, chests and cupboards, with occasionally such extra pieces as chests of drawers and writing-desks.

The chairs and benches were usually the work of the local turner in north Germany, whose influence on styles of furniture was greater in the Middle Ages than in more modern times. Regional conservatism in forms is not surprising, and can be seen in the three-cornered panel and post chairs of the lower Rhine region and Westphalia, or in the armchairs of Schleswig-Holstein, whose construction is equally archaic, the seat being supported between posts at each corner, which also support the back and arm rests. The combined chair and footstool found in central and southern Germany is a less ancient form; the splay legs and the backrest are set into the seat. The back and arms may be curved and the plane surfaces have carved and fretwork patterns on them. Animals are popular motifs: pelicans facing each other in Hesse, entwined serpents on the upper Rhine and everywhere the two-headed eagle in various forms which bear little or no resemblance to the heraldic original. Symmetry is prevalent, though sometimes abandoned under rococo influence. The bride-chairs of Hesse are unusual, with the footrest common to the region added to the kind of panel and post chair found further north. Large numbers of them have survived from the period between the mid-eighteenth and mid-nineteenth centuries. The bride was enthroned on it as she and her dowry were driven to the bridegroom's home.

Tables were generally plain, unless the turner exercised his powers of invention on the legs. These, whether upright or splay, were usually strengthened by horizontal stretchers. North German houses usually had trestle tables.

The four-poster bed with its canopy and tall head and foot boards survived in country districts long after the end of the Middle Ages. It was found in the houses of north Germany, besides the box beds already mentioned. Both kinds were hung with curtains. In the second half of the eighteenth century the four-poster bed was replaced by a newer style from the south, with elaborately shaped head and foot boards. Most babies' cradles had rockers placed crosswise so that the child was rocked from side to side, though in Hesse and neighbouring parts of Westphalia the cradle rocked from end to end. In southern Germany cradles were generally lower and smaller than in the north.

All clothing and linen was originally stored in chests; in some remote districts, the Schwalm region of Hesse for instance, chests continued to serve this function until the twentieth century. They were also used to store corn and flour. The oldest chests were raised clear of the damp earth floors by one of two methods. In northern Germany the posts at each corner were usually extended downward; in the south it was generally the side panels that were extended. The exact distribution of these two methods has not been established. During the seventeenth century a third kind of raised chest was intro-

Page 89 a Powderhorn, Netherlands; *b* Drinking-horn, Salamanca; *c* Powderhorn, Teteven, Bulgaria, 1849

Page 90 Mangle boards and clothes-beaters: *a* Angermanland, Sweden, 1779; *b* Steigerwald, Germany, 1844; *c* Uppland, Sweden; *d* Southern Alps, 1753; *e* Södermanland, Sweden; *f* Northern Frisia, 1790; *g* Sweden, 1784; *h* Netherlands, 1741; *i* Denmark; *j* Northern Frisia, eighteenth century

88

a   b   c   d   e

f   g   h   i   j

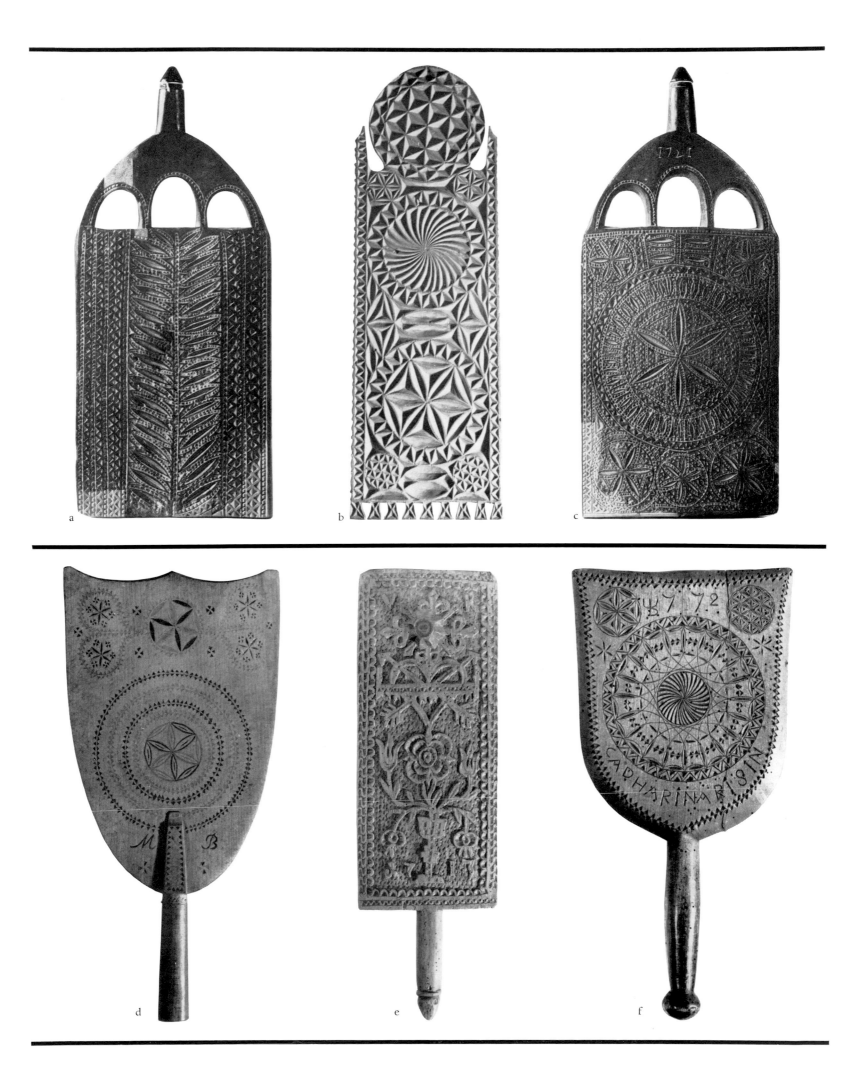

58c, d
40a, 53b

duced standing on stretchers which were connected at the front by a board set at an angle. These stretchers were used on other pieces of furniture in northern Germany, such as dressers and cupboards. The lids of these chests were usually level, perhaps sloping at the front and back edges. The kind of chest with a lid like a gabled roof, which is more common in Switzerland, serves as a flour bin in the Rhön area of Hesse. The earlier mediaeval chests were usually the work of carpenters; the more advanced craft of cabinet making arose in southern and central Germany in the late Middle Ages. The chests they made have dovetail joints and stand on bases which at first were separate pieces, but gradually came to be a part of the chest. The spherical feet of some chests, like those from the Vierlande, near Hamburg, were probably influenced by cupboards made for towns-people. The coffer with a vaulted lid found principally in northern Germany was a form developed later still. It often had iron mountings like those of the very earliest chests.

Cupboards became more common in farmhouses during the eighteenth century. The oldest forms are often as wide as they are high, perhaps to compensate for the limit set on their height by low ceilings. Wardrobes with only one door were common in the south and east; in the north cupboards, even in country districts, were more strongly influenced by the styles fashionable in the Hanseatic cities, with elaborate panelled fronts and top-heavy pediments. In the Oldenburg district, between the Weser and the Ems, cupboards were made in two parts, one above the other, until the eighteenth century, a form which reflects the development of the cupboard from the chest, as does the division of the doors into four panels. Food store-cupboards of a pattern which has hardly altered since the Middle Ages can still be found in Franconia. Tall and narrow, they are raised off the floor and in some cases have separate doors for the top and bottom halves. In north and central Germany earthenware and pewter was stored on the upper shelves of dressers, the lower part of which was a closed cupboard. Round-bowled spoons were placed between wooden pegs. In Hesse the shelves on which plates and dishes were stacked had a wooden rim, while cups and jugs hung on hooks. In some parts of Schleswig-Holstein the more valuable pieces were kept in a *Hörnschapp*, a kind of corner cupboard which is square instead of triangular, and carved on both faces. It is in three parts, the smaller central section forming a recess between the upper and lower cabinets.

The differences between houses in various parts of the country are matched by differences in the furniture. One reason why painted decoration is less common in the north than in the south is that the open hearth and its smoke were banished from the living-room at a later date in the north. However, the existing evidence forbids too facile a division of a south glowing with painted furniture from a sombre, paintless north. Oak was the wood most frequently used in the north and was never painted, while softer woods such as pine often were. Painted furniture is found in eastern Frisia, where the colour often serves to draw attention to the carving, and in Brunswick as well as Pomerania and East Prussia. In the south painted furniture was common from the seventeenth century onwards, though at first the colour was not spread over the whole article as it was later. A particularly fine example of seventeenth- and early eighteenth-century furniture is given by the 'Turkish' style (*Türkenmöbel*), decorated with domes and made in the Schliersee–Tegernsee district of Upper Bavaria, which appears to have been inspired by Renaissance inlay work. Colours and patterns, for which there was most

Page 91 a Clothes-beater, Calabria; *b* Chip-carved spindle, Yugoslavia; *c* Clothes-beater, Calabria; *d* Flax swingle, Rügen; *e* Mangle board, Lungau, Salzburg, 1717; *f* Clothes-beater, South Tyrol, 1772

Page 92 a–c Powderhorns, Salamanca: *a, b* 1848, *c* 1875; *d–f* Drinking-horns: *d, f* Northern England, *e* Hadersleben, Denmark

scope on the larger surfaces of beds and cupboards, are markedly different in the nineteenth century from what they were in the eighteenth. In Tölz, in Upper Bavaria, there was a style of furniture which reached its peak of colourful exuberance in the last thirty years of the eighteenth century, and was sold far and wide. Bunches of flowers, various versions of *rocaille*, and pietistic subjects such as the Sacred Heart, were among the most popular motifs. The community of Exulantes, founded in 1722 at Herrnhut in Saxony, made furniture during the eighteenth century that was painted in the popular style, with religious texts as their basic motifs. The community also made furniture for middle-class customers. Painted furniture reached Silesia at the beginning of the eighteenth century. It also became popular in Franconia, but was less so in neighbouring Hesse. The bride-chairs that have already been mentioned started to be painted at the beginning of the nineteenth century, whereas formerly they had been carved. Inlay, which was superseded further south by painting, remained the customary form of decoration in Hesse until the nineteenth century. Intarsia was used on wall panelling and furniture in the Vierlande, where the style reached its peak around the year 1800. Flowers in antique vases, birds on flowering shrubs, allegorical figures, such as Hope, were among the motifs most frequently used. Plants were commonly given three shoots, which is an identifying characteristic of the style, as is the use of the spiral rosette. The oak furniture of northern Germany was commonly carved in incised technique. The choice of ornamental motifs varied at different times and in different places, as with the painted decoration of the south. In eastern Frisia a tulip with three branches was often chosen. The sunflower and the grape were very popular. In the country lying north of Osnabrück dragons were carved following standard patterns. Human figures were rare.

Smaller wooden articles were decorated in all kinds of ways. There was no end to the different patterns carved and painted on boxes of all sizes. The mediaeval custom of giving little caskets as love tokens persisted for a long time in peasant society. In many parts of the country they were often decorated with chip carving in geometrical patterns. Chip carving also occurs on the mangle boards found in north Germany, the handles of which are carved in the form of fabulous animals and are small works of art in themselves. On the island of Rügen the chip carving of flax swingles was inlaid with coloured wax. The equipment used at every stage of textile manufacture – flax brakes, spinning-wheels, reels – was always elaborately decorated. Salt cellars and spoon racks were usually carved. In Westphalia the backs of spoon racks were carved with a style of fretwork also used on chair backs. Wood was for many centuries the customary material for every kind of household container: drinking-flasks hollowed on a lathe, pitchers and tubs made of slats. The most primitive equipment could at least be of an interesting shape, and some articles were customarily painted, like some types of jug in Hesse and Franconia. Certain objects traditionally connected with particular occupations, for instance the carved and painted cattle-collars with bells on them, were made by the herdsmen themselves. Many of these collars are still to be found in Franconia.

Chip boxes, made of single-ply wood strips bent round an oval base (*Spanschachteln*), were found in every part of Germany. They came in various different sizes and had all sorts of uses. The earlier ones were decorated with marbled patterns, spirals and flowers; in the eighteenth century they might have pictures of ladies and their beaux, soldiers or

Christmas biscuit-mould, Northern Frisia

67b, 68d

134, 3rd row, right

154g

136b

animals, and often a motto as well. Berchtesgaden was a centre of the manufacture of these boxes.

The willow baskets woven by peasants are not only of a pleasing shape but the combination of coloured and natural wood results in most attractive patterns. Among the most decorative is the type made in Bavaria, Baden and Franconia where gaily coloured strips of leather are also woven in. In the Lichtenfels district of Franconia, basket weaving took on the proportions of a cottage industry.

The open fireplaces of the farmhouses of northern Germany called for a wide variety of iron equipment, which was made by local smiths. Pots and kettles were suspended over the fire on adjustable hooks which were secured to an axle. Firedogs kept the burning logs from falling, and curfews banked the fire in at night. The monuments in cemeteries, too, were often made of iron, and in the southern part of the country votive gifts of human and animal figures made of iron were offered to St Leonard, the patron of prisoners and animals. Individual objects are hard to date, though technical criteria allow a relative chronology to be established. Archaic forms, of the kind which have been found in excavations in Württemberg and Franconia, persisted tenaciously. As well as ironware, north German households used copper, particularly for footwarmers and warming pans. The metal was usually decorated with openwork and embossed ornaments.

With rare exceptions earthenware goods were not decorated in the Middle Ages. Coloured glazes began to be used in the sixteenth century. Nuremberg, Cologne, and Annaberg in Saxony were centres which pioneered the production of ornamental pottery, and a folk style evolved in imitation. A mixture of soft clay and metal oxide was piped in patterns through a nozzle, much like the method of icing a cake. With some kinds of ware the pattern was drawn in the glaze. An early centre was established at Wanfried on the river Werra, in Hesse, which sold its goods down the River Weser, in northern Germany. The red-brown ware was decorated with incised figures. From the mid-seventeenth century onwards, display dishes were made in the region north of Krefeld in the Rhineland, which depicted craftsmen at work, or religious subjects, notably the miraculous image in the shrine at Krevekar. These continued to be made into the eighteenth century. Other motifs were horsemen and Prince Eugene, and sometimes there was an accompanying text. Tiles for lining the walls behind the stove were made in large quantities. Silesia was another early centre for folk pottery. The best known ware was probably that made at Bunzlau (now Boleslawiec), with its characteristic dully gleaming brown glaze, with a white clay relief decoration representing flowers or such symbolic figures as the Lamb of God. Relief decoration was also used on the large round pots with handles, the tureens and the cylindrical jugs made in Marburg after about the year 1800. The decoration of leaves, flowers and animals was often applied in many different colours, usually by women and girls.

The shapes of folk pottery are often copied from faience and porcelain ware. Many different types of painted patterns evolved. A luxuriant foliage which spreads all over the article on a white or cream background is typical of one kind of pottery made in Schleswig-Holstein, while the potters of Kröning near Landshut in Lower Bavaria produced some highly original ware, such as trick drinking-vessels which could have been made for a Renaissance hoaxer. They also made knitting and sewing 'baskets', probably modelled on some of the finest pottery made for townspeople. The sides had a pattern of little holes, and often there were animals on them, coated with shreds of fine clay to represent fur. Clay ornaments, jugs in the form of a hedgehog or a mole, would be given a naturalistic coat of this kind. In this part of Germany painting was a less common form of decoration. The plates and pear-shaped jugs of Transylvania used to have tulips and animals painted in blue on a white background, but after 1800 this was reversed and the pattern was outlined in white on a blue ground.

The stoneware made in Höhr-Grenzhausen in the Westerwald, the wooded hill coun-try between the Rhine and the Lahn, was very popular. The range of colours was limited by the extremely high temperature at which the ware had to be baked, and the pots were grey with blue plants and scrolls on them, painted by the local 'blue-girls' (Blau-mädchen). The larger pots and jugs are often relatively late products. In the eighteenth century, besides tableware, clock cases, crucifixes and holy-water basins were among the things made in the Westerwald. This ware is sometimes confused with that made in Hausen, near Giessen, on the other bank of the Lahn, and pots and cans of a similar appearance have been found which were made in Wattenheim in the Palatinate and in Stadtlohn and Warendorf in Westphalia. 147c

Folk painting on glass, particularly on square schnaps-bottles, is similar in subject matter to the painting on the oval chip boxes already described. It is impossible to ascribe individual articles to any one of the several places where they are known to have been made. Painted window panes are a speciality of Lower Saxony, where they were given to a person building a new house by his neighbours. The colours were the same as those used in other kinds of glass-painting; pictures were later replaced by mottoes written in blacklead. 165a, b

When peasant fabrics have a pattern it is often strictly geometrical, like the typical Schleswig-Holstein weaves, or the 'stoned' double linen weaves of Hesse, which were used to make cushion covers and curtains for four-poster beds. Naive representational motifs appear in reversible materials, a simpler version of which was used in dress-making, and in linen damask. Reversible, pictorial tapestries were peculiar to Schleswig-Holstein, where they served to conceal the box beds round the room. There are three types of design: those which are geometrical; those which imitate silken damask with representations of plants and of such animals as the unicorn, the lion and the pelican; and those which depict human figures, in biblical scenes, allegories of the four quarters of the globe, or scenes from the story of Pyramus and Thisbe. 26–7

42, 43

The earliest centres of the manufacture of linen damask in Germany were in Silesia, Saxony and Frisia, followed by Hesse, Brandenburg, Pomerania, Augsburg and the area around Bielefeld. Patterns were at first executed in white on white until about 1700, when blue-and-white or red-and-white fabrics began to appear. Frequent motifs of these coloured damasks were biblical or hunting scenes and panoramic views of towns. Hirsch-berg (now Jelenia Gora), Schmiedeberg and Greiffenberg in Silesia, and Gross-Schönau in Saxony, produced some of the finest examples.

The patterns used in the linen damasks reappear in folk prints. The pattern is drawn in outline and treated with a dye-repellent, and then the fabric is dyed. It is hard to ascribe individual fabrics to particular regions; Hesse certainly produced a large quantity. During the eighteenth century the techniques of calico printing improved under the influence of imported Indian cottons, and, even in country districts, prints largely replaced woven patterns, which were more expensive.

The Mazurian knotted wedding tapestries of the eighteenth century possess a clear ceremonial significance. They are made of wool, dyed in a wide variety of colours. The surface consists of a central field surrounded by a border, which may be broad or narrow. They bear a resemblance to the tapestries of Scandinavia and Finland, although the subject matter is unique: plants, animals, human couples and buildings with three towers.

The kind of embroidery used on domestic articles is well represented by samplers, usually signed with initials and a date. Their designs are based on pattern books and the most common stitch is cross stitch. Samplers from the Vierlande and the Altes Land, which lie along the Elbe, to the south of Hamburg, are distinguished from those made elsewhere by the exclusive use of black thread. Cross stitch was used a great deal in German communities in Transylvania. On large articles like tablecloths and blankets it is often used as an outline stitch, with other stitches to fill in the pattern. Here, too, the use of only one colour was favoured, particularly red or blue, though sometimes they are found together.

Christmas biscuit-mould, Northern Frisia

Franconian embroidery, which also includes a lot of cross stitch, produces a wide variety of pattern in subtle nuances of colour. Often folk embroidery reveals baroque and rococo influences, as for example on the cushion-covers made in Schleswig-Holstein and the embroidered handkerchiefs made in the marshy district between the Lüneburg Heath and the Elbe, around the town of Winsen. One of the most important applications of embroidery was on the traditional folk costumes, particularly the women's caps, shawls and aprons. Tinsel and metal and glass beads are often included in the needlework. In Mecklenburg and Brunswick shawls are bordered with flowers and there is a diagonal division in the pattern. The two halves are embroidered in different colour schemes, so that the appropriate side for different occasions can be turned outermost: a bright side for holidays and celebrations, and a dark one for mourning and attending holy communion. The costume worn in the Schaumburg area includes an apron, with particularly brightly coloured material and embroidery. Men's costumes were also embroidered, notably the fur waistcoats and cloaks worn in Transylvania, made by professional furriers, who also used *appliqué* and braid. In Hesse various kinds of eyelet work were commonly used to embroider shirts and the hems of sheets and handkerchiefs. Other beautiful examples of folk embroidery include the headscarves worn in the Forchheim district of Franconia – the manner of wearing is unique in itself – and the embroidered collars and aprons made of finest lawn worn in Silesia in the Hirschberg valley. The latter were probably derived from the dress of townswomen in the early part of the nineteenth century.

Folk costumes generally tend to preserve upper-class fashions of the past. The costume worn by men in Hesse is clearly based on eighteenth-century dress. The knee-breeches fashionable in the same period are a part of most folk costumes. The kerchief which was formerly worn crossed over the shirt front was replaced by the short waistcoat which

168d

became fashionable among townsmen in the early nineteenth century. It is interesting to note the influence of military uniforms, for example in inland areas of the north German plain. Headgear, again, is generally derived from late eighteenth-century models, the tricorn and the early top hat of the 1790s. The pleated, full, short skirts of the women follow styles fashionable in the eighteenth and nineteenth centuries. By the time folk costumes began to be collected for museums, women's short coats often reflected Biedermeier fashions of the 1840s, while the bodices were still eighteenth-century in style. Headdresses are so multifarious that it is impossible to point out particular influences.

180a–d

By and large it is possible to say that the costumes worn in the Catholic parts of Germany are more colourful than in Protestant areas. This is particularly well illustrated in some of the villages near Marburg and in Franconia. The degree to which the actual wearers were prepared to adopt or reject new fashions, to mix old and new, or to adapt the new to what they already wore, varied from one region to another, even from one village to the next, and the motives behind such variations are often hard to grasp. A young woman's trousseau was usually made up by the village dressmaker, who naturally had a great influence on the costume peculiar to the village. The textiles came from mills which supplied fabrics and trimmings made up specially for peasants, and differing from those required for townspeople. The embroidery was by no means always the work of the actual wearer: there were women who specialized in embroidering headdresses, and in stitching gold and silver thread on caps. The wearing of the traditional costumes has been dying out for the last hundred years; usually men relinquished it earlier than women.

The variations in regional costumes can be studied in picture series which bear witness to a long-established interest in this aspect of rural life, an interest that intensified in the romantic era. Interest in folk art as a whole has been more general since the latter part of the nineteenth century, the initial impulse coming from professional artists in search of new sources of inspiration.

Differences in age and status were reflected in costume conventions, and everyday dress differed from that worn at festivals and celebrations. In many parts of the country brides wore a wreath or a crown covered with fabric or paper flowers, glass balls and stamped tin figures. Churchgoing habits were strong and received formal expression in peasant costume.

186

Metal ornaments were worn, particularly in the north. They were usually silver, except in Frisia and Silesia, where gold was used. The goldsmiths and silversmiths in the country towns made the traditional forms of earrings, necklaces, buttons, buckles for belts and shoes, and scent boxes for the peasants. The *Gadderke*, the pendant worn on the breast in the Saterland region near Oldenburg, is a particularly complicated form. Brooches are often heart-shaped, though some regions developed special forms; in Schaumburg, for instance, they are octagonal, while in Stade they resemble mediaeval ring-shaped fibulas. Filigree was widely prized, not only in the north, but in Franconia and in the south generally, where it was used for the links of rosaries. Amber was popular, not only in Pomerania where it came from, but also in Brunswick and Bückeburg.

The carving of domestic equipment and furniture, chair backs for instance, has been interpreted as an attempt to imbue the object with the qualities of the creature portrayed. The openings of runs of millstones in the mills on the upper Rhine are carved as the mouths of demons and are called *Breikotzer* (literally, 'bran spewers'). Demons also appear on beehives to frighten away honey thieves; they are also said to protect against sickness. Some beehives are made in the shape of larger-than-life human figures; the twenty-one figures formerly in Höfel in Silesia are often mentioned.

Woodcarving was centred around Oberammergau and Berchtesgaden, in Bavaria. Many of the religious images, crucifixes, statues of the saints and cribs found all over southern Germany were made in Ammergau. Besides these religious figures smaller articles for the home were made, clock cases and the toys which are the best and most widely known products of Berchtesgaden. Berchtesgaden also influenced toy production in the Erzgebirge, the mountains on the Bohemian border, where manufacture was centred on Seiffen; both regions shared a distribution centre, Nuremberg, which made an exchange of ideas possible. A wide variety of articles, made partly by hand, partly with the help of the lathe, went all over the world from these mountain villages. The toy industry in Sonneberg in Thuringia was also important. Another occasion for the wood-carver's art was provided by the wooden Christmas pyramids of the Erzgebirge, decorated with biblical characters and pictures of miners. These are known to have been made since at least 1800 and used to be customary in north and east Germany, before they were ousted by the Christmas tree.

Wooden models in glass bottles have long been the delight of collectors. The parts were put inside separately and assembled in the bottle. They were made not only in the south but also in Brandenburg and Pomerania; they depicted religious subjects and mining scenes, and there were also the model ships made by sailors in their spare time.

Peasants' houses used to be full of painted decorations, on the furniture, on the chip boxes and on household utensils. The votive pictures in shrines are the result of joyful emotions seeking expression in brilliant colours. They were the usual means of expressing thanks for answered prayers and they followed centuries-old conventions. The artists usually came from the same station in life as the people who commissioned them.

In the late eighteenth and early nineteenth centuries a new art form evolved in the Black Forest, Bavaria and Silesia. This was painting on glass, a method used for votive pictures, but to a greater extent for religious pictures hung in the home, as well as for non-religious pictures, genre scenes and portraits. The picture was painted on the side of the glass that was to hang against the wall. They were first made by glaziers and later by pedlars and printers. Franz Marc and Vassily Kandinsky published votive pictures and paintings on glass in the *Blauer Reiter* almanac in 1912, which did a great deal to arouse wider interest in this genuinely popular art.

AUSTRIAN folk art is conditioned to a great extent by geographical and historical factors. By far the larger part of what has survived dates from after the end of the Middle Ages. The tremendous upheavals which accompanied the Reformation and Counter-Reformation caused mediaeval folk art to vanish almost without trace, except for such humble remnants as the unglazed household pottery excavated by archaeologists. The religious and political forces of the Counter-Reformation brought Austria into closer contact with the Mediterranean lands, particularly Italy and Spain; their influences can be seen in folk

246e

Carpenter's sign, sheet iron, Austria, *c.* 1800

208b

99

art from costumes to majolica ware. The northern part of the country had more ties with Swabia and Bavaria, to the west, and with Moravia, though relatively few with Bohemia. The movement of travelling workmen, tinkers and toysellers meant lively contacts with Slovakia, then part of Hungary.

Many aspects of folk art were less localized than has later been supposed. Paintings on glass from the Bohemian Forest and Sandl in Upper Austria were carried by pedlars to all parts of the Habsburg domains. The enforced idleness of winter months led to the establishment of domestic industries in mountain areas. Numerous home workshops, turning out woodwork, toys and so on, existed in Gröden and Villnöss in the southern Tyrol and in Viechtau in Upper Austria, while some Alpine valleys, such as the Deferegental in the eastern Tyrol, specialized in making tapestries. Goods made out of horn and bone, like spoons and snuff boxes, had their own centres, Sterzing and Bruneck in the Trentino. With the introduction of the mercantile system in the sixteenth century there was an intensification of small-scale rural industries of this kind, such as the weaving of braids in the forests of Lower Austria and the manufacture of pottery (*Hafner* ware) for everyday use in central Burgenland.

The whole of Austrian folk art can be seen to arise out of the people's way of life and to serve it. It is present everywhere, not just in the external features of the cultural environment, the wayside Calvary, the belfry on the housetop, but in every hand-made article. The very houses and outbuildings are the products of folk art, in outline and in detail: the carved roof beams and the frescoes of houses in the Tyrol, the timbered ceilings, the chimney corners, the crucifix hanging in the corner of the living-rooms and attic bedrooms of Upper Austria. Even the gateways and doors, and the roofed terraces found at the side of houses in eastern Austria, are often decorated with a high degree of artistic skill. On houses with roofs supported by purlins, which had a more gentle slope, it was customary to place balconies on the gable walls, with railings which invited elaborate carving. The fireplace was the most important indoor feature. The gradual replacement of the open hearth and smoking fires by, in most cases, the tiled stove, made it possible to introduce a wealth of shapes and colours into the farmhouse. Carved and painted coffers were customary from the late Middle Ages, as were chests incorporating drawers, from the seventeenth century onwards. Cabinets built into the wall had a long tradition. The ponderous tables were made of thick maple boards, sometimes inlaid with slate, as in the Montafon valley in Vorarlberg for instance, or with a dark wood; or they were painted, particularly in the Enns valley. There would usually be one panel and post chair in the room for the head of the family; the few other seats would have no arms but often had richly carved backs, the so-called 'two-headed eagle' chairs (*Doppeladlerstühle*). Chairs with painted softwood backs are sometimes found in Upper Austria, such as the so-called 'marriage chairs' (*Hochzeitsstühle*), decorated with dancers and musicians. Smaller rooms off the main living-room and attics served as bedrooms; the earlier four-poster beds gave way to beds whose headboards were often elaborately painted and decorated with religious figures and monograms. The wooden rocking cradles and the tall clocks, known as woodcutter clocks (*Holzhackeruhren*), were decorated with similar motifs. Outside in the farmyard there would be beehives, of which there were a wide variety: straw ones in strong basket weave, or wooden ones made of

34a

45b, 46b

39a, b

Page 101 a Wooden loving-cup (cog), Orkney Islands; *b* Wooden beer jug, Island of Rømø, Denmark, 1841; *c* Tankard, Tyrol, seventeenth century; *d* Thread basket, Island of Rømø, 1787; *e* Luggie, Scotland; *f* Small tub, intended as wedding gift, Lower Austria, early nineteenth century; *g* Milk pail, Emmental, Switzerland, 1742

Page 102 a Carved clogs, Island of Marken, nineteenth century; *b–d* Horn drinking-mugs, Sardinia

100

a   b   c

planks and often painted; in Carinthia these were long and low with scenes painted on the front boards. Among the many kinds of carts and sledges the street sledges (*Gasselschlitten*), with their painted figure-heads, deserve special mention. The horses' harness was crowned by the tall hames on their collars, to which the sleigh bells were fixed.

A good deal of Austrian folk art was conditioned by the inherent nature of the material. The natural shapes of particular roots and branches led to their being hung outside a house as a sign, or as a charm against accidents and sickness. Wood was the primary material in all the Alpine regions, for houses and farm buildings and for bridges. The most common method of building houses, stables, barns and granaries was with logs of pine and fir, laid horizontally. Wood was also the basic material for furniture, tools, toys and mangers. The fashioning of drinking-troughs and chests by hollowing out a single log, lying on its side, was a very old skill, as was using an axe to plane logs that were to be used in building and for making furniture.

Twigs, bark and chips could all be put to good use. Basket weaving was a very important craft; the woven basket is used as much today in Burgenland and east Styria as it ever was. Woven firewood-baskets were common in rural areas; in some parts of Carinthia the cupboards for storing food had woven walls. The technique of bending long wood chips to form oval boxes seems to have been known in the Austrian lands since the Hallstatt culture, and is still practised as a cottage industry in some places. The small boxes were always painted with abstract patterns or religious devices, never with representational designs.

The basic materials for the manufacture of textiles were flax and hemp, always spun by women, and wool, usually spun by men. Flax has been grown in Austria for very many centuries and played an important role in the country's economy until very recently (being used, for example, in the paying of rent and other dues). The traditional utensils for spinning and weaving, like other pieces of domestic equipment, clothes beaters and smoothing sticks, often bear decorative patterns that indicate their function as love tokens. Wool was used chiefly to make loden cloth and felt. Other materials of animal origin include the leather of deer, goats, chamois and so on, used particularly in men's clothing, to make breeches and belts for instance, and horn and bone, used for knife handles, buttons, combs and similar articles. In fact the traditional men's costume owes nearly everything to animals: leather breeches, loden jacket and cloak, horn buttons, felt hat and *Gemsbart*, the tuft of chamois hair worn in the hatband.

Austrian folk art drew its materials not only from animals and plants, but from the earth as well. Even in the Middle Ages the potter's craft was well advanced. Unglazed earthenware remained in common everyday use, but from the sixteenth century on it was supplemented by glazed ware, used particularly for plates, dishes and jugs – notably the vast 'guild jugs'. These wares were plain green or brown to begin with, and had patterns in relief from the late sixteenth century. The jugs were sometimes modelled as grotesque figures or faces, or were decorated with paint piped on through a nozzle. Onion dishes and Maundy Thursday dishes were specialities of Upper Austria. In the late seventeenth century the technique of making majolica, with an opaque glaze, reached potters in Upper Austria, in Gmunden for example, and in Lower Austria, in Steinfeld

133a, 134, top row, 147a, 154b, c

Page 103 Gourd with incised drawing, Sardinia, *c.* 1900
Page 104 Spoons: *a, c* Wood, Alentejo; *b* Horn, south Germany, nineteenth century

105

and Fischau, though this had been preceded by the similar 'Anabaptist ware' *(weiss-brüderisches Geschirr)* introduced from Moravia. As well as crockery the manufacture of earthenware heating-stoves had been an important craft since the late Middle Ages. These were faced with various kinds of tiles, the most common being green and slightly convex.

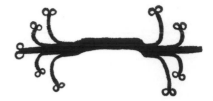

Iron door mounting, Sweden

The most popular metal used in folk art was iron. Smiths plied a brisk trade, producing all kinds of special iron goods such as the human and animal votive figures offered at pilgrimage shrines, as well as domestic firedogs, gridirons and spits, and the signal gongs used in the mountains of upper Styria. Bells were cast of all sizes, from cow bells to the large carnival bells carried in the *Schellfasching*. Other heavy metals were principally used for kitchen equipment. Baking-tins were often made in grotesque shapes of animals and fabulous creatures, particularly those used for the *Gugelhupf*, a cake baked for special occasions. Along the 'iron road' *(Eisenstrasse)*, from the Erzberg to Steyr, the iron and steel implements which most deserve the name of art are the knives and cutlery and the tools of woodmen and blacksmiths. The 'steel' used for striking sparks from flint was made of wrought iron, as were lanterns and holders for pitch torches.

The traditional materials could be shaped in very different basic forms. The shapes of large numbers of utensils were symbols, often sexual. In decoration, besides all the symbolic motifs, plant motifs were the most popular; this links up with the widespread ritual use of trees and branches: the maypole, the Christmas tree, 'St Barbara's branch', the greenery carried in Corpus Christi processions and so on. Some inn signs also originated in bushes, hung out as a universally recognizable symbol, later modified to wreaths or straw crowns. Plant motifs are also common in embroidery and the painting of furniture, and the painted majolica ware of the sixteenth century must in part be viewed as a forerunner of this. Animal motifs also sprang from ritual origins, like the goat, or from heraldry, like the two-headed eagle or the Styrian leopard. Fabrics, furniture and crockery made for newly-married couples are frequently decorated with birds, usually singing birds, and often in pairs. The catching and rearing of singing birds was once widespread, and many artistic birdcages made of iron or wood are still in existence. Human figures occur in all branches of folk art: the realistic 'fountain Turks' of Carinthia, macabre targets, wedding portraits, the 'guild jugs' made in the shape of a practitioner of the appropriate craft, and also in narrative pictures, such as the theme of the 'topsy-turvy world' found on Salzburg majolica.

188b

The figures and ornaments are always meaningful, even though in some cases we no longer know what the precise significance was. It was most often religious. From the household utensil, engraved with the name of Jesus, to the paintings on glass of people and events in the Bible, the tenor of Austrian folk art, even today, is largely religious, essentially Catholic.

207b
208d

CZECHOSLOVAKIAN folk artists operated principally in the fields of architecture and village life: the structure and furnishing of houses, the fashioning of tools and utensils, and finally the whole field of traditional costumes. Contributory features included local customs, the conditions of life in different geographical regions, and the process of adapting artistic styles and techniques to the peasants' own uses.

Wooden Christmas cross, Finland, nineteenth century

10a

19b

On the plains, for instance, houses might be built of packed clay, as in Pannonia, of large rolls of clay fitted together to form an *opus spicatum*, like the grains on an ear of wheat, of fired or unfired bricks; of rubble; or of dressed stone. In size these buildings range from modest two-roomed cottages to the great farmhouses, presenting a street frontage well over 20 yards in length, which are quite common in central Moravia. North-east Bohemia is well known for its timber houses. The white joints between the beams break up the brown surface of the wall with an effect that is as striking and charming when seen on the houses of a whole village as on isolated buildings. In the Carpathians in the eastern part of Moravia, houses are built of unpainted logs with moss in the crevices. The gables found in eastern Bohemia and the Bohemian and Moravian highlands display some skilful panelling. The wooden houses of Wallachia (eastern Moravia) have whitewashed gables and colourful, projecting roofs, and also bear inscriptions with the date of construction, the name of the man who had it built, and wishes for the well-being of the occupants.

The masons who built farmhouses in central and southern Bohemia and south-west Moravia continued to give the exteriors an air of the baroque until well into the nineteenth century. They built imposing entrances, broad, spreading gables and ornate, stucco façades. The porch, known as a *žudro* (solarium), of houses in southern Moravia, is also of architectural interest. It is quite unlike anything found in Bohemia and can range from a simple architectural emphasis of the main door to quite an ornate veranda.

The interiors of houses were well decorated. Furniture might be painted, inlaid or carved in relief, paintings on glass hung on the wall, and even in the houses of the poor there would be faience, carvings or wax models to enliven the corner in which the table stood. While this table was the focus of the room in that people sat down together there, the opposite corner, which contained the stove, was a secondary centre. This was where people sat to work on handicrafts in the winter, to chat and to rest. The appearance and furnishing of this corner was conditioned above all by practical considerations. The bulky stove projected into the room, its mass broken up by cornices and surrounded by benches on which people could stretch out and sleep. It was almost invariably decorated with a tiled relief and crowned with a model of a sleeping cat – an obvious association – a lamb or a dove.

134, bottom row, r.

135, 2nd row, centre, bottom row, r.

136e

141d

146a

155d–f

Earthenware and glass are the materials of a great deal of characteristic Czech folk art, which reaches its highest artistic level in faience. It was the Anabaptists who introduced faience to Moravia, which already had an old-established tradition of excellent pottery. The newly acquired knowledge of what was at the time the very finest kind of ceramic ware was not wasted in Moravia. Whereas previously it had been as expensive as precious metals, it was now produced at prices that were within the means of the middle classes and even of artisans and peasants. Small country workshops took what had been an élite art and turned it, within two or three generations, into a folk art, without in any way impairing its artistic effectiveness.

259a–d

276a

The abundance of timber east of the river Morava provided the raw material both for utilitarian objects and for ornamental carving, particularly in relief. Iron, on the other hand, was used ornamentally only on implements. The blacksmiths who worked in wrought iron combined effective, simple lines with a plentiful use of script in ornamental and figurative designs.

Simple folk fabrics soon disappeared with the introduction of industrial methods. Factory-made fabrics and the vagaries of fashion exercised a strong influence on the styles and colours of folk costumes, which however compensated for the lack of traditional continuity by a wealth of embroidery, in Moravia, and lace, in Bohemia. As one travelled further east, costumes became both more colourful and, surely an allied feature, more varied. Thus, in south-east Moravia, in the early years of this century, an area at most fifty miles square possessed no less than twenty-eight different local costumes. It is therefore hardly surprising if a single local history museum has several thousand examples of local embroidery and costume accessories, while the stock of national museums is between twenty and fifty thousand items.

The traditional folk costumes still survive in country districts, and have not yet lost the importance as expressions of national consciousness which they enjoyed at the end of the last century. In spite of the growth of towns and an urban way of life, the Czech people treasure their costumes as a part of their national culture.

SWITZERLAND's folk art is hard to define or classify as one specific whole, since the Swiss nation is composed of four cultural groups, of which only one, the Romansch, is purely indigenous. Switzerland is a compound of very different parts with mutual ideals, and communities with mutual interests, which formed the Helvetic Confederation for the defence of their common freedom. Artists and craftsmen are not much troubled by political boundaries, and the influences of the neighbouring countries, Austria, Germany, France and Italy, on Swiss folk art are very strong, although by assimilation the results are decidedly and typically Swiss.

The Jura, the Alps and the Swiss plateaux form an impenetrable land of high mountains and narrow gorges and valleys, not only divided into the autonomous cantons but, within them, into tiny, topographically separate communities. Folk art, whether of native origin or foreign inspiration, has a far better chance of survival in such conditions than in areas which are more open to great international movements.

The wooden houses built high in the mountains have a particularly inviting appearance, in spite of the rigorous climate, because of their structural harmony and the grace of their decoration, although this is often obscured at first glance by the weatherbeaten exterior. The Swiss farmhouse, although influenced by town houses, is far more solidly built. On the Swiss plateau, which stretches between the Alps and the Jura, a characteristic feature of the houses is the breadth of the roof which covers both living quarters and outhouses, running to two or four gables. In the rainy hills around Berne the roofs reach almost to the ground, surrounded by galleries bright with red geraniums. Around the lakes and in the Aargau canton thatched roofs are still found occasionally; one well-proportioned example is on a granary near Oberkulm in the Wynental. In the north-east half-timbering in the mediaeval style is still to be found. The red-painted timbers stand out in geometrical patterns against the white rough-cast walls. In the Romansch-speaking areas the simple native house is prevalent; its broad façade is undecorated except for the coat of arms over the door. In the canton of Vaud the houses are in the style of

Burgundy and Savoy, but with the large, Bernese type of roof, whereas in Geneva, the gateway to the Rhône valley, the style is already that of Dauphiné and Provence. In the canton of Neuchâtel houses are built of yellow sandstone, and up in the Jura all but a very few isolated dwellings are free of any kind of ornament, which seems appropriate in this unassertive landscape. In southern Switzerland the houses are built in an Italianate style, of natural sandstone, and often surrounded by wooden galleries, gilded by hanging cobs of maize. In the Mendrisiotto the houses show the influence of Lombardy; the rough-cast plaster is liberally applied. In the Grisons and the Engadine the typical 'Romansch' houses are to be found. Their expansive white façades have no balconies, but massive pillars and thick walls. Small turrets project, and the windows set at an angle in deep niches in the walls are framed by *sgraffiti* and protected by wrought iron shutters. In the mountains this kind of house is replaced by the châlet which the foreigner thinks of as the typical Swiss house. Châlets vary in form and colouring from one mountain region to another; the Grisons and Bernese Oberländer, the Valais, the mountainous part of Vaud, the Rhine valley near St Gall, Toggenburg and the Appenzell all have their own variants.

In the Middle Ages peasants made their furniture in imitation of the furniture in the monasteries, and it was subject to the same kind of changes as architecture. Romanesque ornamentation, geometrical shapes dominated by the circle, persisted for generations on the furniture of country people, particularly on the magnificent chests of beech, maple, oak, larch and pine. Mediaeval furniture is now extremely rare. During the Renaissance, Swiss mercenaries returning home from France, Germany and Italy carried new ideas which enriched the interiors of Swiss houses. Roof beams were replaced by richly decorated cassette ceilings; fine woodwork appeared on pediments, pillars and panels. Furniture too became richer; sideboards began to appear, and tables, while remaining Gothic, acquired more stable legs and a beautiful deep blue slate panel in the centre. Furniture became cheaper, was made of pinewood and was painted with agricultural and allegorical motifs; this art form reached its greatest heights in the eighteenth century, in central and eastern Switzerland. Everything was painted: beds, cradles, clocks, chests, boxes and, above all, cupboards. As well as furniture, village carpenters made sledges, inn signs and the signs craftsmen hung outside their shops, and carved cake moulds. The latter were made of many different kinds of wood, but box was the most popular. The designs were often biblical or allegorical.

In Valais, the Bernese Oberland, the Forest Cantons and Appenzell, the end of June is the time to begin the move to the Alm, the higher Alpine pastures, which is accompanied by ceremonies which have often been recorded by folk artists. One of the most colourful takes place in Appenzell. The cowherd wears a red waistcoat and yellow leather shorts, with braces decorated with pieces of chiselled copper. He is followed by his herds, carefully groomed, with the 'queen' at their head; her horns are decorated and a huge bell hangs from a thick collar of long-haired hide, shining with engraved metal discs. When a boy the herdsman makes his own toys, copying the animals in his charge. When grown he carves his crook, his pipe and all the domestic utensils he needs for his lonely life; milk-measure, cream-spoon, butter-pat, milking-stool, a distaff for his bride. Up to the end of the last century there still existed in some regions the so-called 'herd book',

Miller's sack mark, Berne

19d

278a–d

216b

101g

a triangular block of wood, at least a yard in length, primarily intended to record the number of beasts the cowherd was supposed to tend. This 'book', carved with dates, decorative motifs and proverbs, gives a particularly clear idea of the very individual, symbolic nature of the herdsman's art.

At the end of the Middle Ages tableware was still relatively primitive. Very often people ate off a single common dish placed in the middle of the table, a custom which has persisted on some farms right up to the present day. Small quantities of pottery, however, were made all over Switzerland. Winterthur has been producing tiles for facing stoves since the eighteenth century. The manufacture of round-bellied clay pitchers decorated with incised patterns has been established in Langnau for as long a period. One dish from Langnau or nearby is the colour of ivory and has stylized tulips incised on it; another, now in the Historisches Museum in Berne, has three crossed fishes. Later designs included human figures, framed by mottoes of a moralizing, or perhaps malicious nature, such as:

133d, f
134, 2nd row centre, bottom row, centre, 141f, 155a

> *Bei einem bösen Wib ist warlich grose not*
> *dar vor behüde mich oh lieber her und gott – 1775.*

> ('A shrewish wife brings naught but pain
> dear God preserve me from this bane.')

Plates like these were intended as ornaments and were common gifts. As well as the rounded jugs and the dishes there were bowls and casseroles with lids, coloured dark brown with vivid patterns incised on them. Nearly every house in Heimberg, in the canton of Berne, eventually became a pottery. To begin with their ware was similar to that of Langnau, but an individual style emerged from the beginning of the nineteenth century. Colours ranged from a pale brown to deep black, with anecdotal motifs standing out in light colours against the dark background.

Glass-blowing was established since the seventeenth century in the Jura, in central Switzerland and in the regions along the Italian border. Immigrants from the Black Forest settled in the Entlebuch valley, where they made their iridescent and transparent glass, while in other regions drinking-vessels were made in coloured or plain glass with enchanting engraved patterns. Schnaps-bottles were painted in bright colours. In the eighteenth century houses were decorated with engraved window panes. Processes of grinding or etching produced whole series of coats of arms and scenes of daily life which tell us a lot about the customs of the time. Other windows were engraved, rather in the style of inn signs.

There are still many old inn signs to be found in Switzerland. Since the original inns were mostly stations for changing horses along the pilgrimage routes, it seems only natural that their signs should be placed under the protection of a saint or an angel. The traveller was beset by all kinds of dangers in those days and the sign of the 'good star' would give him a feeling of security. Innkeepers took the devices for their signs from very different sources: mythology as well as animal and plant life. The white horse was very popular, but the most humble articles of daily life also found their way on to the signs. Eighteenth-century signs in wrought iron were particularly fine. Village black-

234a–f

smiths had already brought their craft to a fine art; they were not only farriers but locksmiths and clockmakers as well. They used wrought iron to make delicate spiral ornaments for processional maces, handles for chests, shutters for windows and ornamental mountings for locks. Of course they normally followed traditional patterns, but these left plenty of scope to the imagination of individual craftsmen, as can be seen in the ornamentation of some door knockers and memorial crosses.

174b
175b

Left and above: Millers' sack marks, Berne

It is hardly necessary to describe the traditional costume of the Swiss herdsman, for it is worn by the national hero, William Tell: the hooded tunic of Uri, shorts and rough sandals. This is the classic costume of the Forest Cantons which are the nucleus of the Confederation. The more attractive and varied women's dress came to its full splendour during the eighteenth century, when peasant women adapted for their own use the Parisian fashions which in turn reflected the elegance of the European courts of the day. These traditional costumes have survived longest in the more conservative, Catholic cantons; for example, in Savièse in Valais all the women still go to church on Sundays in their formal black dresses, relieved only by the colours of their silk aprons. The severity of the women of Savièse is in great contrast to the almost sumptuous costume of the canton of Schwyz. The women there wear bodices and skirts of damask and brocade with fine linen flounces; their shoulders are covered by a dainty cloth of embroidered batiste. The fan-shaped, tulle headdress is decorated with a garland of flowers and held together by a metal ring with a filigree clasp in the form of a rose over the forehead. A wide variety of costumes is to be found in the Grisons. All are easily identifiable by the uniform style of ornamentation on the blouses, shawls and black aprons, which are embroidered in bright colours, the carnation being a favourite motif. The headdress is usually very dainty, held by a silver pin. The costumes of the cantons of Geneva, Neuchâtel and Vaud are plain and of little interest. In Ticino the women dress very much in the Italian style and their clogs clatter like castanets. The costumes of central and eastern Switzerland are the least affected by foreign influences. Their dominant feature is the richness of the lace and ornaments: rings, chains and gold brooches gleam against the white pleated bodices. Lace was particularly fine during the nineteenth century in the cantons of Thurgau, Berne, Schwyz, Vaud and Neuchâtel. Embroidery, which was introduced in St Gall and Appenzell in the eighteenth century, is used not only to adorn women's costumes but also, in a wide variety of stitches, on household linen and also on processional banners and vestments.

179b

245a
246a, c
247a

The pagan origins of Swiss folk art, reaching far back to the primitive roots of human traditions, are revealed beyond doubt by, among other things, the use of masks, still current today. In his fear of spirits and death man invented terrifying masks to drive them away. The tradition is particularly strong in the Lötschental region and around Sargans and Appenzell. At nightfall on 13 January, the feast of the Sylvesterkläuse (New Year's Day, Old Style), a very strange play is performed in Urnäsch at nightfall: the powers of good and evil, wearing fantastic, grotesque masks, engage in fierce combat, shrieking and ringing cow bells. The masks and costumes of the powers of darkness are made of brushwood, fir cones and moss, while the good spirits wear masks with a reassuringly impassive expression, beneath an extraordinary headdress made in the shape of a hat with a beaded crown.

a

b

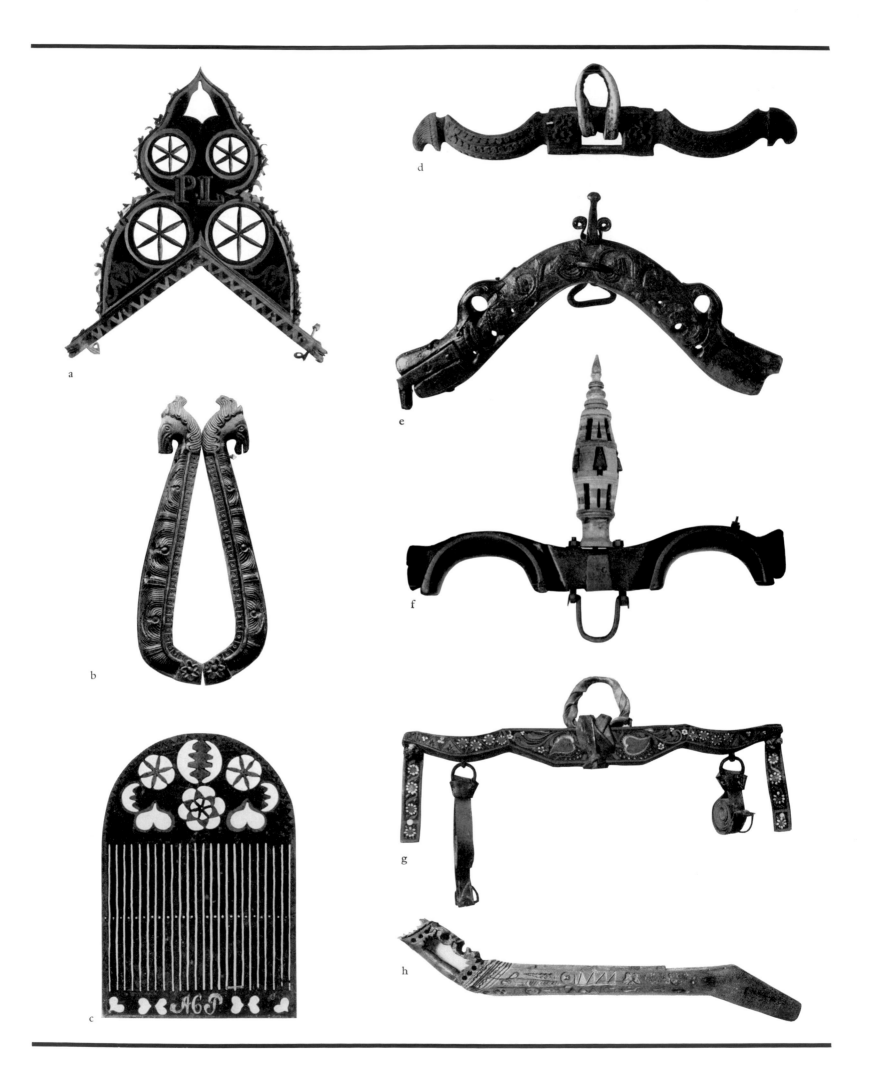

a

b

c

d

e

f

g

h

a

b

c

d

FRANCE is a country where the idea that folk art springs from its native soil and grows in strict isolation is even less true than it is elsewhere. There were always far too many opportunities for the exchange and spread of ideas among vendors and buyers; they changed hands at fairs and markets, and were carried by passing pedlars and itinerant craftsmen, particularly by the *compagnons* on their traditional journey around France, by pilgrims and travellers, by armies returning from foreign parts, and by the prisoners they brought back with them, who were often put to work at a craft.

However old the traditions of folk art in France may be, its period of greatest fullness, beauty and variety coincided with that of French craftsmanship in general, in the years just before and during the first Industrial Revolution, roughly speaking from the second half of the eighteenth century to the last quarter of the nineteenth. The revolution of 1789 hastened the break-up of rural communities and destroyed many workshops which had been engaged in folk art, but other centres developed simultaneously which catered to a large degree for a completely new public, the broad mass of the proletariat. New methods in agriculture, and the technical advances introduced in the second half of the eighteenth century, had so increased the spending power of the Third Estate, both in the towns and in the country, that they were able to bring some beauty into their everyday existence, in the form of attractive furniture and fittings; clothes and utensils could be chosen with an eye to their aesthetic appeal as well as to their usefulness.

60a, e, f

Only from the second half of the eighteenth century onwards is it possible in France to speak with certainty of furniture not only made by craftsmen from among the common people but used by the people. Before that period wooden planks were the most important element in equipping the houses of the poor. Three or four planks laid side by side and covered with straw, either loose or in a sack, made a bed. A board suspended from the ceiling by ropes or rods kept foodstuffs safe from children or domestic animals. Tables consisted of planks laid side by side on a trestle or on empty barrels. Planks supported by long wooden pegs knocked into the wall were the predecessors of cupboards, dressers and the like. But long before the introduction of furniture for the masses, popular art and popular skills had been manifested in the large quantities of furniture made by craftsmen for the more wealthy classes. It is to them that we owe the remarkable chests carved with figures in relief that were made in Brittany in the eighteenth century, or those with geometrical patterns which came from Queyras in the French Alps in the sixteenth century.

Page 115 Bell collars: *a* Central Franconia, nineteenth century; *b, c* Bolzano, Tyrol; *d* South Tyrol
Page 116 Sicilian cart (built by Salvatore Schillaci) with Rape of the Sabine women (painted by Ficano brothers), Palermo, nineteenth century

In the mid-eighteenth century furniture for the common people was made by local craftsmen, whose work was, however, often sold astonishingly far from their place of manufacture at the great fairs or markets in towns like Provins, Tournus, Beaucaire or Orléans. In this way the better-liked patterns came to exert an influence far from the workshop where they were first devised. It explains the popularity of the stylized flowering fern motif, for instance, fashionable on both banks of the central reaches of the Loire, and the convolvulus pattern found on cupboards from Rostrenen. In most of the French provinces craftsmen specialized in particular kinds of furniture. Among those in any one locality there would be the cabinet maker, who was a distinct cut above ordinary carpenters, and the *bâtonnier*, who made benches, stools and chairs; and when the *Directoire* fashion of the very beginning of the nineteenth century brought in chairs with woven straw seats and wooden backs decorated with the so-called *palmette* in fretwork, the *bâtonnier* farmed this work out to specialist woodcarvers. As recently as 1942 there were still two workshops engaged exclusively in the manufacture of this kind of chair in the Loiret, at Orleans and Jargeau. The original *palmette*, which was adopted from the ornamental art favoured by the government of the day, was joined by a great number of motifs from the popular imagination: fountains, flowers and other similar patterns. The straw bottoms were made and repaired in workshops or by itinerant craftsmen. Such men had plied their crafts probably since the Middle Ages and continued to exist, in Brittany at least, until the mid-nineteenth century or later, providing an essential service for isolated farmhouses and hamlets. It was not uncommon for a family to lay wood aside to season at a child's birth, so that eventually an itinerant carpenter would be able to make a bed or a dower chest from it on the spot.

Geometrical patterns appear to have the longest history; they were common all over Europe and occurred in North Africa and Asia as well. In some parts of France they remained the most prevalent right up to the early years of the twentieth century, in the art of mountain farmers, shepherds and the makers of cow bells. They were used as much on furniture as on smaller objects: netting-needles, distaffs and horses' collars. They are usually distributed irregularly, to fill in the whole surface. One very common motif is the wheel, which was originally a solar symbol; although this fact was unknown to the joiners of Queyras when we questioned them about it. They told us it was a very popular pattern and easy to execute, which is of course true of other geometrical patterns. Geometrical ornamentation flourished in the Alps, the Pyrenees, the Landes, Auvergne and even Provence.

Generally speaking even the broad mass of the people had furniture made of the various hardwoods, which look well without the help of paint: oak, nut, cherry, gnarled elm (used in Saintonge). Softwoods, on the other hand, were considered unattractive unless painted, which is one reason why softwood furniture is rare in France, except in Alsace and around Queyras. The workers in the salt marshes around Guérande (Loire-Atlantique) are exceptional in their practice of painting their furniture blood-red all over, but without any ornamental motifs. Joiners borrowed an extraordinary quantity of forms of furniture and ornaments from upper class fashions of the seventeenth and eighteenth centuries. But even though elements taken from the 'official' *Louis-Quinze* style of *rocaille*, shells, doves and baskets of flowers, are plain to see on the cupboards of both Caux (Normandy) and Rennes (Brittany), the styles of the two towns, in spite of their common borrowings, are quite distinct; their works are totally different in spirit and could never be confused. The Rennes 'flower style' is a byword, which reveals the

Above and right: Sheet-iron votive figures, Alsace

60c

33c

118

strength of the personal style that artists from the people were able to impose on the borrowed elements. Unlike the bulk of mere workmen, they were incapable of making blind copies, because they had something of their own to express. All the same, it is hard for us to understand why certain types should have been more popular with makers and buyers than others. How can we explain the extraordinary popularity of the 'pin-head' motif which remained in fashion from the seventeenth century until at least the middle of the nineteenth, in the Alps, the Pyrenees, Auvergne, Velay and a large part of Languedoc? Why did fluting in the *Louis-Seize* style continue to be employed for so long in the region of Arles? Beyond doubt, Brittany produced the greatest variety of types of furniture, showing complete freedom in their forms. They were even decorated with turned 'spindles' or studded with copper-headed nails (in Cornouaille) until finally too much was made of a good thing and the furniture came to look eccentric rather than decorative.

Quite apart from furniture, folk artists have always favoured wood, if only because it was everywhere available. Sculpture in wood has always been an important form of folk art, and in France, particularly in Brittany, has produced a quantity of remarkable statues, usually religious in nature. They were mostly intended to adorn churches, but also filled niches in the outside walls of other buildings, particularly of houses on street corners in small towns and villages. Since the self-appointed 'cultivated' classes looked down their noses at these figures, particularly in the second half of the nineteenth century, large numbers of them have been deliberately destroyed, where they had not already fallen victims to woodworm and damp, but all the same many of them have been rescued and put in museums in the last thirty years. It is very difficult to date wooden objects of this kind, since they were very little subject to changes of style.

The whole population used a large array of domestic utensils made of wood, decorated with carving, turning or fretwork: the turned spinning-wheels of Brittany, which were often painted, the board looms for weaving braid and the netting needles used for making lace in Puy-de-Dôme, Velay and Manche, to name only a few objects. The wooden spoon became a prized possession of the Bretons, who flaunted it on a waistcoat button. So far as can be judged from known, dated pieces, the custom was current between 1675 and 1869. The spoon might be flexible or rigid, carved or inlaid with coloured wax or tiny pieces of shell; it was always decorated with loving care. Among kitchen equipment we should mention the containers for salt, spices and flour, casks and bushel measures, butter-pats, shapes for aniseed cakes (Alsace, since the seventeenth century), and milk churns (Pyrenees). Shepherds made charming necklaces, carved walking-sticks, crooks and all sorts of things to give to their sweethearts: washing beetles, bedsticks, with which to smooth the made bed, and boxes of all sizes for every kind of purpose.

Until the twentieth century every French village possessed at least one basketmaker, who furnished baskets of all kinds: deep ones for gathering the grape harvest, shallower ones for carrying grass to feed rabbits, woven cheese-forms (often a heart shape), muzzles to prevent calves from pestering their mothers unnecessarily, and cradles. Basketwork cradles were common all over France, and where the proper materials were not available locally, the cradles were imported from areas which specialized in basketry, such as Haute-Marne, Thierache and elsewhere. Willow was by no means the only material

54a

256

59g, 84b

used; there were also black dogwood (in the Brière), honeysuckle vines and wild vine, chestnut splints, Provençal cane and the durable wood of the Mediterranean myrtle, which is ideal for wicker fish-traps and crab-pots.

There are a few blacksmiths and farriers, even today, scattered about France, who have retained a feeling for iron and copper and take pleasure in occasional creative work that springs entirely from their own imaginations. They are the last survivors of a profession that flourished for centuries when the horse was its chief *raison d'être*. Their pride in their craft was reflected in the ancient sign of the smiths' guild, which was composed of shoes for horses, mules, donkeys, draught-oxen and draught-cows, and is sometimes crowned by the picture of their patron, St Eligius. It is to the smiths that we owe most of the weather-vanes on church towers, which were cut and chased from sheet iron or copper. Weathercocks, which are supposed to be a reminder of Peter's remorse on hearing the cock crow, are sometimes so stylized that they could almost have come from tropical Africa.

The smiths' work was also needed in the home. They made the iron hooks on which pots were suspended over the fire. The level of the hooks could be adjusted by cogs, in northern France, or by rings in the south, though there was no firm demarcation line, and there were methods which employed both. The hook was a symbol of hearth and home and even today the expression 'to hang up the hook' is used in France, meaning that a housewarming party is to be given. The cooking-pot could also be placed on an iron tripod, which was often made of a continuous piece of iron, bent into shape. The blacksmith also made firedogs large and small, gridirons, waffle irons, forks, spoons and the bars and hooks on which butchers hang their sausages and sides of bacon.

Coppersmiths produced cooking-pots, frying-pans, warming-pans, coal-shovels and cake-forms – the well-polished pride and joy of kitchens and inns. Cast metals were used only exceptionally in the folk crafts, for waffle irons, for example, which had iron handles, or for the curious mantlepiece plates, which were not used very much except occasionally by newly-weds, moving into their own house. Pewter utensils, pots and plates only became popular with the common people when the upper classes had given them up. Yet the characteristic shapes of pewterware recurred in a lot of faience, for instance in that which came from the Loire valley.

The simplest kind of French pottery was black, as the easiest way to render the surface of a vessel as waterproof as possible was to smoke it in firing, which was done by stoking the kiln with green broom and juniper. If greasy rags were put on the fire they brought out iridescent lights in the matt black. A better degree of impermeability was achieved with glazes of various lead oxides, which gave rise to a range of yellows, or of copper oxides, which produced the marvellous shades of green on earthenware from Provence, Languedoc and Saintonge. The potters got a complete range of browns and reds from iron oxides, while manganese produced shades from violet to a dull blue-black. These coloured glazes were always applied to the outer surface only, and often, for the sake of economy, only to the upper half of the vessel.

Towards the end of the eighteenth century and continuing up to the early years of the twentieth, the use became widespread of the kind of earthenware that is glazed inside with an opaque, white enamel, produced from tin oxide, which mostly came from the

Illustrations of French ceramic ware: 127c, d, f; 136c, d, f; 141a, b, c, e; 145a–d; 146d; 153b–f, h; 154d–f; 156a–d

Page 121 Painted carts, Alba de Tormes, Spain
Page 122 Horse brasses, England
Page 123 Cart, Lincolnshire, 1829
Page 124 Staffordshire pottery, c. 1820–50: a Cavalier in a tent; b Highland couple with clock case; c Fob watch case; d Cow and milkmaid

120

a

b

c

d

a

b

c

d

e

a

b

c

d

e

f

Limousin, while the outer surface was nearly always coated with a cheaper black enamel made of manganese oxide. Sometimes the plates and dishes had a small ornament, such as a basket of fruit, or flowers, in the centre and occasionally the rim was decorated too. This popular ware was made chiefly in Orleans (Loiret), Argent-sur-Sauldre (Cher) and Blois (Cher) until the end of the eighteenth century, when Rouen became the principal centre. Technically it is a heavy form of faience, in that an enamel decoration is fixed at a low temperature over a glaze containing tin. Ordinary earthenware was for everyday use, while the faience, for fear of breakages, was reserved for special occasions.

Stoneware is made of clay which contains quantities of fine quartz crystals and needs to be fired at a high temperature to produce a homogeneous, resonant substance. Stoneware sherds look almost like glass. It is handsome enough to need no extra decoration, if it is moulded into a good shape. The high firing temperature limits the choice of colours and glazes. In the potteries of La Puisaye (Saint-Armand and Saint-Vérain), Berry and neighbouring areas of Sologne, and in upper Alsace, sea salt was put in the kilns to evaporate and form a glaze; later, with the rise of industries, foundry slag was used, which produced bold yellows, and glazes containing wood ash, which made an effect of grey shading. Cobalt was also used either to give a complete coat of blue, or for ornaments applied by hand, which to begin with (though not later) were pressed into depressions in the clay (Oberbetschdorf, Alsace). Pottery of this kind was used all over northern, eastern and central France in the second half of the nineteenth century, as was the faience of Saint-Clément and Lunéville, which was often decorated by the peasants themselves in their spare time. They bought plain white ware that had already been fired at a high temperature. They applied the pattern and baked it once more at a lower temperature, to preserve the fresh clarity of the colours. Equally popular were the wares from Sarreguemines and Gien (Loiret), which were in use all over France.

It is unlikely that the pottery used by the ordinary people of France derived from the beautiful earthenware, marked with the potter's stamp, made in the Gallo-Roman workshops which have been found at La Limagne (Auvergne) and in eighty other places. There is more than the difference in quality and form to separate them: the techniques employed were also quite different. The Roman ware was shaped in moulds, the later pottery on the wheel or by hand; the Roman ware is smooth and polished, the French ware is coated with glazes containing lead and various other oxides, and so on. It is a matter of interest that vases, from Lezoux, for instance, were exported via Narbonne and Béziers as far as the Campania, a proof that they stood up to long journeys, in spite of their low cost. Similarly, wine jars of the fourteenth and fifteenth centuries, formed on the wheel and decorated with lines or parallel spirals, were for a long time a puzzle to English archaeologists. The racial migrations of the Dark Ages destroyed the Gallo-Roman workshops and thus cleared the way for a new, native ceramic art in France. Its beginnings can be set in the eleventh century, to judge by the decorated, tiled floors of churches and the burial urns from graves which can be positively dated.

A charming custom developed in Provence, which has survived to the present day, of erecting a crib in the house at Christmas, using little figures of baked clay. These were shaped in moulds and painted by hand in vivid, matt distempers. The customary figures connected with the Christmas story are joined by representatives of every trade, wearing the local costumes of early nineteenth-century Provence. Huntsmen, fishermen, even convicts from the galleys, were all there, and so were farmyard animals. All the figures, the tallest of which were at most six inches high and the smallest about one inch, were arranged in a long procession, moving towards the manger in Bethlehem. Most of the workshops producing these figures were, and are, in and around Marseilles, and there are also a large number in Saint-Zaccharie and Aix.

In France, before 1789, a man who made a business out of earthenware, ceramics or faience lost any legal right to call himself a gentleman; this limitation did not apply to the maker of glass. At first glance it is hard to see why glass, whose basic materials are a mixture of silicates with potash or sodium hydroxide, should be considered a more 'noble' material. In fact the prejudices of the *Ancien Régime* against manual labour were not extended to glassmaking for a simple economic reason. France needed to produce glass of her own to compete with that of Venice and other places. The fact that members of the nobility were engaged in the manufacture of glass must not, therefore, be taken to mean that glassblowing was not also a branch of folk art. That would be a quite erroneous assumption, particularly as regards true glassblowing, with a pipe, which is far older than the industrial use of moulds.

A custom prevalent in glassworks everywhere, not only in France, was to let the workmen have any molten glass left over after the manufacture of the specified quantities of a given object, to do what they liked with, allowing free rein to their imagination and creative bent. The glassblower had a marvellous time; he shaped it with tongs, drew it out, painted and enamelled it, added sulphur and other decorative materials, cut it with the engraver's wheel, exactly as he pleased. When finished, the piece belonged to him; he could sell it to visitors to the works or elsewhere, he could give it away. In this way, particularly in the nineteenth century, large quantities of purely ornamental objects were produced: drumsticks with thick knobs, walking-sticks with curved handles, paperweights, bugles and trumpets, animals, monstrances and holy-water basins, complicated vases and drinking-cups, sometimes with 'surprises', and the little imps which bounced in the 'passion meters', in response to the pressure of a finger on the membrane which sealed the little bottle. But the useful wares turned out by the glassworks also owed a great deal to folk art; the manner of execution, the models and the multitude of different shapes, which were influenced by regional traditions. The glassworks of Toulouse produced rings for carriage reins to slide through. In general it is not easy to establish precisely the place of origin of individual objects in glass. The most one can usually do is to state the region: Normandy, Saintonge, Burgundy, the upper Rhine, the Moselle. One exception to this is the output of the Perroto works in Orleans, at the end of the eighteenth century, and the dated pieces from Soultzmatt, which are in the museum at Mulhouse.

Between the end of the eighteenth century and about 1870, the traditional folk costumes reached a peak of regional variety and an often astonishing, thoroughly delightful extravagance. We need only mention the embroidery executed in brilliant red and gold silk thread on black cloth by the men of Finistère, which was intended principally for bodices and waistcoat panels. Festive garments like these, including the mantle or *pélerine*, were worn by men, women and children alike. The costumes represented a

166 c

Iron grille, England

173 c

130

Iron candelabrum, Sweden

considerable part of a family's worldly goods and were handed down for generations, with alterations according to fit. They underwent no more fundamental alterations for over a century, whereas the 'sugarloaf' hats worn by the women of Pont l'Abbé represent an innovation. These lace headdresses are so tall that they have to be reinforced, and even today they tower above the round and often pretty faces of the women. The white cylinder, about ten inches high, developed out of a small cap, no bigger than a fist, fixed over an embroidered hood. We have described it in some detail because it illustrates the way in which some durable traditional elements of regional costumes manage to hold their own side by side with the variable whims of fashion. Vanity played a certain role in determining changes in costume, since every village wanted to surpass its neighbours. But such changes followed a completely different rhythm from the changes inspired by city fashions. Paris fashions were taken up at speed by the well-to-do, or those with pretensions to wealth, all over France, lest they be ridiculed as old-fashioned (the same principle governs the sale of cars today). Costumes in the provinces naturally adopted features of Paris fashions from time to time, but varying amounts and at varying speeds, according to the region. The variety in costumes, shoes, ornaments and hairstyles is too immense to begin describing; the collections owned by museums and serious folklore societies can reflect only a small section of it.

The people of France did not use expensive, imported materials like silk and cotton for their costumes. Wool, hemp and linen were grown and spun at home. Nearly every household, whether in towns, in the country or isolated in the mountains, possessed a distaff (the emblem of the housewife) and a spinning-wheel. The spun thread was taken to professional weavers in the towns and villages to make into cloth. The well-wearing properties of the cloth led to considerable variations between traditional costumes and current fashions. When silk and cotton came within the reach of the purses of ordinary people, there were still many branches of the clothing trade occupied in the production of individual parts of the costumes: lace-makers, hatters, embroiderers, haberdashers and so on. Before the introduction of machine-made lace, the regions of Puy, Alençon and Quimper were particularly famous for their lace; but it was also made in convents all over France.

Bed-curtains and fire-screens were at one time made of woven fabrics in plain colours or striped, and with a narrow border. As cotton came into general use, factories were opened which produced printed cloths and wide borders which could be put to all kinds of uses. Factories in Lyon, Avignon and Tarascon have collections of the wooden blocks, some of them still in use, which were used in printing fabrics. The patterns carved in the wood were coated with dye and the blocks were arranged to form the desired pattern. A blow with a hammer impressed the pattern on the cloth.

Even the poor often possessed carpets, since these could be made very cheaply. Rags were cut into narrow strips, stitched together and rolled into balls, which were then taken to weavers to make up into carpets, counterpanes or curtains. This technique is known all over Europe and beyond. The resulting fabric is patterned with stripes and highly stylized motifs.

Saddlers took great pride in providing ornamental harness for horses to wear in processions. They decorated the leather straps with studs and tufts of elder wood with

196a, b

131

the bark stripped from it. The manes were plaited with coloured wool. Some of the many leather-bound whip-butts of nettle tree wood, the pomponned hoods to cover the horses' ears, and the decorated cruppers, are extremely attractive.

Large numbers of votive pictures have happily survived, thanks to their protected position on the walls of churches and chapels. They are the best examples of what folk art was capable of achieving in the field of painting in oil, gouache and watercolour on wood, paper and glass. If the purely religious subjects are treated all too conventionally much of the time, the *ex-voto*, votive pictures, giving thanks after surviving accidents, show great originality, whether the situation depicted is fire, flood or a fall from stairs, horseback or cart. The often anonymous painters have a style which recalls that of Douanier Rousseau; his work is so well known that it is hardly necessary to enlarge on the peculiar charm of these delightful folk paintings.

Before the rise of photography, itinerant painters used to travel from village to village, from farm to farm, offering their services as portrait painters. There are no official records of their social origins and status, but their pictures speak clearly enough. The bulk of these artists came from the ranks of the common people, but their clientèle was by no means always so humble; more than one noble family living in the provinces is known to have commissioned portraits from the travelling artists. After Daguerre appeared on the scene, however, the painted likenesses were found ludicrous, if not caricatured, and large numbers of them were destroyed. This is why they are now so rare; at one time they could be found everywhere.

Such tradesmen's signs as were not made of wrought iron or wood were painted, as were showmen's posters. The shop windows of *charcutiers* (pork butchers), particularly in Lyon and Mâcon, were shaded by awnings which displayed naive, but often charming paintings of hunting and coursing scenes. *Pâtés* of wild boar or hare, if well-made, were often the butcher's pride, perhaps because they were not so easy to come by as *pâtés* of pork and veal.

Formal watercolour 'letters' for a godparent to send to his godchild originated in Alsace, and were common there in the eighteenth and nineteenth centuries, if not earlier. At the end of his military service the French soldier often had his portrait painted in a warlike pose in parade or battle uniform against a decorative background. These souvenirs eventually took the form of a watercolour background with a photograph of the soldier's head glued to it, to produce a satisfactory likeness. Other kinds of painting connected with the military life were the certificates awarded to singlestick and fencing champions, and the diplomas with watercolour heads for sailors, cavalrymen, gunners and so on.

The art of painting on glass, usually of religious subjects, though the four seasons and portraits of kings and generals also occurred, seems to have reached France from central Europe, probably from Bohemia, Poland or Rumania. A special branch of this art is found in the cemetery ornaments made in Lyon between 1860 and 1900.

As mentioned at the beginning of this chapter, craftsmen wishing to complete their knowledge of their trade, or to seek work, used to take the road on a pre-determined route which led them to places which had been sacred to the crafts from the time when they had rebelled against the privileges held by the guilds under the *Ancien Régime*.

228b

237a, b

Page 133 Dishes: *a* Austria, seventeenth or eighteenth century; *b* Östergötland, Sweden, 1785; *c* Italy; *d, f* Switzerland; *e* Alsace, 1799

Page 134 Dishes, from left to right: top row: Upper Austria, *c.* 1730; Transylvania, *c.* 1800; Upper Austria, *c.* 1740; 2nd row: Makkum, Netherlands, nineteenth century; Heimberg, Switzerland, *c.* 1830; Småland, Sweden, 1778; 3rd row: Horsens, Denmark, 1789; Italy; Lower Rhine, *c.* 1750–60; 4th row: Czechoslovakia; Switzerland; Makkum, 1790

a

b

c

d

e

f

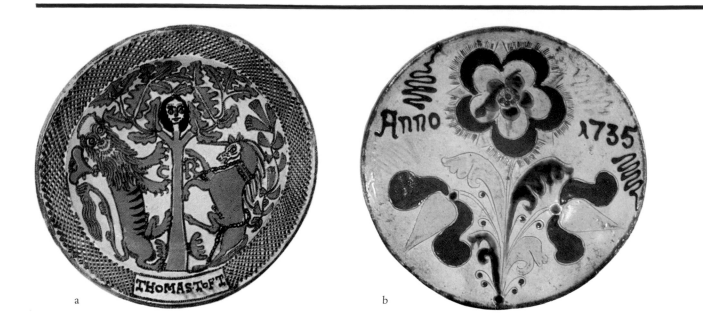

a

b

c

d

e

f

There have survived some splendid nineteenth-century specimens of the letters of introduction carried by the *compagnons du tour de France*, which are decorated with a water-colour or gouache picture of the craftsman setting off on his journey, gaily beribboned, bearing in his hand his formidable stick, both a symbolic and a real counterpart to the sword reserved for the nobility.

There were special workshops, for example in and around Angers (Maine-et-Loire), which catered for the showmen who travelled from fair to fair in the nineteenth century. It was they who made the carved and painted wooden horses and other gaily coloured animals which children and adults rode on the roundabouts. Before 1914 there was a great variety of these exotic animals: stags and boars, giraffes and mermaids, and even fishes, which can still be admired today in La Buissière (Loiret). There were also the carved and gilded carriages, panelled with mirrors, and, at a later date, railway trains. Around 1895 the same woodworkers introduced the mechanical dolls which adorned the *limonaires*, the great fairground organs, and which are among the gayest, most original and most delightful products of folk art.

PORTUGAL falls geographically and historically into three clearly differentiated regions: the Mediterranean, Latin-Moorish south with a hot, dry climate; the Atlantic, Germanic north-west with a temperate, damp climate; and finally the archaic, Lusitanian north-east with a dry climate and fierce contrasts of temperature. This tripartite division is the reason for fundamental differences affecting many cultural phenomena.

There are two main types of Portuguese peasant houses, with one storey in the south and two in the north, where the ground floor serves as storeroom, wine cellar and cowshed. In the southern province of Alentejo the whitewashed house is a compact block with very simple lines and few openings; at one time it had almost no windows at all. It is very often constructed in *pisé* (rammed earth), and the *moirões*, the strong, picturesque buttresses, are intended to prevent subsidence. The gabled roof of reed thatch rests on a lattice frame, which is lashed to the rafters.

The kitchen, which also serves as dining-room and communal living-room, has a rather low fireplace and a tiled floor. Copper and brass pots and saucepans gleam on the spotless white walls, and forks, spoons and glasses add to the decorative effect. Oil lamps stand on shelves against a background of coloured paper and lace, and huge water jugs stand on the *poial*, a kind of table set into a niche in the wall. Town houses, particularly in the southern part of Alentejo, are usually two-storied, with the kitchen on the ground floor, and the house front is dominated by the tall chimney. The houses are narrow and angular, with tiny little doors; the dormer-windows, steps, balconies and arches make a very pretty composition of shapes and surfaces in brick. In the province of Algarve, the white of the houses is heightened by the colours of plants and the intense blue decoration of the façades. In Alentejo chimneys are usually tall and cylindrical, perhaps under Moorish influence, and similar forms recur frequently; often all the chimneys in a street, or even in a whole village look alike. Chimneys in Algarve are very tall, slim and ornate, and there are not two alike in the whole province. The *açoteia*, an open terrace which is used in country districts for drying figs and other crops, is a relic of the centuries of Moorish rule in this region.

Northern Portugal's primeval flint and granite offer a striking contrast to the south. The houses of the tiny, huddled mountain villages, with their steep gables and straw thatch, usually have two storeys, occasionally only one. The ground floor is used as a wine cellar, store and stable, and the family lives on the first floor, reached by an outside staircase of large, roughly hewn stone blocks. In mountainous Minho, tiles have long replaced thatch; the houses are generally less simple than in the south and typically have roofed verandas.

In the bright, clean houses of the south, the smaller household fittings, such as the racks for cutlery, glasses and so on, are generally decorated, or at least fashioned with care. The typical furniture of this region includes chairs with straw seats, settles with ornamental backs, stools of cork and, in Évora, painted furniture, with flower patterns on a plain red, blue or yellow ground. In the more sober houses of the north, in Tras-Os-Montes, for instance, long high-backed settles are to be found grouped round the open fireplace, trestle tables, plain chests, or chests decorated with carving or ornamental iron clasps, comfortable beds and tables with some simple device carved on them, a rosette perhaps, encircled by lines cut with a gouge. The furniture is hardly ever painted, and when it is, then usually in a single colour; but occasionally beds or, more likely, cupboards are found with a rich flower pattern, in which the dominant colour is red.

Alentejo is the province with the most, and best, woodcarving; practically all objects and tools that form part of domestic and agricultural life have been worked artistically. In the other provinces only ox yokes, swingles (*espadeladouros*) for beating flax, and distaffs are carved, though there are no apparent reasons why they should be when other objects are not. In Alentejo the art seems to be closely connected with the many shepherds who spend their long hours of enforced idleness carving. The favourite material for carving is horn, which is used to make containers for powder, oil, salt and foodstuffs as well as cups and many other things. The decoration is naturalistic: bunches of round, triangular and heart-shaped flowers, often in vases; cattle, dogs, birds, fishes; mythological and imaginary beings like mermaids, devils and two-headed eagles; rural scenes and bull fights. Wood is used for spoons, forks, basins, drills, boxes, racks. Cork, which was used a great deal in Alentejo for small seats, boxes, salt cellars, racks and so on, is usually decorated with geometrical or plant motifs. In north-western Portugal woodcarving is confined to ox yokes and flax swingles. But in both these cases the carving takes on some remarkable forms. The yokes, which Frankowski holds to be the most beautiful and the richest in the world, are made of large, high pieces of wood, decorated all over with stylized flowers and branches, geometrical shapes, religious or magical symbols of very ancient origins. In some cases the designs are done in fretwork, in others richly painted in many colours.

Pottery is still carried on all over Portugal, from Estremoz, whose workshops have long produced ware of a very high standard indeed, to Malhada Sorda, where the women turn the primitive potter's wheel by hand as they have for centuries. The *quartas* for water, small, unglazed cooking-pots, and other vessels, often have shapes which are recognizably Islamic, Roman or pre-Roman in origin. They may be made of pale, reddish or black clay. The rough black pots are generally rather clumsy and badly fired. But there is ware of a better quality, from Molelos, Bisalhaes and Vilar de Nantes for example,

275b

104a, c

84f

48b

138

whose smooth exterior is decorated with straight lines, curves or intertwining spirals, which are burnished with pebbles and stand out brilliantly against the matt black background. As well as the old, traditional forms, this style is used for tea-sets, coffee-sets and sugar-bowls, in imitation of middle-class porcelain ware. Unglazed, pale-coloured earthenware is found mostly in the south; the potteries of Loulé (Algarve), Beringel and Estremoz use white clay which makes particularly handsome *amphorae* resembling Roman ones. Estremoz is Alentejo's best known centre for pottery of a particularly fine consistency; its dazzling white outer surface is dipped in a bed of red clay, and on this colourful ground, plant motifs incised with a pebble emphasize the elegance of the object's curves. The traditional forms still hold their own, for instance the two-handled *pucarinhos* for drinking water. Estremoz also produces coloured pottery: extraordinary-looking earthenware jugs which are painted after firing and decorated with ribbons and flowers in slip, with wire stalks. Further north, but still in Alentejo, the potters of Nisa ornament their unglazed ware with small pieces of quartz, pressed into the moist clay. These do not look so rich as the glazed ware, particularly as regards the ornamentation. Barcelos in the province of Minho makes household crockery for the whole of north Portugal, using always the same shapes and bright colours: yellow, green or red geometrical shapes, fishes and lush flowers, on a red or pale background. The pottery of Coimbra in central Portugal is made in similar colours, but the patterns are always geometrical. In Caldas the manufacture of brightly coloured ceramics has taken on the proportions of an industry rather than a craft. The unique shapes that have evolved here are inspired by the paintings of Bordalo Pinheiro with their surprise effects. The typical ware made in the town of Redondo in Alentejo is rather coarse; the pale ground is decorated with flowers, birds and similar motifs in green or other, rather wishy-washy colours. Redondo and Campo Major produce the huge jars, resembling Roman *dolia*, which sometimes hold over 1,500 litres and are intended for wine and oil; they are not formed on a wheel, but built up in spiral layers of clay.

For a long time the fronts of town houses were tiled with *azulejos*. On these faience tiles, geometrical figures were combined with independent, representational figures, inspired by carpet designs. The most popular colours were blue and yellow.

Fabrics of linen and cotton, often with wool threads interwoven, are still made by the traditional methods today in a few places, such as Viana do Castelo, where the women's traditional costume calls for materials of a particular quality and colour. Bedspreads are sometimes made from very thickly woven cotton, and have several broad stripes round a large central motif such as the national coat of arms or a bouquet of flowers. In this context it is apposite to mention the *mantas de farrapos*, blankets, counterpanes and carpets woven from brightly coloured rags. Silk threads were woven into the *colchas* of Urros and into the white linens of Castelo Branco, which were embroidered with patterns of Oriental origin. The carpets of Arroiolos are also inspired by the Orient, using motifs from Persian carpets. Linen was the staple fabric for ordinary people, for sheets, handkerchiefs, tablecloths, underclothes and men's trousers.

Painting, so far as it can be called a folk art at all in Portugal, embraced both religious and secular subjects. Religious pictures clearly betray the influence of academic painting, though votive pictures provide an instructive and realistic view of the furniture, domestic

148 b

153 a

Left and above: Details from a silhouette, England, 1844

interiors and clothing of the people of different periods. The pictures set up on posts near small stone chapels generally depict souls in torment, men, women, priests and bishops burning in purgatory and imploring Christ to release them. The same subject, in a simplified treatment, occurs again on the collecting-boxes inside the churches. Painted furniture is rare; occasionally the head of a bed is found painted with a landscape or a group of people, which also reveal the influence of academic, secular painting. Other wooden objects, trays for instance, may also be painted. The women who sell fish in Lisbon cover their chip baskets with waxed cloths which have geometrical patterns on a plain ground, or pictures of such appropriate subjects as cuttlefish or crabs. The pictures on shop signs are often executed in great detail.

Sculpture in stone, which had a strong folk character, died out in Portugal at the end of the Middle Ages and was replaced by sculpture in wood and terracotta, at first as a purely academic art, but later as a more popular form. The eighteenth-century successors to the *barritas*, the famous mediaeval monastery school at Alcobaça, made figures for cribs, which were taken as models by nineteenth-century craftsmen who made groups of figures from daily life. It is possible to see in the crib groups the origin of modern clay sculpture, which is one of the commonest forms of folk art in Portugal, the chief centres being Barcelos, Gaia and Estremoz. The figures, representing popular types, are moulded in rough outline and painted in bold distempers. The little figurines made in Barcelos are somewhat more refined. At the beginning of this century they were still coated with a thick liquid glaze. That has become rare and the figurines now rely for their effect on oil paints or lacquer, which people seem to prefer. Beyond any doubt the most popular of the traditional figures is the cockerel, which has close legendary connections with Barcelos. Also popular are bulls, yoked oxen, musicians, hen and chicks, mare and foal, monsters and grotesques, demon fiddlers, lizards, donkeys with human heads and many others. In Estremoz figures are modelled by hand and have a more professional finish. Among the older pieces there are some acute caricatures of eighteenth-century types. And of course, in every workshop we find innumerable popular depictions of the Virgin Mary, whose garments on older models are so arranged that they surround her like the petals of a flower.

SPAIN today is a country where folk art is still very much alive. While in other European countries the products of folk art have long found a place in museums as relics of the past, in Spain the people still practise their traditional crafts, encouraged, indeed, by the growth of tourism. It will be hard to cover the variety and wealth of material adequately in so small a space. The variety is easy to explain. Spain is one of the biggest countries in Europe in area. It is the point of contact and conflict between the European and African continents. For eight centuries large areas of Spain were occupied by the Arabs and knew a religion and a culture that were foreign to the rest of Europe. Then, at the beginning of modern times, it was Spain who, from the furthest western tip of Europe, discovered and colonized the new continent of America.

Furthermore, the country's geography contains as many different elements as a mosaic. Spain and France are the only two countries of Europe with both an Atlantic and a Mediterranean coastline. The difference is that the two coasts are divided in Spain by a plateau

Page 141 Plates and dishes: *a* Saint-Zaccharie, Bouches-du-Rhône, 1717; *b* Savignies, France, 1738; *c* Lyon, early nineteenth century; *d* Czechoslovakia, 1674; *e* Sorrus, France; *f* Kloesterlistutz, Switzerland, 1762

Page 142 Staffordshire ware, first half of nineteenth century: *a* Prince of Wales; *b* Pair of lovers; *c, d* Duchess and Duke of Cambridge

Page 143 Dogs ('comforters'), Staffordshire, *c.* 1820–50

Page 144 Sorrowing Christ (Stanislaw Koziarski), Iłza, Poland, 1942

a

b

c

d

e

f

a

b

c

d

a

b

c

d

a

b

c

d

a

b

c

d

e

f

g

h

i

a

b

c

d

e

f

g

h

i

a

b

c

d

with an average height of 1,900 feet. There are towns at 2,500 feet above sea level, like Salamanca, and others at over 3,000 feet, like Ávila. The parallel chains of mountains slice across the face of Spain, isolating the different zones. The northern part of the peninsula is well watered, but the remaining two thirds are dry: the province of Almeira contains the only desert in Europe, and there are regions which go a whole year without a drop of rain. By contrast, Galicia in the north has one of the heaviest rainfalls in Europe. It is for geographical and historical reasons like these that the different regions of Spain have preserved their identities so clearly up to the present. There are still four languages spoken: Castilian, Catalan, Galician and, the only non-Indo-European one, Basque.

The houses of Spain illustrate the variety contained in the country as well as any other branch of folk art: the types of roof range from the flat Mediterranean roof to steep gables, designed to expedite the draining of rain and snow; there are houses built around the hearth and a warm living-room, and there are others where the kitchen hardly exists since people's lives are spent out of doors; on the *huertas* (market gardens) of Valencia and Murcia there still exist the *barracas*, hovels made of reeds and clay. The one province of Granada contains, on the one hand, the Sierra Nevada with peaks rising to 10,000 feet, and a strip of perpetual snow well over 60 miles long, and on the other hand, at sea level on the Mediterranean coast, subtropical plants: sugar cane, orange trees and fig trees.

In recent history, the nineteenth century, the age which saw the industrialization of Europe, went badly for Spain, beginning with the wars against Napoleon and ending with the loss of the last overseas colonies. The isolation and backwardness of Spain did much to preserve the ancient, traditional ways of life which disappeared in the rest of Western and Central Europe. The Civil War (1936–9) dealt them a severe blow, and Spain has now begun to catch up. But now the tourist boom has brought new life to folk arts and crafts, which in Spain are not artificial as they are elsewhere; they are a continuation of traditional forms which were current until very recently.

The common people of Spain have two quite different types of furniture. There is the type designed and made by the people, rather rare, but possessing admirable, functional shapes, which resemble to a surprising extent the modern furniture emanating from Northern Europe. The other type, very popular because of its style and decoration, represents a rustic adaptation of middle- and upper-class furniture. The first category includes, above all else, chairs. These are usually the work of herdsmen and are the principal furnishings found in shepherds' huts, along with small tables and chests. Chairs, tables and chests form the essential basis of the furniture in every peasant dwelling, but they are supplemented by cupboards, cradles, beds, dressers and other useful pieces.

Chests throughout Spain are sumptuously decorated. The most remarkable are the Basque and Navarrese, which have geometrical patterns, and the Castilian which are decorated with flowers and animals; nor should the superb dower chests from Catalonia be forgotten. The choice of wood naturally depends to a large extent on what is locally available. In the north and the mountain regions of western and central Spain the woods principally used are nut, oak and chestnut, whereas pine is preferred in Castile.

There are broadly speaking two kinds of cupboard: those whose pleasing appearance derives from their basic shape, embellished by carving, and those which are decorated with flowers or realistic scenes, painted in vivid colours, sometimes inside as well as out.

It is impossible to write about traditional furniture in Spain without mentioning the *bargueño*, the writing desk, although to do so is to leave the realm of purely utilitarian furniture. Its name derives from the town of Bargas, near Toledo, where most of them were made. There are some beautiful examples dating from the sixteenth and seventeenth centuries, with noticeable Moorish overtones in their ornamentation: the inlay or the ivory on the little pillars. However it must be admitted that the *bargueño* goes beyond the limits of folk art, and was too expensive ever to have been a typical piece of peasant furniture.

Herdsmen make and carve a great number of articles from the horn of the animals in their care, from the minute matchboxes made of goats' horns to the wine flasks from huge cows' horns. In addition to objects which utilize the original shape of the horn, the material lends itself to others: spoons, tobacco boxes and the like. The powderhorns, which were usually made as gifts for the landlord or local dignitaries, showed the highest degree of artistry in their ornamentation, and drinking-horns and the large horns used to carry the herdsmen's provisions did not fall far short. Such decorated horns are to be found all over Spain, but are most common on the northern plateau, particularly in the region of Salamanca. Indeed, it may be said that, as far as folk art is concerned, the Salamanca region is the wealthiest of all Spain.

There are two methods of incising designs on horn: burning the lines in with the point of a red hot knife, or carving the figures in outline or low relief with a cold knife point. Articles are occasionally dated; the oldest known examples are from the beginning of the eighteenth century, but the majority date from the latter part of the nineteenth and the early twentieth century. This branch of folk art has still not quite died out, but the tremendous upheaval in the country's whole way of life, caused by the civil war, brought about its almost complete disappearance.

Herdsmen have shown an equal artistry in woodwork. While naturalistic patterns are the most common on horn, geometrical designs are much more frequent on wood. There are some extraordinarily fine distaffs, on which in some regions woodcarving is combined with delicate basketwork at the top end where the spool of wool or flax fits. In some districts the drawings or carvings at the foot are framed by gilded nails or inlaid ivory. Some of the implements used at various stages of clothmaking deserve to be classed as minor works of art, particularly the rakes and swingles used to separate the fibres; the same applies to the larger rakes with which the women rhythmically threshed the corn. All these articles are decorated in bright colours and usually in excellent taste. Decorated utensils, such as herdsmen would make for their brides, were not generally used, or only on special occasions. They were usually hung on the wall as ornaments, where they served as both a model and an inspiration to later generations.

The crooks the shepherds made for themselves are often very fine; the best have an exquisitely carved animal or some such figure carved at the tip, and nearly all of them are covered with figurative or geometrical ornamental motifs. The same kind of decoration is found on large cooking ladles and on spoons, notably those from the Sayago district of Zamora, whose handles are carved in the form of a church belfry. Of other wooden objects, special mention must be made of mortars and the stamps with which bakers impressed their mark on their bread. Mortars were made all over Spain, but the

89b, 92a, c, 273c

Silhouette (by W. T. Lever), Netherlands

276c

113a, b, 276f

150

Silhouette, clock cover (by G. Datema), Peize, Holland

65

128

151

finest are found in Avila province, around Salamanca and Estremadura. They are nearly always decorated with geometrical shapes. Castanets are also found in every province, but the best examples are those from the Pyrenees and the León area. In the regions with abundant rainfall there is a great variety of vessels, jugs and bowls, for containing water. There is hardly a tool which is not decorated with art and skill. One must at least mention clogs, ox yokes, ploughs and the two-wheeled carts of Salamanca. This cart is a work of art, comparable only to the Sicilian carts. Its wheels, their rims and the square panels of the cart's sides are completely covered with painted hunting scenes, ships at sea, bullfights, animals and landscapes.

Superb wrought iron is to be found all over Spain, even in the remotest corners. The museum at Cap Ferrat de Sitgés (Barcelona) is devoted entirely to the full range and variety of work produced by folk craftsmen in this medium. Estremadura became an important centre of wrought ironwork during the eighteenth century. Its forges produced the famous 'curled' irons, which were sold all over the country and formed the basis, to a large extent, of Andalusian and Castilian work. Alpujarras in Granada has a certain reputation, and in Andalusia there is Seville, famous for its shutters and balconies. Houses throughout southern Spain make a most artistic effect with the ornate wrought iron bars on the doors, windows and balconies set off against the spotless, white-washed walls. No visitor to Spain will ever forget this characteristic sight. Still in Andalusia, there are the beautiful iron crosses set up in the small squares, the most famous being in the Plaza de Santa Cruz in Seville. A purely indigenous rural form of wrought ironwork is represented by the hundreds of elegant weather-vanes, crowned by graceful crosses which are often tipped with a flower pattern or finely chiselled spirals.

Pottery, of a rather primitive kind, has been made since time immemorial all over the Iberian peninsula, with the exception of the Basque provinces and a few districts in the north. In addition the ceramics workshops produced work of a much higher standard, which played an important role in embellishing the homes of the people of Spain. The long centuries of Islamic occupation gave a great impetus to Spanish ceramics, particularly the glazed ware. The main centres of the craft were in the east, in Catalonia and Valencia, the most famous of all, even beyond the boundaries of the province, being the workshops of Manises. For centuries mule trains laden with Manises pottery plodded into Castile, and returned carrying Castilian fabrics. Manises retained its leading position for centuries, until the time of the Napoleonic wars, when its refined decorative style began to lose its popularity in favour of a more characteristically folk style. A great age for folk art ensued. Plates, dishes, bowls, basins and holy-water basins were the articles made in greatest numbers, decorated with graceful flowers and animals in bright glazes. While Manises was the most important centre in ceramics, it was far from being the only one; there were a number of places in Catalonia, where the workshops made plates and tiles *(azulejos)* depicting the various crafts, Teruel, Fajalauza (Granada) with its characteristic dark blue pomegranates and birds on an ivory ground, and the village of Puente del Arzobispo in the province of Toledo. The potters in Puente liked to imitate the art ceramics of the neighbouring town of Talavera, but from the point of view of folk art, their own work is the more important; and although the traditional craft has died out in Talavera, it still survives in Puente. The characteristic ware has a white or ivory background decorated with animal motifs in green, black, ochre or yellow, all in a very pronounced folk style. We must finally make brief mention of a few earthenware articles which enjoy wide popularity: toys, which reproduce ordinary objects in miniature, pipes, the finest of which are found on the Balearic islands, and Christmas crib figurines made in the form of shepherds, washerwomen or, with delightful incongruity, huntsmen complete with guns.

Wool and flax, until recently the two most important raw materials for fabrics, have always been in abundant supply in Spain. Merino sheep, for instance, are world famous. Once again, the centuries of Islamic rule left their mark on the designs of materials and the ornamentation of finished garments. The ivory carving which is such a feature of Muslim art exerted an enormous influence on Spanish art in general, including embroidery. In some parts of Spain today the manufacture and sale of wares woven and embroidered by hand is so well organized that they can be bought in nearly every arts and crafts shop, but this commercialization has in no way diminished their traditional character. Perhaps the two most beautiful examples of this kind of work are the fabrics made in Alpujarras in Granada, and the embroidery from Lagartera near Toledo. The Alpujarras cloths 177b reveal their unmistakeable Arabic origins. Nowadays the industry has reached a stage where it is able to produce cloths by the yard and also made-up articles: carpets, cushions, tapestries, pouches and, a modern variation on the last, handbags. The practice of weaving coloured stripes, green, black, red and white, into cloth is current all over Spain; the woollen fabrics produced in the Granada region are more ambitious, with geometrically stylized plant and animal motifs as well.

The embroidery industry, based on the village of Lagartera, employs hundreds of 187 women in the provinces of Avila, Toledo and Cacerés, making the lovely cotton tablecloths, embroidered in one or more colours, which are so strongly reminiscent of Moorish mosaics. The patterns are either purely geometrical or flowered.

There are a number of examples of such commercialized undertakings, including weaving on the Canary Islands, but peasants still also make and embroider cloths, mostly wall hangings, to decorate their own homes. The techniques and ornamentation are much simpler and more primitive than in the products of Lagartera.

There is no space to describe the wealth and variety of Spanish folk costumes in any detail. Regional differences of cloth and embroidery are accentuated by the artistic design. The most splendid of all is certainly the costume worn by the *charros*, the peasants of the Salamanca region: the men's shirts are very finely embroidered, their jacket buttons are silver filigree; gold thread is used to sew pearls and paillettes in flower patterns on the stiff material of the women's skirts, bodices and vestigial aprons. As if this were not enough they also wear large quantities of chains, crucifixes, pendants, rings and earrings.

Page 153 a Lidded jug, Nisa, Portugal; *b* Tureen, Lunéville, after 1789; *c* Jug, Saintonge, fourteenth–sixteenth century; *d* Jug, Saint-Laurent-les-Mâcon, nineteenth century; *e* Porcelain roof ornament, Tâtre, Charente, *c.* 1800; *f* Jug, Saint-Amand-en-Puisaye, Nièvre, nineteenth century; *g* Jug, Barcelos, Portugal; *h* Tureen, Orleans, mid-nineteenth century; *i* Jug, Borba, Portugal

Page 154 a Wooden water-jug, Schwalm, Hesse, 1901; *b* Flask, Moravia, 1823; *c* Jug, Pustertal, Tyrol, eighteenth century; *d* Jug, Calvados, Normandy, eighteenth century; *e* Jug, France, late eighteenth century; *f* Jug, Normandy, eighteenth century; *g* Jug with handle, Marburg, Germany, 1820–30; *h* Vase, Italy; *i* Wooden flask, Transylvania

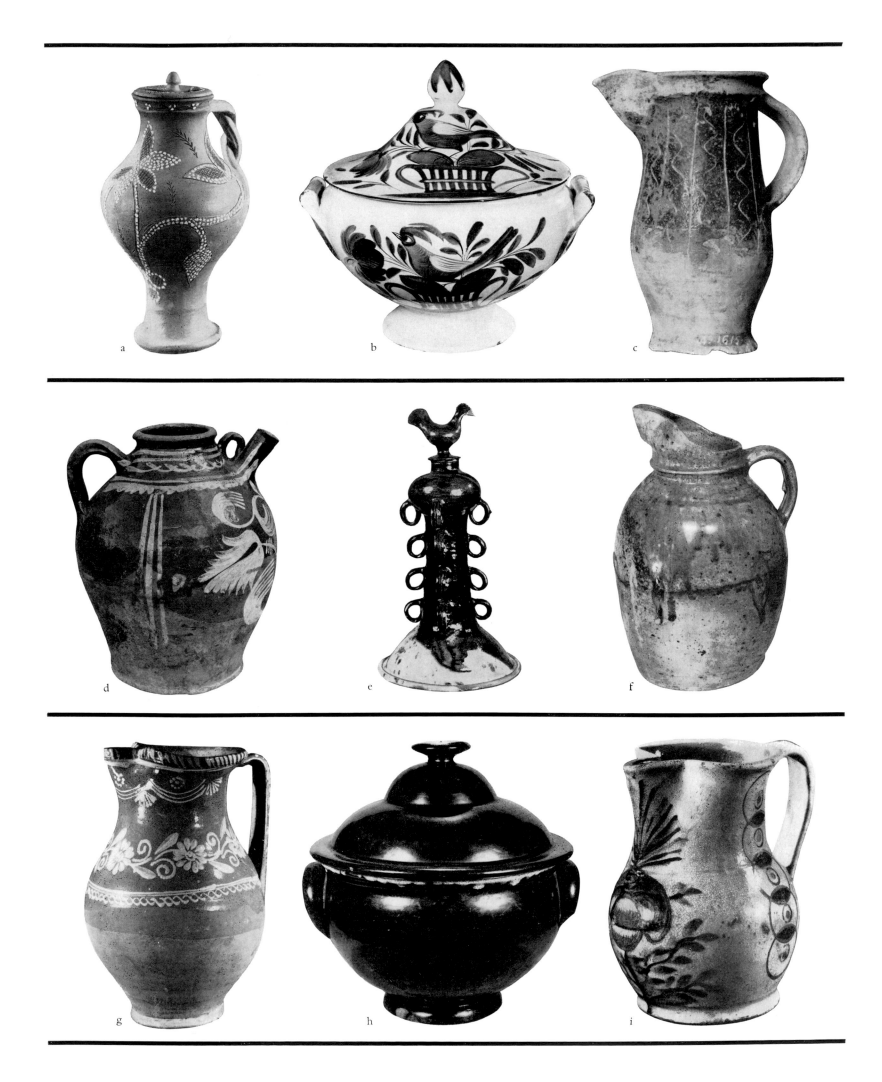

a   b   c

d   e   f

g   h   i

a

b

c

d

e

f

g

h

i

a

b

c

d

e

f

g

h

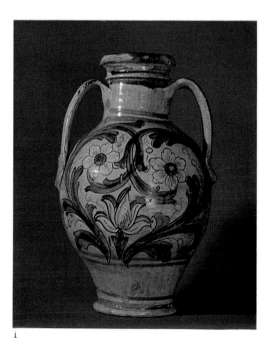

i

a

b

c

d

Southern Europe

Italy · Yugoslavia · Greece

ITALY's geographical situation and the complex historical vicissitudes in the cultural and ethnic life of her people have endowed her with an extraordinary variety of expression in folk lore in general and in folk art in particular.

So far as typical peasant houses are concerned the country falls into three main regions: the Alps and Pre-Alps, the more level country of central Italy, and the southern 'Mediterranean' area which is characterized by the style of architecture best represented in Amalfi and Capri. Obviously, climatic and topographical circumstances in the Alps, which drive the people to spend so much time indoors during the long winters, lead to an emphasis on interiors and furnishing, whereas further south domestic and agricultural activities take place out of doors, and the furnishing of interiors is reduced to a minimum.

Many Alpine houses are built wholly or partly of wood, with balconies all round at ground and first-floor level where maize and other crops are spread to dry. The steep roofs are characteristic of the region. In Carnia the fireplace is not against the wall but far enough away to allow room for a wooden seat to run all round it, on which people may sit to warm themselves, to knit or to keep an eye on the cooking. Roofs in the Italian Alps may be of thatch or stone. The former variety have a steeper slope, and are also found on the *casoni* of the Venetian coastal plain. In order to reduce the risk of fire the chimneys are built up the outside of the house and rise well above the level of the roof.

In central Italy the farm buildings are usually separate from the living-quarters. The family generally lives over the *rustico*, the stables and cart shed, and the first floor is reached by an outside staircase. Naturally there are many variations on this arrangement on different kinds of terrain. On the one hand there is the primitive *casa per terra*, a one-storey building made of rough bricks, on the other, particularly in Tuscany, farmhouses of two stories with numerous rooms show the unmistakable mark of Renaissance architecture and remind us of this region's great cultural heritage.

In Abruzzi there are two characteristic types: the brick farmhouses with exterior staircases found in the Apennine foothills, and the stone houses grouped for safety in villages and small towns higher up the mountains, where the farmers set out early in the morning to walk several miles to work, returning late in the evening. There are excellent examples of houses in both brick and stone in Amalfi and on Capri; hence the general term 'Amalfi-Capri architecture' to describe the style prevalent in southern Italy. It is a Mediterranean style in that structure and function stand in a patent relation to everyday life, to the history and civilization of the people and places on the shores of that sea. There are similar houses both on the coast of Liguria and southern Lazio (Sperlonga) and in North Africa. The eye is first caught by the dazzling white walls and the roof, which takes the form of a dome, a flattened dome or a semi-dome. The entrance is

157

usually at the top of a small flight of steps. The flat roof is often found instead of the dome. One particularly original kind of house is the *trullo*, which is locally believed to be unique to Apulia. A recent comparative study by Rohlfs, however, shows the existence of similar structures not only in Liguria, in the mountains of Istria, in Sardinia and Sicily, but in other parts of Europe also, in the south of France, in Spain and even in Ireland. In its original and simplest form the *trullo* or *casedda* is a stone hut with a conical roof, the upper half of which is often decorated with ornamental *motifs* and good luck symbols.

Some of the furniture found in peasants' houses was made and decorated by shepherds and some, of better quality, by professional craftsmen. Objects in the former category, which often take very ancient forms, include cradles, stools, footstools, chairs and kneading-troughs. The wooden cradles are carved or painted, and sometimes both. The best examples come from the Alps, and employ all the usual kinds of motifs. Flowers are the most popular, but there is nearly always a protective religious device, such as the Lamb of God, a monogram of Christ or, more rarely, a picture of the Virgin. The mountain shepherd likes to decorate the sides of cradles with carvings of the animals in his environment, particularly the stag and the roedeer. In southern Italy and Sicily the *naca* is used, a kind of bag made of cloth, formerly of sheepskin or goatskin, which is hung from a roof beam so that the mother can rock her baby while doing her housework. The wooden frame is often decorated with geometrical patterns.

58b

The six-pointed star is a favourite motif found on milking-stools and many other articles carved by herdsmen. The chairs are most richly decorated on the back and arm-rests, with designs derived for the most part from the work of professional craftsmen. In Sardinia and Abruzzi the backs of chairs are very high. One of the most important and elaborate pieces of furniture found in the necessarily modest homes of peasants and farmers is the chest in which a young wife's dowry is stored. The dower chests of Sardinia are certainly the finest: durable and richly decorated in a style at once severe and elegant, they adhere closely to traditional patterns which yet allow considerable variations. The chest stands on tall, well-made legs, and is decorated with a wide border of circles or rosettes carved in relief around a central rectangle that contains carvings of birds, hearts and similar motifs. There is also a wide variety of ornate dower chests in mountain regions of the mainland, which are lower than the Sardinian since they are used not only for storage but also as seats. They show the clear influence of Renaissance and baroque urban forms.

56i

47a, b

The finest examples of wooden bedsteads come from the Alpine regions, showing great skill in their carved decorations, with elegant simplicity of form and piety in their choice of subject. The head is always adorned with one of the monograms which represent the name of Christ. In the Adige valley the bed, like all the other furniture, is painted all over; and the four corner posts support a wooden canopy which is also painted. A *prie-dieu* stands beside the bed. Peasant furniture – chests of drawers, cupboards, dressers, coffers and caskets – offers much that is the artistic equal of more sophisticated forms.

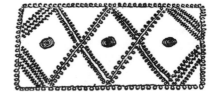

Above and right: Patterns on floor tiles, Scotland

Peasants and herdsmen customarily make objects of everyday use for themselves, carving and decorating them too, and using wood, the material most freely available to them. The decoration lavished on shepherds' crooks shows their love of ornament for its own sake. All the equipment used in tending sheep and cattle is carved; the most

115b–d common motifs are the sun and the six planets, ancient pagan symbols. though sometimes Christian images, ciphers of Christ and the Virgin or the cross of St Andrew, occur in their stead. Ox yokes are also richly decorated. In the Alto Adige common devices are a motif resembling a mitre and dots, like those on a dice; in Sicily they favour carved soldiers or painted saints, in the same style as on the painted carts. Milking-stools, pails and other dairy equipment are also carved and painted. In addition to the kinds of ornament already mentioned, geometrical shapes and hearts are also frequently found. The peasant also carves the *portacote* in which he keeps the slipstone for sharpening his scythe; it is made of cowhorn and sometimes decorated with human figures, wearing the local costume. In the dairy the object most certain to be decorated is the butter-pat.

273a, b
280c In the Val d'Aosta they are carved with cows and edelweiss, in Ticino with blossoms, a burning heart or the carver's initials. The forms for bread and cakes are also carved:

277e–h the finest come from Lazio and Abruzzi, bearing symbols of love and marriage. Spoons, forks and ladles have animal and human figures carefully carved on them with the point of the knife. Among the many varieties of wooden drinking-vessel we must single out the *grolla*, found in the Val d'Aosta and used only on special, festive occasions. This huge cup, shaped like a goblet, probably turned on a wheel, following ancient models, has a lid which, like the cup itself, is decorated with bas-reliefs. In Sicily is to be found the *appizza-bichieri*, a kind of carved wooden rack to hold cups, which are usually decorated with geometrical patterns or human and animal figures. A young woman's distaff was usually given her by her bridegroom and was therefore carved with particular grace and using a particular range of motifs: entwined hearts, a female figure, 'the bride', or a man and woman embracing, as well as the usual geometrical patterns. Distaffs are to be found everywhere, but the Calabrian model, shorter than those of the mountain regions, is the most interesting to the archaeologist and the anthropologist.

102b–d Horn and bone are other materials worked by folk artists. Sardinia has produced some very fine drinking-cups, flasks, tobacco boxes and powderhorns. The carved ornamentation follows characteristic archaic patterns, reminiscent of Byzantine art, though translated into the primitive formal language of shepherds. The form is not confined to Sardinia: some of the Sicilian *gotti*, a kind of goblet, are decorated in a classical style, though they may also depict contemporary scenes and customs. Carved gourds are taken to the fields as drinking-flasks by huntsmen and farmers. The most interesting are found in Sardinia, Sicily and Calabria. They usually depict religious themes, but sometimes

103 everyday scenes and people, always in the same, precise, archaic style, like a classical vase, which can have a comic effect when the figures are in a more modern dress. Straw vessels made in Sardinia are of artistic interest for their shapes modelled on classical vases, or for the agreeable use made of straw in different colours.

However, all these articles are on a primitive level compared with metalwork: utensils made in copper, iron or pewter, and brooches and pins in gold and silver. All metalwork calls for a proper workshop, however small, and a trained craftsman. Copper objects are often of the highest artistic value: jugs, dishes, basins, pails, kettles, warming-pans, braziers, tankards, cake tins and many others. The elegant lines of Tuscan and Umbrian jugs are particularly remarkable. The typical large dish, the *conca*, found in Lazio is no

less elegant. It is certainly more attractive and more practical, and less slavishly copied from older models, than the round *conca* of Abruzzi, of which examples have been found in graves of Roman date. The ancient models are typically decorated with simple flowers or abstract motifs, while the later ones from Lazio have embossed ribbon patterns on them. The copperware of northern Italy, buckets, warming-pans and footwarmers, is embossed and chiselled with particularly elaborate care.

Wrought ironwork has a long and splendid history: it is at its best in Carnia and the Trentino, in shutters, fire-irons, inn signs, memorial crosses on graves, and in the grates of open fires. Locks, hinges and clasps were chiselled, engraved and hammered, to particularly good effect in northern Italy. Pewter was considered to be a more special material than copper and iron and was used for vases, plates, dishes and platters; they look extremely well on the dressers of farmhouses throughout the Italian Alps from Piedmont to Carnia. Golden ornaments in the same designs are often worn by members of the same family for generations. This practice is particularly prevalent in Abruzzi, notably in Guardiagrele and Pescocostanzo. Earrings in the form of boats or gondolas, pins, hairpins, engagement rings and little perfume flasks are made in filigree silver and engraved.

The earliest Italian ceramic ware originated in the south. The most important centre in Sicily is Caltagirone (Catania); others are Collesano, Terranova and Canicatti. The simplest, and probably the oldest, forms are the bowls and basins, of various depths, like the *limmiteddu*, which are used principally for washing dishes; such basins sometimes have two or four handles. The best known come from Patti, and exactly resemble pieces found in Caltagirone which can be dated several centuries before Christ. Oil lamps, too, preserve traditions which are thousands of years old. The larger ones are in the form of human figures (women, huntsmen or brigands) with hollow heads to hold the oil. There are numerous vessels to hold water, notably the *quartare*, made in the shape of rounded *amphorae*, with either smooth or twisted handles, and the flasks, *fiaschi*, of all shapes and sizes.

133 c
154 h
155 g–i

125

Sardinia's most important ceramics centres are Oristano and Dorgali, where the *brocchete*, jugs in the forms of cocks and hens, are made. The typical Calabrian terracotta ware comes from Seminara; it is glazed in green, yellow or orange and painted with horses, birds of flowers. Another interesting item is the flask in the shape of a fish, the symbol of the early Christians and of pilgrims to the festival of St Rock.

Apulia has been producing pottery since Roman times; as well as the *quartare* there are the *giara*, a cup with two handles; the *ziru*, a tall, massive vessel for holding oil; the *ugghiarolu*, a small oil cruse; and the *trufulu*, an earthenware wine bottle. Sometimes the *giare* have a 'secret', a device which makes it impossible for those who do not know the secret to drink from them. The dark brown pots and jugs with spouts from Basilicata are lacquered and shiny but have no decoration on them. Things are very different in Abruzzi. A local style of ornamental pottery has developed over the last three or four centuries in Castelli (Teramo). The brilliant colouring and original shapes of the pots and painted statuettes reflects the love of the local people for bright colours, unusual subjects and formal exaggeration. The chief centre for this ware is Palena; among the most common forms are jugs with trefoil-shaped lips, flat or circular flasks patterned with flowers, and painted flasks and oil lamps in the form of human figures.

In Molise the art of the vase makers *(vasari)* flourishes. The most important centres are Campobasso, Venafro and Guardiagrele. The ornamentation is fairly simple and the

Silhouette (by W. T. Lever), Netherlands

160

Silhouette, Holland, 1834

colours muted. Pontecorvo in the southern part of Lazio, a region where the population is closely related to that of the Campania, is still today the home of a kind of pottery which is one of the most interesting in Italy. The whole population practises the craft, mixing the clay, shaping it on the wheel, smoothing and burnishing, painting it while still moist with stylized animals, birds, flowers and abstract ornaments. Still in Lazio, Arpino produces a form of earthenware, using the simplest methods, in robust colours and crude shapes, which is yet extremely effective, for example the plates and dishes decorated with comic drawings and pictures. Deruta in Umbria still makes its famous majolica. In the Marches the highly artistic majolica of Pesaro exists side by side with a simple peasant pottery in dark colours and brillant glaze. This is used for all kinds of domestic crockery: baking-dishes, pots and pans and the typical *trufa*, a drinking-vessel with a very narrow neck which harvesters take to quench their thirst in the fields. In Tuscany, too, peasants still make their own earthenware, at Monte San Savino (Arezzo), at Montelupo, known for its jugs, and Signa and Impruneta, known for their terracotta. Faenza in Romagna has been famous since the sixteenth century for its excellent ceramic ware, so that the word 'faience' is synonymous with 'ceramics' in many countries; but the true folk pottery of Romagna comes from Imola. In the three Venetian provinces pottery still follows eighteenth-century styles, adapted to the popular taste and painted with such traditional subjects as the seasons and the months of the year. The chief centre in Liguria was formerly Savona, where a high standard was achieved, but it has been superseded by Albisola.

The technical processes involved in glassmaking require properly equipped factories and workshops and it has never been a significant branch of folk art in Italy. We will just mention the nineteenth-century Neapolitan liqueur bottles with pictures of historical personalities like Victor Emmanuel III and Queen Elena, and also fishes and paraffin lamps made of glass.

The nature of folk weaving is conditioned by the use of the handloom, which was still
194 general all over Italy up to fifty years ago. The best carpets come from Abruzzi, Calabria and Sardinia, and there are also some fine examples from Apulia, Sicily and Lazio. The material used is sheep's wool, and the dyes are extracted from plants: pale green from beech and ash leaves, blue from the indigo plant, yellow from saffron, red from grape skins. Patterns follow certain conventions which make the most of the potentialities and limitations of the material and methods. Since weaving is fundamentally an arrangement of threads at right angles to each other, patterns and styles are necessarily based on straight lines. The centre of an Abruzzi carpet is generally divided into a pattern of rhombuses which frame the imaginative symbols and figures: centaurs, mermaids, the fountain of love, the Lamb of God, the unicorn, the griffin, the two-headed eagle, various plants, or even the swastika and the solar wheel. These are all mediaeval motifs, still used on carpets of more recent origin. The striped rugs of Sardinia are spread over the dower chests. The patterns woven into the stripes include horsemen and extraordinary, stylized birds, flowers and imaginary beasts. The large blankets which cover the high Sardinian double beds are made using the *a piloni* technique. The central pattern usually consists of stylized flowers which run in from the four corners, surrounded by a single strip of border. In Erice in Sicily carpets are made in simple patterns with horizontal

161

stripes and geometrical shapes. Peasants also weave their own carpets in Lazio, Campania and Sannio Beneventano, where they are very thick and the colours most intense.

Perugia has been famous for its fabrics since the Middle Ages; they can be seen in countless Renaissance pictures, for example the tablecloth in Leonardo da Vinci's *Last Supper*. The linen cloths are usually square, with a pattern executed in a single colour, often turquoise, and sometimes portraying mediaeval symbolic animals, such as the griffin, which appears in Perugia's coat of arms, or dragons, unicorns, hounds pursuing a fox, stags and so on. Unusual and attractive products of folk art are the blankets, either printed or dyed a russet colour, made in Romagna originally to protect cattle against the cold of winter.

Painting occupies a very special place in Italian folk art. Its subject matter falls naturally into three main groupings: life on the land, life in the small towns and popular piety.

The chief feature in the first category is the farm cart. In Emilia and Romagna this is large, has four wheels and no side boards, and is drawn by two oxen. The carts of Emilia, which are often carved as well, have a picture of the Madonna of San Lucca, who is honoured in Bologna, on the front board, and St Antony on the back board. This order is reversed on the Romagnese carts, where St Antony appears on the front and the Madonna of Fire, honoured in Forlí, on the upper half of the back board, surrounded by appropriate agricultural motifs, with St George below her, in the act of killing the dragon. The carts typical of central Italy are less massive and less painted, but have side panels, which facilitate the transport of hay and straw. In Tuscany carts are simply painted brick red, whereas in Abruzzi and the Marches the painting is more elaborate and colourful. The carts generally used for carrying wine in Lazio are painted rather crudely in one or two colours. They are drawn by horses and have a kind of round thatched roof to shelter the driver. By far the finest painting is found on the two-wheeled carts of Sicily, covering 116 every square inch of surface, including parts that have already been carved. The sides, usually divided into two square panels, have scenes from tales of chivalry or well-known traditional puppet plays, or episodes from history or the lives of popular heroes. All the 216a characteristics of true folk art are here: the folksong-like thematic simplification, which 227 concentrates on the really important facts, the exaggeration and simplification of line and colour; the stylization of the figures; and the repetition of lines and areas of colour, which enhances the total effect and emphasizes the rhythm.

Even the insides of the carts are painted, perhaps with the red sun in splendour, or panelled with little pieces of mirror glass, and the total effect is rounded off by the horse's harness, studded with patches of red. For a long time it was believed that the origins of the Sicilian carts must lie in classical antiquity, but the hypothesis has had to be abandoned for the simple reason that until the end of the eighteenth century Sicily had no roads on which the carts could have been driven.

The blankets worn in winter by cattle in the Verona region are held in place by a wooden framework which is brightly painted with geometrical patterns and six-pointed stars. Carved and painted yokes are typical of the Marches, decorated with ears of corn, 114a hearts, flowers or figures.

The main sphere of folk painting in country towns was on the signs outside shops and inns, the posters put up by travelling salesmen and the sheets displayed by ballad singers, illustrating their songs. The best are the signs and placards of the Florentine melon vendors with their witty slogans and rhymes, the Neapolitan inn signs, depicting Pulcinella and scenes of everyday life, and the huge placards of the Sicilian ballad singers, on which the main episodes of their often gruesome narratives are illustrated in a sequence of drawings. They bear a stylistic resemblance to the posters displayed by puppet-showmen, whose art is still very popular in Sicily; and in their vivid colours and their subjects, inspired by the romances of chivalry, they are reminiscent of the painted carts of the island.

226

214a, c, d

But the most eloquent field of Italian folk painting must be the votive plaques (*ex voto*) which survive in great numbers in all the pilgrimage churches of Italy from the Alps to Sicily. In the church of the Madonna dell'Arco near Naples alone, more than four thousand have been counted, dating from the sixteenth century right up to the present day. The custom of dedicating a plaque to a divinity, to ask for a blessing or to give thanks for one, is extremely old and was described in detail by Roman writers such as Cicero and Tibullus; it has persisted, uninterrupted even by the transition to Christianity. The earliest extant painted votive plaques date from the second half of the fifteenth century and the most interesting, from an aesthetic point of view, are those in the pilgrimage church of the Madonna del Monte near Cesena (Forli). The *ex-voto* are usually painted on wood, but linen, sheet metal, cardboard and tiles, particularly in centres of ceramic manufacture like Deruta and Castelli, are also found. They usually measure twelve to twenty inches wide by eight to twenty inches high, but some are as big as a good-sized oil painting. The general scheme of composition has the Virgin or the appropriate saint among clouds in the top part of the picture, looking down on the scene of the miracle, and below that an abbreviated inscription such as v. f. g. r. (*Voto fatto, grazia ricevuta:* 'vow taken, grace received'). Often the votary's name is also given, with the date and a short description of the miracle. The most common calamities include falls, accidents on journeys, robbers, shipwreck and the like; illness, operations and miraculous cures; and preservation in time of war, right up to the age of tanks and aircraft. Modern ones, not surprisingly, deal mostly with railway and road accidents. The painters manage to imbue the scenes with high drama, often to a grotesque extent, particularly by their use of colour. In scenes of shipwreck the sky and sea are pitch black and midnight blue, riven by lightning flashes; red blood washes round a haemorrhage case as if in a slaughter house; dead white sheets, transparent wax candles and white nightcaps frame the bloodless faces of bedridden invalids. Ochre, bottle green and garish blue vibrate in sudden accidents which threaten a festive occasion but are averted by the miraculous intervention of the saint, whose benevolent, childlike face peers down from the top of the picture, his head ringed by a flickering halo.

Popular sculpture also makes its most telling effects, like the painting, in religious subjects, particularly in the Alpine regions, from the Val d'Aosta to the Venetian Alps and from the Trentino to Carnia. The stylistic affinities of the statues made all over this wide area are remarkable. They are made in wood or stone and occasionally in metals. Stone is used in the Monte Lessini (in the provinces of Vicenza and Verona) to make statues of saints, the Virgin with the Infant Jesus, and the *Mater dolorosa* bearing the dead Christ on her lap, and also simple crosses decorated with symbols of the Passion.

Above and left: Ornamental leaves, wrought iron, England

163

The primitive wooden figures from the Val d'Aosta include colourful Madonnas, bishops and monks at prayer, and there are also bas-reliefs depicting the lives of the saints or gospel stories. Wood sculpture is prevalent throughout the Alps.

A special branch of this art is the crib. Around the Nativity, the figures of Mary, Joseph, the Child in the manger, the ox, the ass, the shepherds and the three kings, there gradually grew up a crowded scene involving dozens of people occupied in all kinds of everyday activities against a background of usually classical architecture. From the seventeenth century on, the Neapolitan crib with its vivid and original scenes was a model for many others. In Calabria the figures were set in motion by unseen machinery, and in Liguria the brightly painted figures were made in terracotta.

265b

A minor form of *ex voto* art consisted of silver or wax votive models of people at prayer, soldiers or babies, and also of parts of the human body that had been afflicted or cured, such as arms, legs, hands, heads, eyes or breasts. It is quite possible that these offerings represent the survival of practices that stretch back to Roman and Etruscan cults.

A more profane note is struck by carnival customs. The carnival of Viareggio is one of the richest in this respect. In some regions, notably in the Alps and in Sicily, carved wooden masks are worn, of demonic or bestial aspect.

YUGOSLAVIAN folk art is the expression of a people who live at the point of intersection of east and west, on the busiest crossroads in Europe; they have lived through migrations, crusades and Turkish invasions. The ancient cultures of the Balkans flourished here, and the Greek east met and mingled with the Latin west. All these influences have been absorbed and transmuted in a highly original way.

There is a wide variety of architectural styles and materials. In the heavily wooded areas of Bosnia, Slovenia and part of Serbia, houses are built of logs *(brunara)*; on the broad plains they are constructed in *bondruk*, a kind of half-timbering with fired or unfired bricks between the timber framework, or simply in packed clay *(vaboj)*, with thatched roofs of straw or reed. In the Karst region along the Adriatic coast, houses are built of stone. There are also transitional zones where materials are mixed. Turkish influences are apparent in the buildings of the eastern part of the country; the style could be called a Balkan one, and is most marked in the *kuće moravke*, the houses in the region of the Morava river, with their arcaded galleries. In Croatia, Slovenia and the Voivodate, village houses display exuberant baroque features.

19a

While it is possible to speak of different architectural styles that are characteristic of particular regions, all that one can say of the furniture is that it is very simple. The most prominent piece in any house is the bed, or rather sleeping-platform, of oak or whatever wood is available, which is completely covered by a woven blanket, the *sarenica* or *gubera*. Chests and coffers are the most beautiful pieces of furniture, and are always decorated with elaborate carvings or painting. They are used for storing clothes and all kinds of household linen. The three-legged tables and stools found in mountain areas give way to more usual forms of tables, chairs and benches on the plains. A wall cupboard *(dolap)* for storing crockery and food, and a baking-trough where flour is kept and dough kneaded, are the most important things in the kitchen, apart from the fireplace, of

Page 165 a, b Painted brandy-bottles, eighteenth century: *a* Alsace, *b* Swabia, Silesia; *c* Glass rolling-pins, Nailsea, early nineteenth century

Page 166 a Drinking-measure, Scotland; *b* Schnaps-bottle, Szentgál, Hungary, 1841; *c* Bottles, Toulouse, late eighteenth century

a

b

c

a

b

c

a

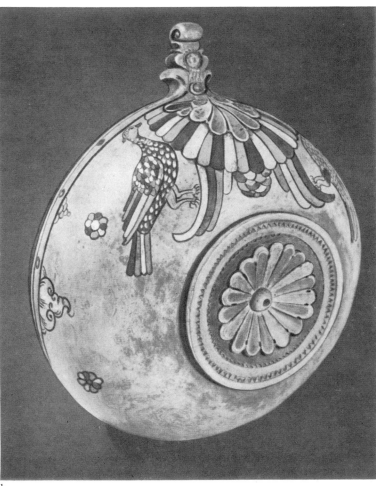

b

c

d

a

b

c

d

course. Earthenware and copper pots are ranged beside it and a tripod always stands over it with a copper kettle on the simmer. It can be said that all the spoons and knives, which comprise the total stock of cutlery, the various baskets for wine and spirits bottles, the wooden containers for water and many other simple pieces of kitchen equipment, are each and every one unique, because they will usually have been made by the man of the house. The metal domestic vessels are an exception, being the work of professional craftsmen. Their forms are typical of the Balkans, introduced in the main by the Turks, but there are some which copy wooden and clay vessels. They are used in cooking and baking, but there is a larger type, rather like a tray, called a *sinija*, which is used as a kind of table. They are hammered, engraved and sometimes chiselled. The ornamentation is of Oriental origin, portraying stylized flowers, and sometimes animals in relief.

Pottery is still widely practised as a folk craft, principally for making cooking-pots and containers for water, grain and beans. The most primitive techniques still exist beside highly sophisticated modern methods, and there is a great variety of styles, shapes and patterns. There are three main techniques of making pottery: by hand, without any kind of tools, the results being known as 'women's ware' (*ženska keramika*), since it is a method used only by women; moulding on a wheel turned by hand; and thirdly on a wheel driven by a pedal. Each of these methods produces its own peculiarities of form and ornamentation. The first, most primitive method is used for making cooking-pots and a kind of oven for use on open fires, which is made in two parts, a base (*crepulja*) and a lid (*vršnik*), in which bread or other food can be baked. Apart from the variety of their shapes, round, oval or conical, these ovens have no kind of decoration and are becoming as rare as is the use of open fireplaces for cooking.

The wheel turned by hand is the tool of village craftsmen. They use a mixture of clay and quartz, producing a rough finish. To strengthen them and render them waterproof, the pots are dipped after firing in a paste of flour and soot, which makes them black or at least very dark. They are made in different sizes, and decorated with horizontal, straight or wavy parallel lines or with short, vertical notches. Larger vessels have circles raised in relief, which serve both as reinforcement and decoration. Such pots have the maker's seal on the base, a cross, a circle, a star or any combination of these devices. They are nearly all used for cooking.

Ceramic ware made on the pedal-driven wheel is smooth and carefully coated with a thin glaze that does not stand up to great heat; it is used primarily for vessels intended to hold liquids, and in addition for a wide range of miscellaneous objects: musical instruments, toys, ornaments for house façades, pipes and so on. These pots and jugs, like those made of metal and majolica, often copy the shapes of wooden vessels. Earthenware produced in this way is found all over the country, with ethnic and territorial variations in form and ornamentation. The typical Macedonian ware is made in classical forms; in Kosovo and Metohija it copies the shapes of the metal vessels which are common in this region; in the Voivodate it closely follows Pannonian earthenware, adding late baroque ornamentation to primitive shapes. The best-known centre of earthenware manufacture, Pirot in Serbia, deserves its reputation for its great variety of forms, using three-dimensional ornaments, and for its vessels in human and animal shapes. The stylistic and

Page 167 a Wooden beer-ladle, Telemark, Norway, 1781; *b* Bowl for drinking wine, Russia, late eighteenth century; *c, d* Jugs, Gzel, Russia: *c* late eighteenth century, *d* 1792

Page 168 Embroidered jackets: *a* Bulgaria; *b* Bridal bodice, island of Marken, Holland, eighteenth century; *c* Rumania; *d* Transylvania, 1888

formal characteristics of this ware developed under Byzantine and Turkish influences; it is coated with a good polychrome glaze.

All available natural fibres are used to make cloth for all purposes; wool, hemp and flax are very common, cotton and silk less so. Besides the very simplest technique, weaving the weft in and out of the warp with a shuttle, producing stripes and checks in four shades from two basic colours, there is the more complicated technique whereby the individual threads of the weft are knotted into the warp with the fingers, a method which allows far greater freedom to execute imaginative patterns. Cloth woven in this way is characterized by a wealth of colours and of traditional, geometrically stylized plant and animal motifs. The heavier kinds of weave, such as bedspreads and carpets, 195b are not only attractively coloured, but also remarkably hard-wearing. The wide variety 197a, 198a of Yugoslav folk textiles is increased by fabrics specially woven for the traditional 174c costumes, cloths embroidered in different stitches and styles, knitted stockings and 176b gloves, various kinds of lace, and the use of *appliqué* on skirts, jackets, waistcoats and cloaks.

Folk painting is found on eggs, gourds, and, in Slovenia, beehives and wooden chests. 235b The designs executed on eggs are very rarely realistic, usually consisting of extremely stylized representations of butterflies, peacocks, turtles, snakes and human beings. A number of different techniques are used, chief among them batik. The background colour is likely to be red, yellow, blue or black. The patterns on gourds are always plants or geometrical shapes. Lines are carved with a small knife, and then darkened by rubbing with charred nut. The other colours used are also of plant origin. The wicker doors of beehives in Slovenia are completely covered with naively realistic drawings illustrating legends and proverbs. Chests are always decorated in oil paints with plant motifs which are equally naive and realistic. The background is painted a dark colour; a similar style of decoration is used on children's cradles.

There is a plentiful use of carving as a means of decoration. Herdsmen take great pride in carving their belled wooden collars for rams and bulls, guzlas (one-stringed fiddles), crooks, whips, spindles and mugs. The crooks usually terminate in a human or animal head, and snakes, oak leaves and blossoms twine round the staff, copied by the herdsman from his surroundings. The spindles made as gifts for sweethearts and wives are decora- 91b ted with geometrical patterns and stylized plants and with naive portraits of humans and animals in relief. Reliefs are also often carved on fences, doorposts, wicker granaries, and, particularly along the Adriatic coast and in some parts of Macedonia and Serbia, on chests and coffins and on doors and ceilings. There are all kinds of different wooden containers for liquids. Gourds are carved with reliefs or with beading, which also occurs on rounded beakers, wooden spoons and the like. Carnival masks worn in the Alpine regions are made of wood and often carved with grotesque expressions.

It is customary in all parts of Yugoslavia to decorate cakes baked for religious festivals 257b, c with shapes moulded in dough. The traditional shapes are of native origin but similar forms are found all over Europe.

Gravestones occupy a special position in the folk art of Yugoslavia. The vertical stone 255a, c, e slabs bear a carved portrait of the deceased with the dates of his birth and death, his profession and pious texts.

170

Left and above: Embroidered caps, Karelia, eighteenth century

GREECE, long exposed to the influences of both east and west, has assimilated something of both in her folk art without sacrificing anything of its national character; the topography of the country, with its numerous islands and its regions isolated from each other by mountain ranges, has resulted in a multitude of local artistic styles. The influence of Oriental art is most apparent in weaving and embroidery, while ornamental silver (particularly in churches), sculpture and painting are more subject to the influences of European baroque.

There are three main areas of activity in Greek folk art, each with its own individual style. There is, firstly, village art, or herdsman's art, the naive, spontaneous decoration of all possible utensils and tools in general daily use, done by the peasants in their own homes; secondly, urban art, which can also be the work of amateurs, but is for the most part executed in the workshops of professional craftsmen and is characterized by a greater degree of refinement. This is the area of folk art most open to foreign influences and innovations. The third area is ecclesiastical art, carried on exclusively in workshops, which unites western influences and the artistic traditions of Byzantium.

The decorative subjects of Greek folk art can also be grouped in categories, four in all: the purely ornamental motifs, flowers, vases, geometrical figures and linear compositions; subjects drawn from everyday life, ships, pastoral scenes, weddings, hunting, dancing; symbolical subjects with a special significance in custom and superstition, such as cypress trees, eagles, stags, serpents, the slaying of dragons; and finally subjects with centuries of artistic tradition behind them: rosettes, curves, swastikas, spirals, vine leaves, heraldic compositions and mythological figures.

Apart from architecture, those fields of Greek folk art which show the greatest amount of local variety in style and character are weaving and embroidery on silk. Both are exclusively feminine and domestic arts and each style is restricted to a single locality. For this reason embroidery and weaving, in their use of specific basic materials, colours and types of ornamentation, are the purest expression of an individual local style.

In contrast to this diversity, sculpture, woodcarving and metalwork all show a great degree of similarity, not only all over Greece but often throughout the Balkans as a whole. This is due to the fact that they were all practised by itinerant professional craftsmen who travelled for chiefly economic reasons through all parts of Greece and often beyond her borders. Comparable technical and aesthetic similarities are also to be found in those areas of Greek folk art in which output was concentrated in workshops established in particular places; this is true of silverware, for example, and, to a certain extent, of gold embroidery. Economic and natural local reasons, such as the availability of specific raw materials, led to the establishment of centres where workers in a particular craft joined together in professional associations. Because of the high standards resulting from their specialization, the work of such craftsmen was much sought-after outside their own region. A leading centre of artistic activity and creation in all media was the district of Epirus and its chief town Ioannina; the outstanding work of its artists was sold not only throughout Greece but all over the Balkans and large areas of the rest of Europe.

There are two main styles in domestic architecture, one typical of northern Greece and one prevalent on the Aegean coast and on the islands. Houses in the former style have two or more storeys, tall projecting bays without windows, and dormer windows with coloured glass, like church windows. Houses in the Aegean style have only one storey, their external proportions are based on the cube, and the roofs are tiled and have a shallow pitch or are flat.

Woodcarving and painting are inseparable adjuncts of building. In peasants' houses they are not merely decorative, they are an integral, organic part of the whole. Every wooden fitting and piece of furniture is decorated with carving: cupboards, window frames, doors, ceilings, tables, stools and chests. The four walls of the 'best room' are painted with friezes along their whole length and for most of their height. These paintings are predominantly naturalistic representations of such scenes as harbours, walled towns and subjects copied from the Western European copper engravings which, published at one time in editions of thousands, made their way as far as Greece.

218b

Carving in stone had equally close connections with architecture. As represented on buildings of the eighteenth and nineteenth centuries, folk sculptors were affected by the attitudes of the Muslim world, which forbade portrait sculpture, and restricted themselves to ornamental reliefs, in which eastern, western and purely local elements are happily combined.

258b

Embroidery falls into two main categories: one embracing all domestic linen, particularly that brought out on special occasions, and above all the sheets and covers of the wedding bed, and the other including the whole wide field of traditional Greek dress.

179a

173b

One of the most important arts practised by professional craftsmen in Greece is the fashioning of silver, for ecclesiastical use and for the personal ornaments worn by men as well as by women.

The liberation of Greece from Turkish rule opened the doors to the products of western industrialism, which progressively killed Greek folk art. The gradual disappearance of traditional costumes from the towns, in particular, resulted in the decline of two of Greece's greatest arts, embroidery and the making of silver ornaments. Today there only remain, in some remote areas, weaving and the woodcarving done by shepherds.

Belt and dagger, western Finland

Page 173 a Costume, Bulgaria; *b* Hungarian coat, Huedin, Transylvania; *c* Woman's costume, Pont-l'Abbé, Brittany, *c.* 1880; *d* Woman's tunic, Dodecanese, Greece

Page 174 Women's costumes: *a* Dalarna, Sweden; *b* Appenzell, Switzerland; *c* Prizren, Yugoslavia; *d* Sliven, Bulgaria

Page 175 Women's costumes: *a* Bujak, Hungary; *b* Düdingen, Fribourg, Switzerland; *c* Norway; *d* Cork, Ireland

Page 176 a Bead embroidery, Russia, late eighteenth century; *b* Embroidered purse, Dalmatia; *c* Cushion cover, northern Slesvig, *c.* 1800; *d* Wax intarsia, Somogy, Hungary; *e* Embroidery, reception of the King and Queen of Denmark in Sonderborg, 1840

a

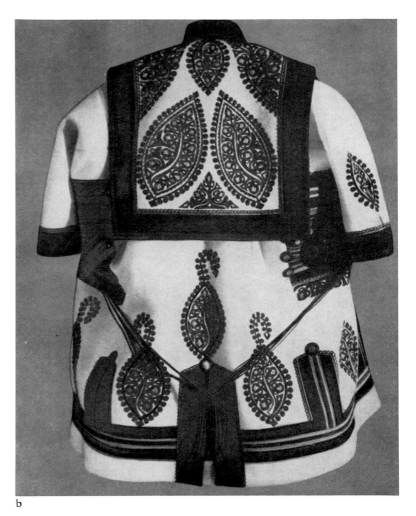

b

c

d

a

b

c

d

a

b

c

d

a

b

c

d

e

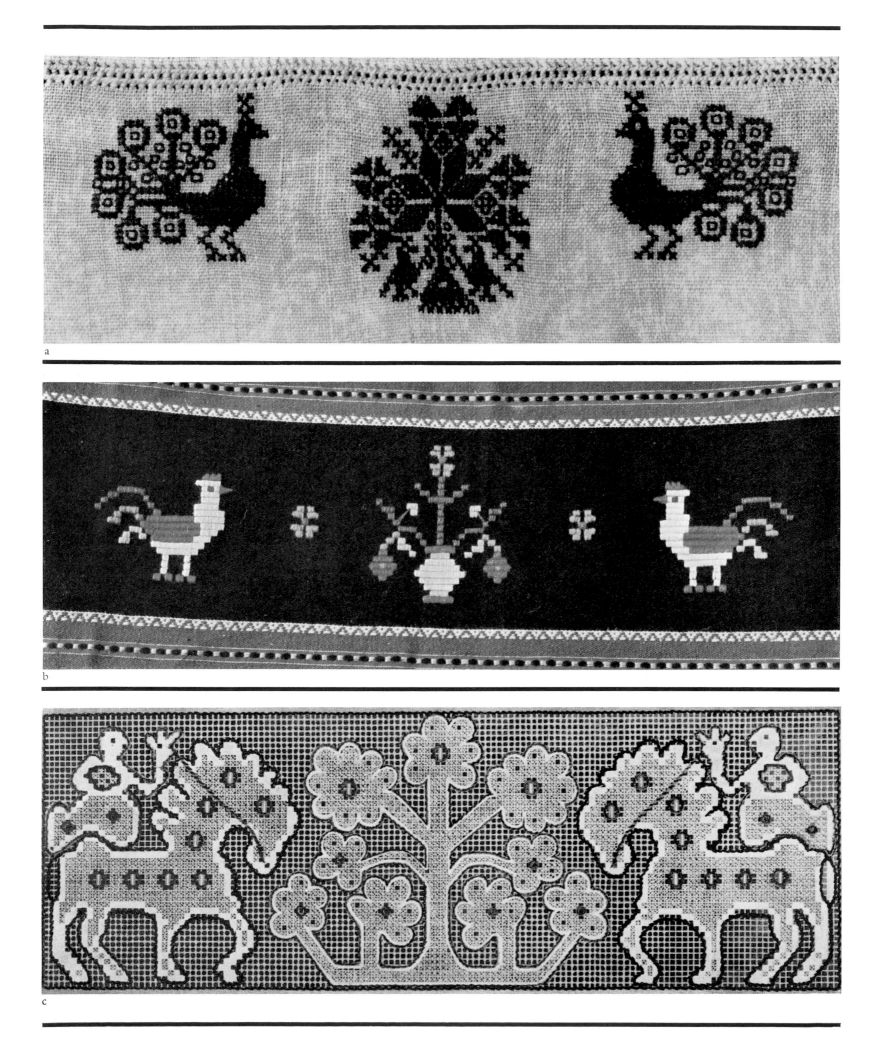

a

b

c

a

b

c

a

b

c

d

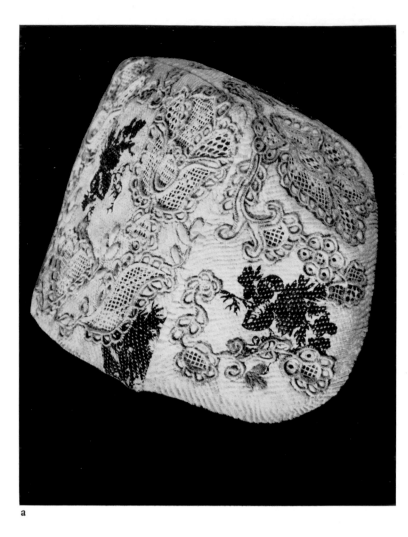

a

b

c

d

Eastern Europe

Hungary · Bulgaria · Rumania · Poland · the Soviet Union

HUNGARY's people have no ethnic ties with their neighbours, but their art nevertheless takes its place in the general picture of the folk art of the other European peoples. Their extra-European origins are revealed only in the richness of their expressive range, in their love of pomp and colourful splendour, and in their preference, to a certain extent, for Oriental, particularly Turkish, motifs and forms.

10b

Houses are usually one-storied and built of clay, stone or wood. Roofing materials vary, according to the region, between reeds, straw and shingles. Street fronts are decorated, with carving on the beams and timbers of gable walls, ornaments in rough cast on stone walls, and ornamented door frames, window frames and shutters. An open porch or veranda runs the whole length of one side of the house; the roof extends over this veranda and is supported by pseudo-classical wooden pillars or, in some regions, by arches, which rest on slim posts or squat columns. All this woodwork is carved.

Passing across the veranda, one enters the house by the kitchen. Even this room is resplendent with often more than a hundred gaily painted dishes, plates, cups and jugs on the walls, but the living-rooms surpass this with a wealth of pottery, embroidery and fabrics. The room where guests are entertained is furnished in a style that became customary only during the last century, and attention is focussed on two features, the bed and the table. The bed, in one corner of the room, is piled high, even to the ceiling, with cushions and quilts and with two or three gaily-embroidered blankets thrown over them. The walls around the bed may be hung with bright tapestries or, more often, with dishes and jugs. In some places the tapestries are hung in the corner round the table instead. A mirror hangs in the middle of the wall between the bed and the table, ringed by gay earthenware plates, and along the wall there are hung, in Catholic households, row upon row of pictures of the saints and, in Protestant households, plates painted with roses.

Beds, benches, chests, plate racks and sideboards were made of carved hardwood or painted softwood. The linen brought to the house by women on their marriage was stored in massive dower chests, and there were smaller chests to hold writing equipment and caskets for trinkets, combs and hairpins. Furniture was usually made, carved and painted by professional joiners, organized locally in guilds, which also arranged the sale of their work. Regional variations are manifested less in forms than in the basic colours (yellow, red, dark green, dark blue, black or white) or in the motifs (wreaths or bunches of flowers). The styles of painted furniture have an ecclesiastical origin, and even today the ceilings, galleries, pews and pulpits of Protestant churches are painted.

Herdsmen used to do some very fine carving, making useful and ornamental objects both for themselves and for others. They used wood and horn, and decorated them with

Page 177 a Cross stitch, Holland; *b* Wool embroidered tablecloth, Alpujarras, Granada; *c* Drawn-thread work, silk and wool, Russia, nineteenth century

Page 178 a Embroidery on linen, Skåne, Sweden; *b* Cross stitch, England, 1852; *c* Cross stitch, England

Page 179 a Embroidery, Patmos; *b* Embroidery, Chur, Switzerland, 1696; *c* Tapestry, Gudbrandsdal (?), Norway, second half of seventeenth century; *d* Tapestry, Herod's feast Gudbrandsdal (?), Norway, second half of seventeenth century

Page 180 Women's caps, Germany, nineteenth century; *a* Bavarian Forest; *b, c* Silesia; *d* Ermland

46f
57c, 59c

engraving, chip carving and intarsia. They lavished particular care, not surprisingly, on their own staffs, crooks, whip-butts and drinking-vessels. The handles of these last are often carved in the shape of some animal, a dog, a ram or a snake. The cup itself is decorated with relief pictures of pastoral and hunting scenes. On other utensils, such as mirror frames, razor-cases, salt cellars, ointment boxes, horns and drinking-horns, the herdsmen employed, in addition to engraving and chip carving, another technique: wax intarsia. After carving the article they pressed the wax into the notches with a knife blade. The earliest examples are in one colour, but later a wider range of colours and improved techniques made it possible for them to execute quite elaborate pictures. Other peasants did not reach the same high degree of artistry as the herdsmen but they used to make utensils for their womenfolk, such as washboards, washing-beetles, distaffs, shuttles, spinning-chairs and so on, which they decorated with chip carving, reliefs and occasionally with metal intarsia.

84c
73a
176d

Utensils in fired clay were made by professional craftsmen in potteries, each of which had its own range of shapes and a characteristic style. Some potteries are famous for their white ware, decorated with blue, which resembles porcelain, while others are known by their use of a single basic colour, greenish-brown, ochre or ivory. In some places black pottery was produced, with a pattern incised by a pebble. Common ornaments consisted of pairs of continuous, broken or dotted lines with plants, flowers or leaves, or birds. Comic verses or sayings were often written on drinking-vessels before firing. The many guilds and societies used to have remarkable wine jugs of great size, which were generally glazed in green and ornamented with an appropriate symbol of the particular trade: a pair of scissors, a weaver's shuttle, a plane and so on. Sewing-baskets, inkwells, brush cases and holy-water basins were also made in earthenware.

135, 3rd row, r.
146f
147d

Large amounts of embroidered work have survived and can be divided by and large into two categories, the garments, such as the typical Hungarian peasant cloak, the *szür*, made and finished by men, professional tailors, who worked in leather and woollen cloth, and the household linen, cushion covers, counterpanes, tablecloths and curtains, embroidered by women in their homes. Eyelet work, or *broderie anglaise*, on linen is one of the oldest kinds of embroidery, usually executed in one colour, red, blue or black. The oldest work is done in wool thread, but cotton has been used in more recent times. Polychrome embroidery forms a category of its own, worked by the professional tailors in silk or wool threads, in patterns that are partly geometrical. Perhaps the most typically Hungarian form of embroidery is that in which the design is a freehand composition of stylized plants and flowers. Domestic and professional embroiderers alike were fond of using *appliqué*, often in combination with embroidery stitches; the women sewed figures in linen or silk on to linen, the men sewed chamois leather on leather or cloth.

173b

197b

Iron door mounting, Sweden

The most striking element of most of the Hungarian regional costumes is the short blouse with embroidery on the collar and wide sleeves. Women wear a close-fitting bodice (*pruszlik*) over this blouse; the bodice is sometimes richly embroidered, but where a shawl is also worn the embroidery appears on the shawl instead. In some regions the people wear short skin jackets with the fur side turned inwards or short cloth cloaks. Women wear aprons over full, pleated skirts and layers of petticoats. Men's clothes are

Silhouette, detail, England, 1844

made of linen or woollen cloth. Linen is used to make shirts with wide, often embroidered sleeves and very wide trousers, which are also embroidered and trimmed with lace. Woollen cloth, usually frieze, is only used for outer clothing; even here underclothes and shirts are always of linen. Cloths may be woven by hand, at home or by local craftsmen, or be factory made. The trousers worn by Hungarian men have a characteristic fly and very narrow legs with only one seam, and are worn with the ends inside the boots. The short, sleeved jackets and the long *szür*, resembling an academic gown in cut but in white, home-made frieze, are usually worn tossed over the shoulders. Another overgarment is the *suba*, a sleeveless, sheepskin cloak which reaches to the ground and is worn in the same fashion. The *szür* and the *suba* are the characteristic wear of Hungarian men, and may be richly embroidered according to the wearer's social standing.

BULGARIAN folk art reveals its enduring Slav nature in an archaic linear and geometrical style of ornamentation and in the constant tendency to fit all motifs both in original designs and in those copied from other models into a geometrical framework. While traces of the original Turanian culture of Bulgaria are very rare, ancient elements of both Oriental and Occidental origin have been assimilated, particularly in jewellery, woodcarving and copperware.

198d

200b

The principal art forms of the Bulgarian people are embroidery and weaving. Every house used to have its own, home-made loom, used above all to make clothes, but also for blankets, carpets and cloth for all domestic purposes. The characteristic patterns on all of these are stripes in harmonious, rich colours, arranged in symmetrical groups and often enclosing geometrical or stylized figures. Warm colours are favourites, and all shades of red are particularly common. The motifs in the pattern are entirely composed of such basic geometrical shapes as triangle, square and rhombus; this is largely due to the technical limitations of the loom. These elements are combined and manipulated to represent plants, animals and human figures, and the result is a distinctive primitive stylization.

168a

173a

174

Embroidery, which is used principally on clothing, follows much the same conventions in pattern and colour as weaving. All embroidery was originally worked on hand-made linen, and the particular structure of this weave, with the regular crossing of threads at right angles, imposed certain limitations on the forms of motifs and a need for geometrical outlines, though not quite to the same extent as in weaving. Natural motifs such as plants, animals and heavenly bodies are somewhat easier to execute in embroidery than in weaving. Embroidery uses the same range of colours as weaving, but with far more telling effect since it is easier to introduce individual colours to enhance details. The greater technical freedom of embroidery also allows outlines to be filled in with a mosaic of different coloured stitches. Such embroidery has a compositional rhythm, the result of repetition and variation of individual motifs, and of a regular, repetitive colour scheme. In general it can be said that Bulgarian embroidery and weaving are characterized by the stylization of their patterns and the absence of the realism which is found both in Oriental work and in other European tapestries.

There are two kinds of woodcarving in Bulgaria: shallow engraving or incising, which is common and within the capabilities of anyone, and the deep carving of professional

183

woodworkers. The first technique is found on all kinds of objects of everyday use: distaffs, spoons, mugs, walking-sticks and so on. The work of the professional wood-carvers is seen principally on buildings, on pillars, capitals, ceiling panels, banisters and railings, doors and built-in cupboards. Shallow carving employs simple straight lines or zigzags, either running parallel or arranged in squares, stars or triangles. Deeper, more elaborate carving is found on everyday articles only when their natural shape lends itself to that sort of treatment, for example snakes on shepherds' crooks and heads of birds or beasts on the handles of walking-sticks. The fine examples of professional wood-carving which survive show the influence of western Renaissance, baroque and rococo styles. Some are mediaeval, but most date from the nineteenth century. Monks used to carve innumerable miniature icons, crosses (not crucifixes) and other devotional objects; this art too was rooted in Western European art.

202
280 b

Potteries flourished all over the country, being concerned mainly with the production and decoration of articles for domestic use. Jugs and jars usually have well-rounded proportions and elegant necks. All types of earthenware generally have decorative colouring and glazes on them. The simplest form of decoration is white slip or a plain green, red or yellow glaze. Other common forms of embellishment include vertical lines, either in isolation or grouped together, lines radiating from a central point, broken lines, incisions or impressions round the rim, and rope-like bands of extra thickness round the body of the vessel. Plant motifs are relatively rare on coloured earthenware, but human and animal figures occur very frequently on wedding jugs.

The blacksmiths who made tools and agricultural implements also produced everyday domestic utensils – fire-irons, candlesticks, hooks, door-handles, locks and crosses – of great artistic merit. Styles of decoration ranged from simple hammered strokes, indentation and turning of rims to complete models of dragons' heads, horses, snakes, birds and other motifs which are often masterpieces of artistic realism.

Copper was widely used for pots and containers in daily use, but decoration in the form of the pale, silvery gleam of tin plate, or engraved or embossed ornaments, was not neglected. The basic shape of many copper vessels and their ornamentation – ornate arabesques with plants, architectural motifs and, though more rarely, animals – betray Oriental influences, but these have been absorbed and assimilated over the centuries by the Bulgarian craftsmen, to produce a native art.

Classical traditions of artistry in gold and silver reached their peak in mediaeval Byzantium and found their way from the imperial court to the poorest levels of the Bulgarian people. Gold and silver ornaments set with enamel and coloured stones – rings, necklaces, bracelets, earrings, buckles – are still made today in all the larger towns in Bulgaria. There is an impressive variety in decorative styles, from the ancient style of linear and geometrical engraving, similar to that found on wood and ceramics, to intricate, naturalistic arabesques and plants derived from Oriental and other European styles.

185 a

Decorated Easter eggs are the most popular form of folk painting in Bulgaria. The pattern is first painted on the egg in liquid beeswax, and it is then dipped in red dye. The patterns are composed of linear plant and animal motifs, and Bulgarian women have made a fine art of depicting familiar models. The figures and lines stand out brilliantly against the red background.

Page 185 a Silver buckle, western Bulgaria, nineteenth century; *b* Brass ornament from a side-saddle, Iceland, eighteenth century
Page 186 Bridal crown, Black Forest

184

a

b

a

b

The symbolic figures which decorate ritual loaves at weddings, the New Year, Christmas and other festivals, take the same naive forms as those on Easter eggs. In spite of the ritual significance of these loaves, the women who bake them take homely, familiar things as their models: ploughs, shepherds and doves. All the figures, especially the birds, are presented in a naive, often schematic fashion, which exactly corresponds to the personal vision of the baker. The uninitiated will probably be baffled by them, but their significance is clear to their maker.

RUMANIA may claim artistic traditions thousands of years old. There are traces of artistic activity in pre-Roman and Roman times, and both material and documentary evidence from the dawn of Rumanian history in the ninth century. Even today the ancient origins are still visible at times in the forms that Rumanian folk art has evolved over the centuries. While there is an underlying stylistic uniformity inherent in all Rumanian folk art, the varying pace of development, and differing conditions in many parts of the country, have brought about a multitude of local forms.

19c

There are three basic traditional types of house construction in Rumania: the low, clay houses with reed thatch on the plains; the two-storied houses with cellars, built of stone and wood and with shingle roofs, in hilly country; and the stout timber houses with steep roofs of thatch and shingle in the mountains. The mountain houses are of particular architectural interest; in some cases the roofs are half as high again as the rest of the house. Doors, window-frames and roof beams are carved with geometrical patterns. Where the beams project beyond the walls they are often carved in the shape of a horse's head. The pillars supporting the roof of the porch (*prispa*) or gallery are always carved with great care and skill. Particularly in the lower hill country and on the plains, the gables and wooden parts of the porch and gallery used to be decorated with fretwork flower patterns. On the plains in the southern part of the country, where wood is less common as a building material, walls are decorated with geometrical motifs in plaster which imitate woodcarving. Roofing shingles, or straw or reed thatch, can also be laid to add to the total decorative effect of a house. Colour does not play an important part in external decoration except in some parts of Transylvania where blue paint is used. The regions of Oltenia, Mures, Suceava and Maramures all have a great deal to interest the student of architecture; the main gates of farmyards are worth particular attention. In Oltenia they are decorated with fine chip carving, in Maramures with rosettes and powerful linear patterns which copy the twists of a thick rope. Yet in spite of regional diversity, they all retain a certain uniformity in a geometrical style which is typical of all Rumanian woodcarving. Among the most striking buildings in all Rumania are the wooden churches found in Transylvania. In spite of their impressive height, which may be as much as 185 feet, the spires, soaring above the shingled roofs of the churches, blend harmoniously into the landscape.

35b

Apart from minor regional variations, the living-rooms of houses all over Rumania are laid out in much the same fashion: as you stand in the doorway, the fireplace or stove is against the wall to the left; the bed is in the corner against the left-hand wall; a table and chairs stand in the corner formed by the facing and right-hand walls, with benches right against the walls; the dower chest stands beside the bed or against the same wall;

Page 187 'Charra' in traditional dress, Salamanca
Page 188 a Wall-hanging, Spain; *b* Wall-hanging, Austria, 1820

and there is a cupboard on the right of the door. There will be one or two windows in each of the facing and right-hand walls. On the walls you will see gaily coloured crockery on a high shelf which runs all the way round the room, icons painted on glass and framed by rich damask or embroidered cloths, tapestries on either side of the benches and above the bed. All these articles create agreeable splashes of colour, well set off by the white walls and the natural dark shades of the furniture and roof beams; although each has merits as an isolated piece, they blend together as a stylistic unity.

Essential components of this scheme of interior decoration, both for their practical and their ornamental role, are the pieces of furniture, which show great imagination, as much in their strictly functional design, considered individually, as in their total fitness for the house in which they stand. Chairs, tables, shelves set with hooks for jugs, plate racks, corner cupboards, wall cupboards and dower chests are all deserving of serious aesthetic consideration. The same types of furniture are found throughout the country with the exception of tables; in the south they are low and circular while in the north they are higher and rectangular. The design of both chairs and beds is an indication of Rumania's position between the Balkans, where furniture is generally closer to floor level, and the Carpathians and Central Europe, where it stands higher. There are regional differences to be seen in formal details and in ornamentation. Woodcarving in geometrical patterns, particularly ornate on dower chests, is prevalent throughout Rumania, except in Banat, and some parts of Transylvania, where wooden furniture is painted it patterns of flowers and plants which clearly reveal Central European influences.

In addition to its use in building and in furniture, many utensils and tools are made of wood. It can be decorated in numerous ways: bending, coating with strips of bark, paring, incising, chip carving or chiselling, drilling, inlay, combining two or more different woods, framing or inlaying with metal, branding, painting or turning. The most common and the most important from an artistic point of view are incising, chip carving and chiselling. All three methods are used in the geometrical patterns which are the characteristic feature of Rumanian woodwork and its stylistic uniformity, rooted in primeval traditions. Among the most artistically successful objects are distaffs, spindles, the stretchers of looms, ladles for drinking water, caskets, nutcrackers, musical instruments, saddles, yokes, and the unusually beautiful cheese forms. The same technique of chip carving as in wood, and using the same ornaments, is found on powderhorns made from hartshorn.

The artistic treatment of metal implements, locks and clasps also carries on an old tradition which archaeological discoveries have shown to date from pre-Dacian times, and which is still current in Rumania today. The technique most commonly used by village smiths is wrought iron, with the addition of punched geometrical motifs. Following the tradition of casting in bronze, small ornamental objects are nowadays made of pewter, cast in matrices of stone or wood. In some parts of northern Rumania small axes are made of copper.

Ceramics form one of the most important categories of Rumanian folk art. Their development can be traced in broad outline from the Neolithic Cucuteni culture up to the present day. Centres of production arose generally in the mountainous parts of the country where the raw materials were most readily available. There are over a

46c

280e

Iron candlestick, Valkeala, Finland

190

hundred villages in Rumania where pottery is the chief means of livelihood. They are distributed all over the country and each has its distinctive style. Pottery is most used for domestic articles, plates, pots, jugs, pitchers and beakers, as well as larger vessels; all of them can also be ornamental. There are other articles connected with various customs and habits: children's toys, such as clay pipes, a special kind of jug intended as a gift at weddings or funerals, wedding flasks and similar objects.

134, top row centre
135, 3rd row centre
147g, i

Tools and techniques are simple and vary little from one place to another. Shaping is done on the wheel, driven by a pedal. Different styles of ornamentation and methods of firing lead to a greater variety: black ceramic ware fired in a completely closed kiln, ornamented with stamped impressions and burnished; unglazed ware painted in black and white on a terracotta ground; glazed slipware which is fired twice with a painted or relief decoration; polychrome glazed ware, decorated in *sgraffito*.

There is a certain degree of uniformity in the ornamentation and the stylized floral patterns; there is a tendency for all patterns to be geometrical, even when the dominant motifs are flowers. The range of colours is rather limited everywhere, consisting in the main of red, green, yellow, black and white.

Textiles for domestic use as handkerchiefs, tablecloths, or soft furnishings are made of hemp, flax or cotton, with patterns incorporated in the weaving, particularly in geometrical shapes, rhombuses of all shapes being a clear favourite, with broken and wavy lines. Exceptions to this rule are found in central Transylvania, where floral patterns predominate, while in the south, in Oltenia, Mutenia (Wallachia) and Dobruja, plants, animals and even human figures occur. Colour combinations are usually restricted to black, red and blue. The fabrics of northern Moldavia are very fine; patterned borders are woven in white on white handkerchiefs and tablecloths and on the side panels of upholstery.

Gridiron, England

Tapestries of wool or wool and cotton woven by women in their homes serve a number of purposes in different regions: as bedspreads; as tablecloths; as hangings at the head of the bed; hanging from a rod against the wall as an ornamental panel; or in the form of long runners. They come in all shapes and sizes according to the part of the country and the purpose they serve. All these different woven cloths, hung on the wall or spread over benches, tables and beds, are alike in that they are nearly always patterned with checks or stripes and geometrical shapes. It is quite a different matter with woven carpets and mats. The provinces which produce the finest carpets are Moldavia, Maramures, Banat and Oltenia. Carpets are divided into a central field surrounded by a single border in Moldavia and by a double or triple border in Oltenia. The central field contains flowers and the tree of life (Moldavia) or ornate compositions of bird and plant motifs which are repeated in the borders. Favourite colours are pale shades of terracotta, green and ochre in Moldavia and vivid blue, red, white, yellow and green in Oltenia. Carpets from Maramures are in deep, rich shades of brown, yellow and blue and are characterized by the rhythmic disposition of variously emphasized geometrical motifs, enriched by schematic representations of human and animal figures, and are imbued with a powerful and original feeling for realism. The vivid red, white and green carpets from Banat have geometrical motifs arranged in wavy or zigzag lines down the sides which have the effect of extending the width of the central field. While the lines of carpets made in Moldavia,

200a

Maramures and Banat are broken up in rectangles by the nature of the weave, an effect which is even more emphasized by the holes in the weft produced by the Karamani technique used in Banat, Oltenian carpets, woven on vertical looms, have a quite different character, one of graceful curves and wavelike stylization; the technique, very close to that used in the making of Gobelins tapestries, allows more subtle nuances of pattern and colour.

The *cerga* which serve as decorative bedspreads are woven by a method which is found almost exclusively in the Carpathian-Balkan area. Woven in coarse wool in one colour or in stripes, long threads, either knotted in or drawn out by combing, give this cloth a shaggy appearance. It is found in every sheep-rearing area and enhances the simplicity and warmth characteristic of living-rooms in houses in the mountains.

Weaving of all kinds in straw, rush and twigs is used to make a wide range of articles in everyday use, and woven straw also serves in some farming regions to make harvest crowns and ornaments for the house.

Painting on glass, which was so widespread in Central Europe up to the end of the nineteenth century, was also popular in Rumania, particularly in Transylvania, where there were several villages – Nicula, Gherla, Kronstadt-Schei, Mühlbach and Cârtisoara for instance – in which artists specialized in painting icons in this manner.

The splendid and sometimes strange personal ornaments worn by Rumanian peasants had a number of different significances over the centuries, from talismans to badges of status, age and sex, but they were always meant as adornments. In addition to actual costume accessories which could be ornamental as well as useful, such as pouches, belts and braces of leather and wool, handkerchiefs, gloves and over-sleeves, there were also articles which were purely ornamental. The magnificent costumes worn in parts of southern Rumania, in Banat, Oltenia, Wallachia and Dobruja, were often completed by a particular kind of necklace made of heavy gold or silver medallions. Women throughout Rumania wear necklaces with beads made of glass or stone, coral or amber, bone or shell. Many pre-Dacian traditions linger on in the mining regions of the western Carpathians, including the making of some remarkable gold ornaments, delicate earrings, brooches and necklaces. In the Hunedoara region ornaments are cast in tin and rings and other articles are made of tin and copper. One of the most widespread articles of female adornment is a neckband made of small, coloured beads woven in a multitude of geometrical patterns. All the different regions and ethnic zones of Rumania, even individual villages, boast unique and original headdresses. The dozens of different kinds fall by and large into three main groups: headscarves or veils of linen, cotton or un-twisted raw silk in various shapes and sizes, prevalent in Oltenia, Wallachia, Dobruja, Moldavia and southern Transylvania; caps and hoods of various kinds, found in the Hunedoara region and Banat; wreaths, crowns or similar headdresses worn on special occasions, particularly by brides, and most common in Transylvania.

Folk costumes show a remarkable variety. In general women's costumes consist of a blouse reaching below the waist and a gaily-patterned woven belt. The garment worn from the waist down differs greatly from one region to another; the *ɀadïi* or *catrinte* of Transylvania, Banat or Oltenia takes the form of two aprons, one in front and one behind; the *vilnic*, also found in Oltenia, is a richly patterned, brightly coloured pleated or gathered

Silhouette, detail, Lowice, Poland, nineteenth century

207 c

Page 193 Sampler, Netherlands, 1750
Page 194 Tapestry, Calabria, nine-teenth century
Page 195 a Ryij, Satakunta, Finland, nineteenth century; *b cilim*, Pirot, Yugoslavia; *c* Reversible rug, Warsaw Voivodate; *d* Carpet, Iceland
Page 196 a, b Borders, hand-printed from wooden blocks, Provence, nineteenth century; *c* Woollen carpet, Alberca, Spain

192

a

b

c

d

a

b

c

a

b

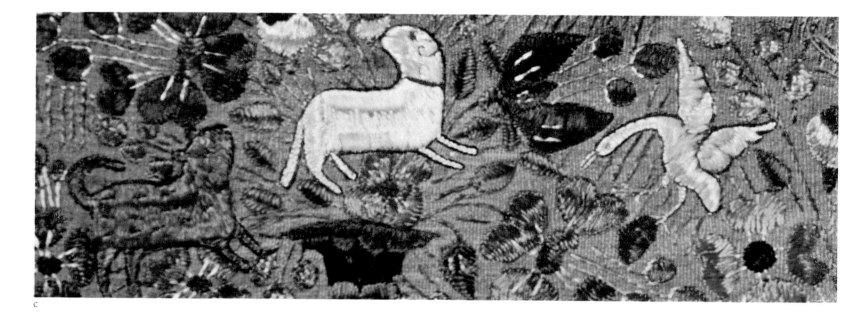

c

a

b

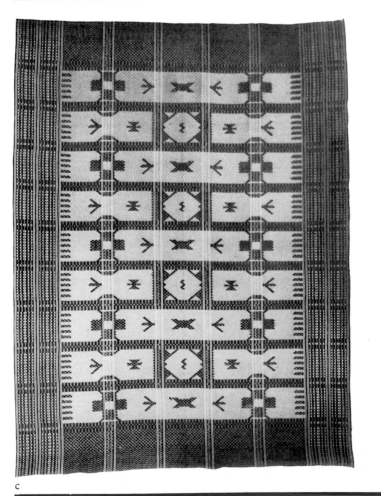

c

d

a

b

c

skirt; the *fota* of Wallachia and Moldavia is a single piece of cloth wrapped round the hips; the *opreg* of Banat is narrow and fringed. They are all made in woollen cloth and range from the plain black of Hunedoara to the bright patterns of Oltenia. The blouses have an overall similarity, with decorative panels on the shoulders, sleeves and fronts sewn in various colours.

The men's costume of shirt and trousers is much simpler. The shirt, which is long in the south and shorter in the north and west, is held by a narrow, woven belt, the *brîu*, or a broad leather belt, the *chimir*. The home-made linen trousers worn in summer are long and narrow in the south and east and shorter and fuller in the north and west; the thicker winter trousers are long and close-fitting.

168c, d Both men and women wear handsome cloaks made of cloth *(sumane)* or fur. They also wear short tunics of sheepskin with the leather turned outwards and embroidered.

POLAND possesses a highly developed, strongly characterized folk art which still survives as a living tradition in a number of places even today. For centuries the difference between the cultural levels of the court, the nobility and gentry and the urban middle classes on the one hand and of the broad mass of the peasants on the other was exceptionally great. As a result of the social circumstances the common people, the people without history, were driven back on a pre-literate culture, based on oral traditions, practical techniques and compositional schemata of great symbolic significance, which was passed on from generation to generation. This culture was the common property of the whole population, apart from the court and the clergy, up to the sixteenth century, and only then did a specifically folk art, an art of the rural population, begin to evolve. There are practically no surviving traces of this art earlier than the end of the eighteenth century, apart from isolated examples of the architecture.

Polish peasant houses are generally made of wood and show relatively little variation throughout the country with the exception of those found in the mountains in the south. The oldest surviving cottages have only one living-room, a lobby and an alcove or bedroom behind the living-room. During the nineteenth century two rooms became customary with an entrance hall between them and sometimes alcoves at the end of it. In the Vistula basin to the north of the Carpathians there are houses with a so-called *wyzka*, a single room or attic built over the entrance. Apart from the western provinces where walls are sometimes built with vertical posts, walls of horizontal timbers are the rule throughout the Polish heartland. All kinds of roof are found; in the north and west and in the northern part of Mazovia they are pitched, while in central and southern Poland they are hipped.

Carving, particularly ornate in the Vistula basin, used to decorate beams, gables and the frames of doors and windows. It was also found on furniture and domestic utensils: cupboards, chests, tables, chairs, spoon racks, salt cellars, sieves, candlesticks, washing beetles and looms, as well as sledges, carts, dairying equipment, cooking-ladles, cheese forms, butter-pats and brandy-casks. The motifs are predominantly geometrical and hardly differ from those found all over Europe.

We know from archaeological excavations that pottery is a very ancient craft in Poland and there were professional guilds in practically every small town. Some particularly

201

important centres, even today, are Iłza, Urzędów in central Poland and many smaller places in Rzeszów province. One of the oldest and most interesting techniques is that used to make the black *siwaki*, which employs ancient shapes for jugs and pots, such as are also found in Byelorussia. Glazes have been used in Poland since the thirteenth century, on tiles from the Mazurian and Cracovian lake districts, terracotta figurines made in especially great numbers in Iłza near Radom, and many other things. 135, 3rd row, l.
144

Handweaving continued to flourish until very recently, particularly on the right bank of the Vistula. It was, and indeed in a few places, Lowicz, Kurpie and around Lublin, still is, the usual method for making woollen fabrics for clothing and the brightly coloured sashes *(pasiak)* which are a characteristic feature of the folk costumes of very nearly every region of Poland. Wool and cotton are also used to make slippers *(kraciaki)* and bed-curtains. Wool sashes are also woven on primitive board looms in the Suwalki district. Another kind of weaving for specifically decorative purposes comprises the complicated 'carpets' made of wool or a mixture of wool and linen. They have purely geometrical 195c patterns, woven in two or three colours, and are native to Podlasia and some parts of Lublin province. From a European point of view the most interesting of all are the double-weave carpets, which were once known all along the Baltic coast and which are still made in Podlasia and on the right bank of the Vistula.

Traditional embroidery was closely connected with local costumes; chain stitch was used to embroider geometrical patterns in red and black on blouses and shirts. This is still customary around Kurpie and its decorative potentialities have been developed further. Linen embroidery of the Richelieu type is found in Little Poland, and there is rich embroidery done on velvet in Masovia on the left bank of the Vistula.

Distaff, western Bulgaria, nineteenth century

Among the most interesting products in metal are the cast iron pipes from the Podhale, patterned with punched geometrical shapes, and buckles and axe-heads *(ciupagi)*. In the district of Cieszyn buttons and belts are still made in silver filigree, while around Cracow there are to be found old brass rings set with coral. Around Kurpie and in Kashubia, amber necklaces used to be made which were an essential part of women's costumes in many parts of Poland.

Sculpture in wood is still widespread throughout the country, partly as a shepherd's pastime, but principally as a full-time craft carried on in villages and small towns. Its religious subject matter marks a continuity from the old guilds. The artistic quality of this carving is very high and it is distinguished by a tendency, rare in folk art, to individual expression. The most common wood is lime, less common are oak, elm and maple. Favourite subjects are Christ at the whipping-post or stumbling under the weight of the 253 cross, a theme typical of Little Poland, and the Madonna and Child or the Deposition, 254a, b the Mother of God in triumph or in sorrow. The most popular saints are John of Nepomuk, Antony, Florian (the patron saint of Cracow), Francis, Joseph, Barbara and Hedwig, and Adam and Eve are also popular.

The main centre of popular painting is Czestochowa, where at the beginning of this 55a century there were still about a hundred workshops employed in producing pictures 207a, h on paper and canvas for the millions of pilgrims who came to see the *Black Virgin of* 208a *Czestochowa*, a portrait attributed (falsely!) to St Luke. The artists used stereotyped, stencilled outlines and exercised their imagination chiefly on the painting of bunches

Horse and rider, painted on a chest, New Mexico, early nineteenth century

of lush flowers which were placed in the background of pictures of saints. Paintings on glass were a speciality of Silesia, Zywiec, the Podhale, Kashubia, the province of Lublin and along the Lithuanian frontier. There is little difference in technique between paintings on glass from these places and those found in Bohemia, Slovakia or Germany, but there are notable stylistic differences, and the Polish are of a very high artistic standard. As well as the religious subjects common to other fields of folk art, scenes involving robbers and brigands, similar to Slovakian paintings, occur, especially in the country to the north of the Carpathians.

Early traces of the Polish custom of painting Easter eggs (*pisanki*) have been found in excavations. The original geometrical designs have everywhere been replaced by plant motifs, occasionally enlivened with animal and human figures. There is a technical distinction between *pisanki* proper, which are decorated in batik, dyed in bright colours after the design has been picked out in wax, and *skrobanki*, on which the pattern is scratched with a pin after colouring; and there are finally eggs decorated by sticking coloured paper or elder pith to them.

210, 211

240c

A characteristic branch of Polish folk art which came into existence only around 1870 is the art of cutting shapes out of coloured paper. These silhouettes were pasted on to the walls of houses. The earliest patterns were done in one colour and formed by folding the paper a number of times on different axes. This produced various stars, trees and friezes of figures and flowers. In the Lowicz and Kurpie districts this effect was enhanced by sticking paper shapes in contrasting colours on to the silhouette, and sometimes whole pictures, called *kodry*, were composed in this manner, always portraying secular subjects.

Finally we must mention a very new field of Polish folk art, one which did not really develop until after the Second World War. This is the painting of wall hangings, in oil on canvas, to hang over the bed, which are now made all over Poland east of the Vistula. As well as religious subjects this unusual art form covers such subjects as deer in the forest and swans on lakes, and comes undeniably close to fairground *kitsch*, but it operates within the formal schemata of older folk art and often achieves a considerable artistic standard.

RUSSIAN culture is more properly defined historically as the culture of the East Slavs, an ethnic group covering an immense geographical range. A quick glance at a physical map of the European part of the Soviet Union is enough to explain the two chief types of Russian, or to be more precise, East Slav house; that is, the wooden houses of the north and north-east, where pine forests abound, and the clay houses of the south, where timber is scarce. As well as the differences in climate and economic conditions it is above all the nature of the available materials which determines the differences between the two types of house.

The log house is typical of Northern Europe from Scandinavia to the Urals and indeed beyond, though becoming less common until it peters out in Siberia. The Russian version is, however, quite distinct both in its basic form and its ornamentation. Archaeological discoveries and recent research have allowed Soviet historians to collect an impressive quantity of material, covering a wide area in both time and space, which presents a very accurate picture of the evolution of the Russian log house. Chronicles and archives, from

Wrought-iron toasting-fork, Sweden

203

the later Middle Ages onwards, becoming more plentiful in the sixteenth and seventeenth centuries, have yielded numerous verbal and pictorial records of popular techniques of log construction and their achievements.

The simplest form had four walls of split logs, a pitched roof of planks, an earth floor, and windows which could be closed from inside, the whole effect being rough and ready; inside it had two rooms, sheltering men and beasts under the same roof, but at least possessed the minimum refinement of one room which could be heated. This was always black with smoke which had to make its way out of the doors and windows, since the stove had no chimney. (The East Slav cooking-stove unites the three functions of the Central European hearth, oven and heating-stove.) This primitive form was soon enlarged with an entrance hall in the middle, between the main living room, the *izba*, which had a stove, on one side, and an unheated storeroom, used as a bedroom in summer, on the other. Up to this point the width of the house was limited by the natural length of the roof beams, but with the need for more space an extension was built on in front, with a partition wall to support the ceiling. In the north the house and the farm buildings lie in a row or a double row beside a covered yard, while further south the buildings enclose the open yard on three sides. In a village the houses present their gable ends to the street and have the richest carving on that side. Indoors, living-rooms are always arranged in the same way, though with regional variations. In a typical room, the stove stands against the far wall in one corner, and the platform on which the whole family sleeps, in winter at least, stands in the other. Benches and a table stand in the corner diagonally opposite to the stove, beneath an icon on the wall, and the fourth corner, often curtained off, is the kitchen area.

The house of the steppes and the treeless plains of Byelorussia and the Ukraine is fundamentally different from the north Russian house. Houses with wooden frames and half timbering are still found in the northern part of the steppes but further south the *ssaman* brick, a mixture of clay and manure bound with straw or fibre, is the chief building material. Instead of a pitched plank roof, roofs are hipped and thatched. The door of the north Russian wooden house is approached by steps, while the Ukrainian *chata* is more or less level with the ground. Its walls inside and out are smooth and whitewashed, doors, window frames and the roof cornice are often painted, and occasionally walls are decorated with murals. The clay houses of the Ukraine are welcoming, bright and well proportioned, though not as richly decorated as the wooden houses, where the carving is often very ornate. The layout of the interiors is similar to that of the wooden houses. In villages the long side of houses is turned to the street; within the yard, the house and the farm buildings are separated from each other. Nowadays artificial building-materials are increasingly replacing the old natural ones in northern and southern Russia, as elsewhere in Europe, and a modern architectural style, with little or no regional character, is replacing the traditional styles, except where architects are deliberately including elements of the popular style in a conscious attempt to keep the tradition alive.

The abundance of timber in parts of northern and eastern Europe is the reason for the popularity of wood as a raw material in Russian folk art. We have already mentioned in passing the decorative carving which found its way on to all parts of the wooden houses: gables, cornices, corbels, window frames, shutters, steps, balconies, fences, doors

Silhouette, Poland, nineteenth century

Page 205 Votive picture, Styria, 1760
Page 206 The Robber's bride, Frajerka, Poland, nineteenth century

204

a

b

c

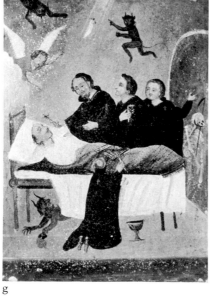

d

e

f

g

h

i

a

b

c

d

258b
and gates provided permanent sites for works of art in relief carving and fretwork, which were not without influence on the more generally acknowledged spheres of art, such as the 'line by line' arrangement of the ornamental stone reliefs of Russia's ancient cathedrals, which show the inspiration of the native art of woodcarving not only in their sense of form, but also, in spite of the different material, in their technique. The interior of the wooden houses also attracted the woodcarvers to decorate walls, ceilings, doors and pieces of furniture, particularly the frames and panels of chests and coffers, though these were sometimes painted instead. A large variety of agricultural and domestic utensils

167b
were made of wood and decorated with carvings: mugs, drinking-bowls, dishes, spoons, ladles, salt cellars, toys, mangle boards and moulds were often particularly fine. Cheap, mass-produced articles caused the hand-made objects to disappear abruptly in the latter part of the nineteenth century; the decoration on buildings was more enduring. Recently, schools of arts and crafts have been trying to revive the old traditions.

176a
177c
2
The manufacture and decoration of fabrics is one of the other chief fields of Russian folk art. Russians and Ukrainians are both masters of weaving, knitting, embroidery, lace-making, linen-printing and making carpets. Every region has its own variations in detail, and the multitude of techniques, colours and forms, the abundance of motifs and ornaments are a continual source of amazement. Embroidery is particularly rich in variety, from the working of sacred images in a Byzantine style on linen and silk cloth and the embroidery of shrouds to the adornment of curtains, tablecloths, sheets, handkerchiefs and the various components of the brilliantly coloured costumes worn by both men and women. There is a great variety of such costumes throughout the lands occupied by the East Slavs, differing from one ethnic group to another and from district to district.

167c, d
There are points in the production of fine ceramic ware when the distinctions between art and folk art become meaningless. The potteries of Gzhel, which flourished in the eighteenth and nineteenth centuries, are a good example, turning out plates, jugs and carafes in most attractive shapes and colours, and figurines and painted clay models of delightful humour. One peculiarly Russian folk art is the manufacture of small, lacquered boxes of *papier mâché*, painted with miniatures in vivid colours. The decoration of Easter eggs is particularly popular in the Ukraine.

If one were asked to single out one characterizing feature of Russian folk art, it would have to be the remarkable wealth of motifs and ornamental devices which, although they later became of purely decorative significance, must originally have sprung from the figurative world of popular superstition: such exotic beasts and mythical hybrids as griffins and lions, panthers and basilisks, unicorns and mermaids. There is still no absolute certainty about the origins and spread of these motifs, but even a cautious interpretation must admit Far Eastern elements as well as native images, reaching far back to very early times, as basic sources for the ornamentation, particularly in carving and embroidery. We may be quite sure that folk artists had long lost any awareness of the symbolic nature of double cross and rosette, mermaid and naiad, horse and bird, and that these images offered no more than an opportunity to prove their own artistry, time and again, by containing them within the geometrical severity of a stylized ornamentation.

Page 207 Devotional and votive pictures: a Madonna nutrix, oil on paper, Poland, nineteenth century; *b* Painting on glass, Austria; *c* Painting on glass, Brasov, Rumania; *d* St Martin, painting on glass, Alsace; *e* The Flight into Egypt, painting on glass, Switzerland; *f* Painting on glass, Spain; *g* Oil painting, Mexico, nineteenth century; *h* Our Lady of Gidlo, Czestochowa, Poland, oil on paper, nineteenth century; *i* St Michael, oil painting, Mexico, *c.* 1800

Page 208 a Madonna of La Saletta, Cracow; *b* St Genevieve, painting on glass, Silesia, nineteenth century; *c* St Florian, painting on glass, Moravia, nineteenth century; *d* Temptation of Eve, painting on glass, Upper Austria, early nineteenth century

83a, b

The New World

North America · Latin America

Diana, iron weathervane, Lahaska, Pa., early nineteenth century

IN THE AMERICAS, early European settlers were from the very first obliged to make the greater part of their housing, furniture, utensils and all the other requirements of their simple daily life for themselves. Craftsmen sailed with Columbus, and once in the New World they had to put the skills they had learnt in the Old World to good use. Clearly even the functional shapes of the things they made expressed something of contemporary European styles, quite apart from any decoration that would doubtless be applied occasionally. These early hand-made objects must be looked on as the beginnings of American folk art of European origin, and already they bear the characteristics of all later folk art in America, whether at first in the central and southern parts of the continent settled by the Spanish and Portuguese, or later in the Dutch, French, English, Norwegian or German colonies in North America. These characteristics are techniques, shapes and decoration from the settlers' European birthplaces; American materials; and social equality between makers and users, at a level equivalent to that of the European folk artists.

There were of course contacts between the indigenous Indian art and the art of the colonists. In North America the influence was almost entirely one-sided, from the settlers to the Indians, while in Latin America, particularly in those areas where the proportion of natives is still very high today, an autonomous folk art of Spanish or Portuguese cast evolved. Indian folk art by itself has, of course, no place in a survey of the folk art of the European peoples. On the other hand the work done in America by the settlers of European origin should not be ignored.

NORTH AMERICA is a wide field, embracing the popular arts and crafts of colonial New England, the folk art of the mainly German and Swiss settlers in Pennsylvania and the southwest, furniture and utensils of the pioneers in the Mid-West and Texas, the textiles of the early Mormons in Utah and all kinds of popular crafts in Ohio, Illinois, Iowa and other parts of the continent. Quite a lot of this folk art has survived in New England and the central states on the Atlantic coast, but examples from the south and various parts of the west are rare. It may at first seem surprising that the early settlers and those who followed them in the next two centuries should have made more than plain utilitarian articles, that their work is above the crude level one might expect in a primitive frontier station. We must remember that even in a virgin wilderness they could draw on the ancient traditions of their homelands. As people from different parts of Europe settled in separate communities in America, the techniques, crafts, arts and ornamental styles they brought with them survived and continued to evolve for many years, even centuries. Most of the settlers were from the lower classes of society, and so

211

the arts and crafts of European origin that developed in America were far more exclusively 'folk' art than they were in Europe. There was no art commissioned by courts or nobility in America and only a small amount of upper-middle-class, patrician art, which arose at a relatively late date; it should perhaps be called an early capitalist art.

But this folk art lacked any common, specifically North American forms; the population was composed of far too many groups of marked individuality and disparate origins. Even the English majority was composed of heterogenous elements, and in addition there were Dutch settlers along the Hudson; Russians who, although they later withdrew to Alaska, set up their samovars in California where they built houses and churches in the style of their homeland; Finns, who built their saunas in North Dakota; the Shakers who settled in Lebanon, Pennsylvania, after their sect was banned in England, there to construct their simple furniture and weave carpets with bold geometrical patterns; Swedes along the Delaware river and elsewhere, who wove colourful fabrics with stylized designs composed of human figures reduced to squares and triangles; Norwegian settlers whose convoluted dragons and serpents on chairbacks and benches are reminders of their Viking forebears. But no other national group remained so faithful to the customs of their homeland as the Germans, who settled above all in eastern Pennsylvania, where they are known as the Pennsylvania Dutch. The Pennsylvania Dutch have lived in America since the seventeenth century; the large farmhouses were built by Pietists from the Rhineland who first came over in 1683, in William Penn's lifetime. For two centuries the furniture, tools, utensils, crockery and textiles made by these communities were very similar to those made in Hesse, the Palatinate, Alsace and Switzerland.

240a
46e

Gradually American traditions did evolve. After the attainment of independence, symbols of a new, American patriotism became popular ornaments on furniture, pottery and glass: the arms of the Union and the various states, the Stars and Stripes, the bald eagle, figures of Columbia and Liberty, and naive portraits of national heroes like Franklin and Washington.

While English traditions were the strongest, the influence of immigrants of other nationalities can be traced in the work of even the earliest craftsmen, and the interchange of ideas was probably increased by movement about the continent, which was always considerable. Thus the folk art of Pennsylvania, New Jersey, New York, Virginia, North and South Carolina and the early colonies immediately to their west shows great variety from the very beginning. Pennsylvania Dutch later settled in several of the New England states; immigrants from Moravia and the Palatinate travelled up the Shenandoah valley through Virginia to North Carolina and westwards along the Ohio, leaving behind them, wherever they went, the influence of their typical crafts.

That the English tradition itself was by no means a narrow one is already clear in the work of those artists and craftsmen who had crossed the Atlantic before the mid-seventeenth century. They brought with them practices which derived from mediaeval or even earlier developments in England, France and the Netherlands. The mediaeval traditions survived for a long time in England and the early colonists who took them to America were often both masters of one craft and, if necessary, 'Jacks' of several others, able to turn their hand to whatever was needed. Ships' carpenters, for instance, could also build houses and make furniture, tools and utensils.

Page 213 St Antony, painting on glass, Spain

Page 214 Votive pictures: *a* Italy, eighteenth century; *b* Mexico, eighteenth century; *c* Italy, nineteenth century; *d* Italy, 1905

Page 215 Paintings on glass, England: *a* The Agony in the Garden; *b* The Lord's Supper; *c, d* Scenes from the life of Queen Caroline, early nineteenth century

Page 216 a Scene from a romance of chivalry, from a Sicilian painted cart, eighteenth century; *b* Painting of a farmyard, Appenzell, nineteenth century; *c* Beehive front board, oil on wood, Carinthia, 1910

212

a

E.X. GRAZIA

b

c

ANNOLFO . . FRANCESCO

d

ROSARIO STRANO E DOMENICO STRANO IL 7 NOVEMBRE 1905

a

b

c

d

a

b

c

a

b

c

a

b

a

b

28a, b, f

66

The simple construction of even the very oldest houses, such as those in Plymouth, shows that they were built by professional craftsmen. The first settlers in New England brought two main types of house with them: the two-storied, mediaeval, timbered house found in East Anglia, where the beams supporting the upper storey overhang the ground floor; and the simpler, one-storey house with a very steep roof and low eaves, introduced into England in the fourteenth century from Flanders and taken to the New World by the Puritans. Both types were, of course, constructed in the wood which was available in such great quantities, even those parts of the building such as floors, pediments and foundations which were normally built of stone or brick in England. In this way the houses of colonial America, however closely they followed European models, were at once stamped indelibly as American. For all their bare severity, they resemble the more ambitious buildings that went up as settlements became towns, in being so well proportioned that their architectural merit is undeniable. Constructed of massive logs, the houses were boarded inside and out with horizontal planks of even size; the roofs and, at a later date, part of the outside walls were shingled. It was not long, however, before brick tiles, made in the colonies, were available, and stables and barns, in particular, were often thatched. About sixty wooden houses dating from the mid-seventeenth century still stand in various parts of New England. There were stone houses as well, of course, in Pennsylvania for example, where the Hessian settlers built in the style

28c

of their homeland. The kitchen and living-room of the Kershner house, built *c.* 1755 near Wernersville, are preserved in the Winterthur museum. The furnishings may be taken as typical in their juxtaposition of pure German tables, coffers and chairs with the English Windsor chair, copper kettle and pewter jug. While in general styles of furniture derive from European fashions and the traditions of the settler's own district, close contacts with neighbours of different origins brought a mixture of European traditions

46e

under one roof. One and the same house might hold a typical German chest painted with brightly coloured birds, and slender unpainted Queen Anne cupboards, or rural Chippendale might be found beside pure south German peasant rococo. This continued to be true until the end of the nineteenth century, as long as true folk art was practised, and it applied also to utensils, crockery, dress and fabrics. There were German painted wooden boxes for women's caps and ribbons, and English tea-caddies, coffee-pots and trays painted with flowers, and zinc washtubs; there were brass warming-pans with engraved flowers and birds, and charcoal footwarmers, similar to those found in Holland, England and northern Germany.

Pottery played an important role in the folk art of Pennsylvania, where several masters are known by name from between 1770 and 1880: David Spinner, George Hübener, John Monday and John Neesz. Various kinds of textile production include the fine embroidered or woven wall hangings; the handkerchiefs with strictly symmetrical patterns, usually worked in cross stitch, of German origin; the tablecloths and bedspreads decorated in the English style with flowers, the Tree of Life, the Fall of Man or scenes of harbours or markets, all done in *appliqué*.

American folk painting began as an untutored expression of the seventeenth-century settlers. Amazingly, it has persisted as an acceptable and even a treasured mode of representation long after photography began to satisfy the need for simple imagery. In

Page 217 a The constable and the fishers of Broadsea welcome home the laird and his wife, Aberdeenshire, 1840; *b* Votive picture, detail (by Camille Chapnis), Bonfol, Berne, 1845; *c* Sign of a painter and glazier, Netherlands, eighteenth century

Page 218 a Two pairs of lovers, painting on a distaff, Nizhgorod, nineteenth century; *b* Harbour scene, mural, Thessaly, nineteenth century

Page 219 a St Maurice, oil painting (by C. F. Brun), Switzerland, nineteenth century; *b* Sowing, oil painting (by Olaf Krans), Bishop Hill, Ill., *c.* 1880

Page 220 Girl with red shoes, believed to be Magdalene Douw, grandmother of Herman Melville, Albany, N.Y., *c.* 1780

contrast to handicraft traditions which usually derived from European skills and continued older decorative forms, painting generally reflected the unskilled and unsophisticated while portraying the new. Although urban portraits, landscape decoration and much genre painting of the eighteenth and nineteenth centuries did borrow from European prototypes, specifically English and Netherlandish, the most fundamental level of folk painting was independent. Thus it developed its own idiom, and one might hazard the conclusion that unskilled primitivism itself became a kind of national sub-style, or folk style, which was capable of satisfying something more than the desire for mere representation.

Weathervane, Monterey, Pa., early nineteenth century

Just as ships' carpenters who went ashore to build dwellings and fashion furniture would also sculpt adornments, so the house-painter would frequently turn to decorative signs and even portraits and landscapes. Obviously the sign was not considered a work of art, but in its emphasis on silhouettes, relieved only by a few well-placed nails, it chose to advertise the honest essentials and not the luxuries of applied ornament or rich materials. The same economy pervaded the majority of portraits made by the travelling 'limners', also users of outline and plane. One need only read these craftsmen's advertisements for simple and correct likenesses, rendered in either flat or modelled versions, to understand the basic but undemanding needs they served.

But it would be against the innate nature of the brush if decorative details were not forthcoming. Even so austere a group as the Pennsylvania Dutch (mostly Germans from the Lower Palatinate) ornamented with traditional motifs and bright colours their birth, marriage and death certificates as well as their more ceremonial furniture; these were often inscribed, even after two centuries, in a loose German *Fraktur* script. As in much Pennsylvania work, there is a combination of looseness of execution with a relative fixity of pattern.

The *Portrait of Magdalene Douw* (Albany, New York, eighteenth century), on the other hand, is a more professional combination of the conceptual and the decorative. It reveals, too, a reasonably skilled artist who has looked at European portraits and engravings, but there are the same tendencies to compartmentalize, flatten and project shapes on to the background as are found in the tradesmen's signs. The varied but impersonal shapes of the shoes, table, fruit, dress and windows almost conflict with the more sensitive, softer and sweeter face. Somehow the whole work retains something of those wallpaper and mural decorations which dignified many of the more wealthy homes of the eighteenth and nineteenth centuries. As in Europe, portraits according to formulas were quite acceptable, but underlying the American folk likeness was the directness of the unsophisticated and almost untrained artist. These factors infused the portrait with a self-consciousness that perfectly matched the patron's sense of individuality. One sometimes feels that a certain austerity compensated for the limner's inability to obtain a truly photographic likeness. While Magdalene may be enhanced by her luxurious surroundings, their formal qualities transcend their class significance and present an image of the restrained and moralistic American settler.

220

Brutal by comparison is the *Portrait of the John Wagner family* (Aurora, Illinois, *c.* 1840). The rugged plasticity of the faces, despite its derivation from professional portaiture, serves to strengthen the individual and collective identities. The prosaic grouping, the

Indian, weathervane, Pennsylvania, eighteenth century

219b

bare setting, the inclusion of only the simplest chairs, the accentuation of heads and the near-suppression of hands and feet, still embody the essentials of the American primitive style. The self-consciousness of the sitters, only an undertone in the portrait of Magdalene, is asserted with such vehemence that we must conclude that it mirrored their deepest wishes. Surely this is obvious in Mr Wagner's ostentatious self-declaration as an upright citizen in a land of liberty! It was this insistence on isolated Protestant individualism, as echoed in the stiff postures, flattened shapes and exaggerated features, which made the primitivism of folk painting an American style that persisted, far beyond its necessity, down to Charles Sheeler, Edward Hopper, John Kane and Grandma Moses.

Many groups of Americans, especially the English Shakers, the German Mennonites and the Swedes, prided themselves on a severe, almost ascetic existence. When it allowed itself expression beyond utilitarian tools and furniture, it contributed elements that strengthened the almost abstract ground forms of American folk painting. This is still visible in so late a work as *Sowing* by Olaf Krans (Bishop Hill, Illinois, 1875–95). The line of ploughing teams in the background and the three sowers in the foreground are not just unskilled renderings of a scene but an expression of the harmony of human beings working in unison. It is a record of group work with which the single worker might identify; for when confronted alone with the vastness of the mid-western plains, as shown by Krans, he could only feel his isolation and helplessness.

238–9   A more individualistic satisfaction with New World accomplishment may stand behind the typical over-mantle scene of which the *Farmhouse of Marten Van Bergen* (Leeds, New York) is an example. Once again, a variety of roughly-differentiated forms is unified by the primitive's layered composition, which respects the front plane of the picture. The small wandering figures recall those in sixteenth- to eighteenth-century engraved views, but here each group has a specific ideational purpose, enabling the owner to inventory the life surrounding his farm house. The building itself, unimposing and simple, is small in scale and off to one side. The artist instinctively avoided a symmetrical arrangement and favoured little indications of life and motion – the grazing cattle, the horse-drawn carriage, the frolicking dog and the gently blowing smoke. All this is set against a natural background whose peace and harmony reflect the well-deserved repose and satisfaction of the owner. The entire atmosphere, like the hearth it overhung, is friendly and warm; the artist has devoted particular attention to the calm peaceful reflections in the water of the middle distance; neither man nor nature is an enemy. It hardly taxes the imagination to grasp the purpose of this kind of painting. Like the portraits, genre scenes and occasional still-lifes, landscapes were a relief from daily work; they provided a mirror in which to contemplate the modest accomplishments of the dedicated individuals who first came to America. If the mirror itself was uncomplicated and unpretentious, it admirably suited the simple pride of its viewers.

230, 231, 242, 263   Iron and copper weather-vanes were widespread in the eighteenth and nineteenth centuries, and as well as forms also common in Europe, such as horses and cockerels, the Red Indian with bow and arrow was particularly popular. Folk sculpture, mostly in wood, also produced some notable works which are purely American in nature, though some types of figures were also known in Europe. There were cigar-smoking Indians outside tobacconists' shops and sailors outside ships' chandlers, ships' figureheads, horses

223

and all kinds of other mounts for merry-go-rounds, all of which were often made in the same workshops in spite of the different uses to which they were put. Another group of figures, which almost certainly originated in America, are the wooden models of ducks and other game birds used as decoys by hunters. Stylized and often painted delightfully, decoys are nowadays very fashionable and are being made again in the traditional way by hand in numerous workshops, destined for the ponds and gardens of country houses and suburban villas; they have even spread to Europe, where they threaten to expel the plaster gnome.

Decoy duck, mid-nineteenth century

LATIN AMERICA, apart from Brazil but including the former Mexican states of California, New Mexico and Arizona, is an area where Spanish cultural influences predominate. The British, French and Dutch made little mark, however much the canals and tall narrow houses of Curaçao may remind us of Amsterdam; for one thing they occupied relatively very small areas, and for another there was far too great a social gulf for them ever to have influenced the art of the native population. Neither the Indians who were settled in the Caribbean at a later date, especially on the British-held islands, nor the Chinese who crossed to the Pacific coast, Peru in particular, exercised any influence, mainly because they kept to themselves. The influx of African slaves had a far stronger effect throughout the Caribbean area, especially on Haiti and in the coastal regions of Colombia, Venezuela and above all Brazil. In some parts of Brazil, particularly in the north-east, the Negro influence far outweighs the Portuguese.

When the *conquistadores* began to invade the Americas in the early sixteenth century, they were most attracted to those parts which were believed, rightly or wrongly, to possess the greatest wealth: the Caribbean, Mexico, and the Andean countries now known as Ecuador, Peru, Bolivia and Colombia. Brazil, Venezuela, Chile and Argentina were of minor importance to begin with, though the Río de la Plata became the main port for traffic to the Spanish empire of Peru.

The European culture made its first impact on the Indian inhabitants of the highlands of what are today Mexico, Guatemala, Colombia, Ecuador, Peru and Bolivia. The *conquistadores* were followed by missionaries, the most influential being the Jesuits in the area covered by the Argentinian state of Misiones and neighbouring parts of Paraguay and Brazil. A third stage was the introduction of cattle-rearing, by *gauchos* in the vast pampas of Argentina, by the *guasos* in southern Brazil, Uruguay and along the Chilean coast, and by the *charros* on the plains lying to the north of the Amazon and Orinoco basin, on the *llanos* of Venezuela and Colombia and in northern Mexico. The cattlemen were exposed, particularly in the far south, to attacks by the Araucanian Indians, the only Indian nation never completely conquered by the invaders. Since both sides were evenly matched in such acts of war as carrying off each other's women, there were not the same psychological tensions as assailed the *mestizos* further north. There was no other real barrier to the conquest of the endless plains and low hill country, while in the Andes the Incas' network of highways proved their undoing.

It must be made clear that the 'European' influences on South American folk art were themselves mixed forms. Arabian and North African elements were already strong in Spanish art and even stronger in Portuguese, which is probably why the latter found it

Page 225 Prize bull, oil on canvas, England, early nineteenth century
Page 226 Scenes from a ballad of chivalry, Sicily, c. 1800

224

so easy to absorb the new influences of the African slaves. They are particularly noticeable in articles concerned with the riding and breeding of horses.

Latin American houses were built of the available materials – wood, bricks of sundried clay (*adobe*) and stone – following the traditions of Iberia, which of course included Arabian traditions. In Chiapa de Corzo, Oaxaca, Mexico, for instance, there is a 'Spanish' fountain which is in fact an example of pure Islamic construction. The poorest houses are built in the Indian style, but with African traces as well. Stables and cattle sheds generally have European origins, since the pre-conquest Indians were ignorant of animal husbandry as we understand it. The plough was introduced from Europe; draught animals were unknown in the Americas. The introduction of the wheel, which had also been unknown, revolutionized transport. The stable, two-wheeled ox-cart came into use in many parts of Latin America. There are still some very fine examples in Costa Rica, where the wheels and bodywork are covered with brightly coloured paintings, usually stylized flowers. The whorled containers for cocoa, found especially in Mexico, where the Aztec chocolate (in Aztec, *xocolatl*) came from, and the mortars used for crushing maize on the South American continent may have been introduced both from Africa, in Brazil, and, via Spain, from Arabia; the fine, turned whorled spoons of Mexico certainly suggest Arabian models.

40b

The hovels of the Indians had practically no furniture. Beds, tables and coffins were of woven matting. Their few articles of clothing were hung on the walls. There were chests, which later came under the influence of the conquerors' wood and leather coffers. The hammocks were certainly not of European origin, but all the other pieces of furniture were: chairs, simple beds, cupboards, tables and chests. Folding stools made of a single piece of wood are obviously copies of Arab stools. Indians squatted on the ground, so the few native chairs derived from the thrones of princes, as can be seen from some examples in the state of Michoacán in Mexico. The settlers' love of luxury made inlaid furniture popular; this is most common in Santa Maria del Río in Mexico, and is also found in Lima.

126d

127a

147h

252

The native traditions in ceramics were so very strong, particularly in Mexico and Peru, and of such a very high standard, that many pre-conquest conventions and techniques have survived to the present day. The Spaniards introduced the potter's wheel, but this is now used almost exclusively where pottery itself was introduced by them, notably in the Talavera centres in Puebla, Mexico. All other ceramic ware was shaped by hand or in moulds. European patterns prevailed above all in those areas where the settlers demanded them, in Puebla and in Michoacán, for instance, and near Mexico City. Glazing was introduced from Spain to some areas, mostly the earliest colonies in Mexico, Guatemala, Peru, Chile and Argentina.

While all manner of European styles were adopted, the clearest examples of European influence are the Talavera pottery of Puebla in Mexico and the wine jugs with pointed bases of Peru and Argentina. The wheel was also used in Brazil, at Carrapico in Sergipe. The clay models of Latin America have yet to be studied in detail. The figurines made in Carrapico suggest a connection with Galo de Barcelos in Minho province in Portugal. The *tanguyús*, figures of horses and riders from Tehuantepec in Mexico, are based on Spanish models.

Page 227 Scenes from ballads of chivalry, painted panels of Sicilian carts (by Giuseppe Genova), nineteenth century

Page 228 a Painted New Year's greeting in the Romansch tongue, Switzerland, 1747; *b* Painted letter from a godparent to his godchild, Alsace, 1832; *c* Painted inscription, 'The Father's Grave', England, 1847

It is perhaps in the field of textiles that European influences are strongest. Before the Spanish conquest leather, bark and plant fibres were used in different regions. The wool of the llama and vicuña was reserved for the Inca élite. We know from frescoes and codices that Peru and Mexico produced some textile masterpieces. Andean weaving has probably never been surpassed. There were blankets and cloaks (called *tilma* in Mexico) from which the poncho (*sarape* in Mexico) developed. The Spaniards introduced wool-bearing animals, sheep in particular, and weavers who brought with them European table looms and stylistic conventions, a considerable number of which derived from Islamic influences. Barely fifty years after the start of the Spanish conquest the first twenty looms were set up in the Argentinian missions, and the first to reach Mexico, in the state of Tlaxcala, were also very early. But as in the case of pottery, although the European techniques took root and have survived, in other parts of the country the more primitive Indian techniques also still survive. The *rebozo*, a stole-like wrap of Arab-Spanish origins, spread into many parts of Latin America, but was nowhere more popular than in Mexico. Examples of it are found in all kinds of designs and in techniques ranging from the very simplest to the magnificent *Ikat* weaving of Tenancingo and Santa Maria del Río. There are also signs of strong European and Arab influences in lace-making, such as the fine Ñanduti work from Itauguá in Paraguay. Lace-making was unknown in Brazil until introduced by the Portuguese.

Pouch, made by Otomí Indians, Mexico

The headscarves worn by women in one part of the Mexican state of Chihuahua are an interesting curiosity. This was an area settled by Mennonites and the scarves, white for girls and black for married women and embroidered with flowers, can be traced from the Vistula and previously from Frisia.

It was a characteristic of folk dress in the Andean highlands and in Guatemala that costumes showed distinct variations from one village to the next, so that a man's home was at once apparent from his dress. When the Spaniards conquered these regions they managed to impose their conventions of dress on the natives, and yet, strangely enough, the tradition of local variations was retained. Even today there are traces of the Spanish influence in the dress of mountain Indians who had hardly any contacts with the conquerors, not least in the various kinds of hat, such as the leather helmets worn in the Sucre region of Bolivia. In the south of Mexico classical, pre-Spanish elements, notably the *huipil*, a straight tunic, persisted in traditional cut and materials. In Yucatán, Mexico, which was more accessible, the *huipil* survived, but was adulterated at an early stage with European flowered patterns and Arabic lace. The traditional wrap-round skirt also survived in Guatemala and on the Pacific coast of Mexico, but European embroidery came to be superimposed on its plain coloured cloth, as at Chilapa in Guerrero, Mexico. In the early colonies in Mexico and the Andes, and later in Chile and Argentina, the long skirt worn over many petticoats was introduced, which, together with her bowler hat, lends the *pollera*, the Indian woman of the mountains of Ecuador, Peru and Bolivia, her unique appearance. The dress of the Negresses of Bahia bears traces of Portuguese influences and there are Spanish elements in Guatemalan costumes, as at Chichicastenango.

Basketry and weaving with straw were already well established in pre-Columbian America, so European influences made little impact, except in hat-making. The Spanish sombrero became a great success in the tropical sun: some Indians wear two, one on top

230

of the other. The first hat-making workshops were opened by monks, often in places, such as San Francisco del Rincón near León in Mexico, which are perversely far from sources of raw material, which had to be carried hundreds of miles on rough tracks.

A favourite pastime was making reproduction of all sorts of everyday objects. These toys ranged from clay figures no bigger than a coin to dolls' clothes and glass miniatures. In the oldest Mexican colonies, in Bajio, toys of wood and tin are to be found, and in Michoacán miniature stringed instruments. In various parts of Mexico there are animals, small baskets and so on made of vanilla, in Papantla, of chicle, the basic material of chewing-gum, in Yucatán and Tabasco, and of chilte, an arboreal resin, in Jalisco. Some curious toys are made for the Day of Death, including skulls made of candy, particularly in Mexico City and Toluca.

207g, i, 214b

Although the pre-conquest Mexicans are known to have been great lovers of flowers and gardens, it seems likely that the floral pictures carried in processions are composed under European influences. Pictures made of seeds, like those made by ladies of society in the colonial era, are still to be found as the fertility festival in Metepec, Mexico, and once again European influences seem probable. They are certainly present in the highly colourful votive pictures, in the fine primitive oil paintings which photographers use as backcloths, in seventeenth- and eighteenth-century painted chests, and in Mexican lacquer work of the kind found in Uruapan, Chiapa de Corzo and Pátzcuaro, and formerly also in Quiroga and Olinalá. The lacquer work probably also has some pre-Spanish elements, since both here and in Peru, lacquer of an early date has been found.

European influences are everywhere very strong in sculpture and ornamental carving, particularly in churches. The best is to be found in Brazil, particularly in the work of the colonial era in the museum at Bahia and in the work of the mulatto sculptor O Aleijadinho. Colonial-style sculpture is still done today, partly to meet a genuine demand and partly for the benefit of tourists, and *santos*, figures of the saints, are still carved in traditional styles for churches.

A decree of Philip II forbade Indians to own or work precious metals. They were driven back on tin, and copied European styles in church candlesticks, censers and the like. The casting of votive objects in silver, also after European models, is a more recent art; they usually played the role of talismans, and were expected to heal sickness, protect children and ward off robbers and ill-fortune. Some types of metalwork, usually in silver, from the colonial era are well known, such as the crosses from Yalalag in Mexico and Otavalo in Ecuador, brandy casks from Bolivia and brandy spoons from the Andes. The forging of iron, unknown in South America before the conquest, tends to follow Islamic models particularly in spurs, stirrups and other appurtenances of riding, and the technique of using iron and silver beaten together is probably also of Arabian origin. The working of horn began with the introduction of Spanish cattle. There are some fine examples of carved drinking-horns, particularly in Argentina. Some regions of Mexico produce decorated combs made of horn. But the most remarkable work of this kind is the tortoise-shell carved in ways that go back to Spanish and Islamic models, found on the coast of Mexico (Veracruz) and Colombia (Cartagena, Barranquilla).

Leatherwork existed before the Spanish conquest, but horse riding gave it a particular boost, especially in cattle country; saddles, bridles, lassos whips, sheaths for knives and

Design from a stoneware jug, New York State, *c. 1800*

machetes were made in most parts of Latin America, often with great artistry, and in Argentina there were the *botas de potro*, very soft leggings made of kid leather.

Masks show a close mingling of Indian and African strands – in the devil dances of San Francisco de Yare, Venezuela – as well as European elements, which are most prominent in the masks worn by Mexican quadrille dancers, which have fair skin and hair, blue eyes and moustaches.

In sum, the Spanish and Portuguese conquerors brought to Latin America a wealth of highly developed forms in all fields of art, and an original, colonial art was quick to develop, which contained some elements of the new religion. It has not been possible here to illustrate the complex interplay of the techniques and styles of the two worlds in any detail. The position of the Indian has altered very little in some states from the time of the *conquista* to the present: he remains a servant, though his masters have changed. It was only after years of doubt whether Indians were men or beasts that a Bull of Pope Paul III in 1537 pronounced them to be men. But for a long time they were denied any independent artistic activity, and materials like precious metals were forbidden. It is therefore all the more surprising that they were able to weld the immensely strong Spanish and Portuguese influences into an original style.

Heathen idols were banned, but the old gods lived on in the Indians' hearts. The cross was already a symbol of the Tree of Life to the Maya, and with typical flexibility the subject race adopted many elements of the new religion in which they saw a significance undreamed of by the missionaries. The old gods still stand in the magnificent church of Santa Maria Tonanzintla in Mexico, hand in hand with the new.

Design from a plate, Tzintzuntzan, Mexico

Wrought iron griddle, Netherlands

Page 233 Solomon and the Queen of Sheba, painted paper wall-hanging (by Daniel Andersson), Rovgärdet, Dalarna, Sweden, 1843

Page 234 Swiss inn signs: *a* William Tell, Hauenstein, Solothurn, early nineteenth century; *b* The Sun, St Johann, Toggenburg, *c.* 1702; *c* The Bear, seventeenth century; *d* The Cross, Sachseln, Obwalden, seventeenth century; *e* The Red Cock, Geneva, 1605; *f* The Menagerie, Aarwangen, Aargau, 1697–1771

Page 235 Beehive front boards: *a* Yugoslavia; *b* Yugoslavia, 1889; *c* Carinthia, 1910

232

rottningen af rika Arabia kommer till Konung Salomon. Till att för söka honom med gåtor. hafvandes med sig guld och ädla stenar. 2 Chroni6o.B.C.9

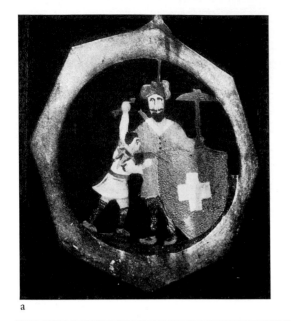

a

b

c

d

e

f

a

b

c

a

b

a

b

c

d

Wrought iron griddle, Netherlands

Page 236 Birds and flowers, water-colour by a country priest, near Beauvais, c. 1840
Page 237 Portraits of soldiers, so-called 'souvenirs militaires', Alsace: a 1846; b first half of nineteenth century
Pages 238–9 The Farm of Marten van Bergen in Leeds, N.Y., painted by himself. Mural from the house in the picture, c. 1750
Page 240 a Painted design, Pennsylvania, c.1800; b Appliqué motif from a patchwork quilt, Pennsylvania, nineteenth century; c Coloured paper cut-out, Poland; d Painted wooden plate, Norway, early nineteenth century

241

THE ILLUSTRATIONS in this book may well give the connoisseur and the dealer the impression that they are walking round an antique shop with a widely varied stock from all periods. But it would have to be a special kind of antique shop, because for all their variety the objects are all of a very special nature. Not very long ago, many of them could have been bought quite cheaply. Furthermore, unlike various other, as it were 'orthodox', *objets d'art* and antiques which have always been recognized as such in the art trade, there is still a considerable lack of agreement in assessing the products of folk art. For a long time there were no standard prices. With the increasing scarcity of antiques and the consequent general rise in prices, however, the prices (if not always the value) of works of folk art have also risen.

That they have always been collected is proved by the museums and older private collections, and, above all, the open-air museums which needed a comprehensive stock to furnish the old buildings they preserved. The well known Dutch collector Dr Wiegersma acquired many of the specimens in his collection, which now forms a large part of the collection in the Arnhem Openluchtmuseum, from the patients in his country practice. Similarly, in the early years of this century, the German physician Professor Häberlin let his patients pay him with old pieces of furniture, pictures and utensils, which today form the very valuable nucleus of the Häberlin-Friesen-Museum in Wyk on the island of Föhr. In many countries of Europe and America, there are now open-air museums, often with a number of old buildings, even enough to form a small village, and museums of local history with complete reconstructions of rooms. Some are up to a hundred years old, and they all paid very little, by modern standards, for their collections; the converse of this is that to start or re-build institutions of this kind today requires enormous financial resources. In the meantime a specialized trade in folk art has grown up, whose main function is to supply a large circle of amateur collectors.

In spite of this development, some art dealers still look down on objects of folk art on the grounds that they have little or nothing to do with 'real' art. It is true, they say, that antiques which today are sold at high prices are nothing more than the useful articles of an earlier age, but they are usually the work of artists, sculptors, silversmiths and other professional artists. Folk art, on the other hand, is the work of peasants, shepherds and simple craftsmen.

Whether that is a valid distinction – or prejudice – or not, the fact remains that there is a market for all these objects nowadays, even if it is easily overlooked on the international front and has not established anything like the relatively uniform standards of evaluation that prevail in the 'orthodox' antique trade. For this reason what follows can consist only of generalized indications, and of examples that are fairly typical and may give the collector a practical criterion in specific cases. The page numbers in the margin refer to illustrations of the *type* of thing under discussion, never of the actual article.

The demand for antique farmhouse furniture is very great everywhere at the present time, and by and large it can be said that simple, well-preserved old furniture that can still be put to use will always fetch a higher price than comparable modern pieces; this 33, 36–9, 54 a, 60 e, f applies to presses, chests of drawers, tables and seats of all kinds. On being re-sold after five or ten years they will fetch at least the same price (often much more), while new furniture always depreciates considerably. Current prices in Europe for presses and chests of drawers range between £ 30 ($ 75) and several hundred pounds. Large, unpainted oak furniture dating from before 1800, even of only average quality, is relatively dear; painted Alpine softwood furniture is cheaper, unless it is particularly beautiful. The kind of chests which were found everywhere in peasant houses from the sixteenth cen- 40, 45 b, 46, 47, 53 tury on and hardly changed up to the end of the nineteenth cost up to £ 100 ($ 240) or so, depending on their carving and ornamentation, though larger, especially splendid pieces sell at considerably more. Early nineteenth-century coffers, with rounded lids and, often, ornamental iron mountings, can be bought in Germany, Holland and Scandinavia for as little as £ 15 ($ 36). Four-poster beds have become very popular recently, in the simple 54 style which changed very little up to the last century. Later examples of the plain oak beds were painted, and if you want to buy an English or German four-poster today you must be prepared to pay at least £ 100 ($ 240). Cradles which are to be found in every 58 country vary between £ 30 and £ 300 ($ 70 and $ 700). Simple chairs which once cost a few 56 shillings are now ten times as much. Tyrolean pine tables of the early nineteenth century cost about £ 20 ($ 50), older ones comparably more; seventeenth-century tables are unobtainable at less than £ 60 ($ 150).

Mahogany grandfather clocks, which are much sought after, cost between £ 40 and £ 50 (about $ 100) in England, but this does not include the cost of repairing the works, which is often considerable. With a certain amount of luck you may come across one in a second-hand shop in a small town for half the price, but in Dutch, German, Danish or American antique shops you will not find one in working order for less than three times the price.

Weather-vane, Pennsylvania, nineteenth century

Old cake forms and moulds have become internationally popular over the last few 278 years. The prices vary, according to size, age, subject and quality, between about £ 10 and £ 50 ($ 25 to $ 125). At an auction in Copenhagen in 1963, for instance, five cake forms ornamented with human and animal figures fetched £ 60 ($ 150), and seven cylindrical carved moulds fetched £ 90 ($ 225). Chip boxes, in which caps and ribbons were kept, 74 were once widespread in Europe and America, painted in a style typical of Berchtesgaden, while in France they had copper engravings pasted on them. Today these may cost as much as £ 30 ($ 70). Other kinds of caskets and trinket boxes are equally popular. A Danish sewing box, decorated with chip carving and dated 1834, went for £ 14 ($ 35) in 84 Copenhagen in 1963, while another box originally made to hold shaving tackle, with a sliding lid and dated 1805, fetched £ 50 ($ 125). A weaver's reed of 1807 with ornate fret- 114 c, 59 f work decoration was sold for £ 34 ($ 85), but plainer reeds cost up to £ 10 ($ 24) at present. The typical Danish fob cases cost between £ 25 ($ 60) and £ 30 ($ 75). Scandinavian mangle boards, most of which date from the eighteenth and early nineteenth centuries, fetch between $ 25 and $ 250 if they are in good condition, and without regard to their age. The sum of £ 1,200 ($ 3,000) was recently offered (to no avail) to a Berlin collector for a magnificent carved and painted Sicilian cart of about 1800. Carved, engraved and painted tobacco boxes are available in wood, copper, bone and whalebone; with these their origin plays an important part in evaluation. They will cost at least £ 10 ($ 24) – and this also applies to Russian lacquered boxes. Silver ones will cost up to £ 200 ($ 500).

116
273 d, e

Ceramics have long been a favourite field of private collectors in every country. There is considerable variation in prices according to age, quality and place of origin. To name a few 'cheap' examples: an ordinary grey Westerwald jug, with the usual bold blue pattern, holding about a litre and a half, and a good hundred years old, costs at least £ 2 ($ 5), an average Staffordshire dog of the same age costs about £ 5 ($ 12), and an Upper Bavarian dish of the late nineteenth century, painted with stylized green foliage, costs about £ 4 ($ 10). On the other hand, some of the most expensive items are dishes by Thomas Toft which never fetch less than £ 100. Good, painted brandy bottles of the late eighteenth and early nineteenth centuries cost at least £ 10. Nailsea rolling-pins are keenly sought after, because of the variety and brilliance of their coloured glass. Although they were made in the nineteenth century and in great numbers, they cost between £ 1 and £ 6 in England and are almost unobtainable on the Continent.

143

136 a
165 a–c

In the wide field of folk painting, it is even harder to give definite or even relative prices than in the rest of folk art. It is almost entirely a seller's market, and yet it is in this field that, given the necessary taste and knowledge, one can most easily find a bargain. For works of real originality, particularly in America, prices of $ 250 are by no means rare. With certain genres standard prices have evolved. For instance, paintings on glass before 1900 are unobtainable at less than £ 10 ($ 24), and the same is true of votive and devotional pictures in good condition. Older examples of particularly high quality can cost up to ten times as much. The front boards of old beehives from Carinthia and Slovenia are very rare and cost up to £ 100 ($ 240).

207 b–f
208 b–d
213, 216 c
235 a–c

Even the old houses of peasants and fishermen are much in demand nowadays as homes or holiday cottages. This is a very welcome development as many valuable old buildings, often with some if not all of their original contents, are preserved in this way as memorials to old folk arts, which would otherwise be demolished and irrevocably lost.

The time for buying bargains in the folk arts is, generally speaking, past. Prices are too high, and nowadays a lot of what is on sale is of inferior quality or, quite simply, trash. Another factor which makes evaluation difficult is that many objects are unusual and there are great differences in quality. Certainly there are still treasures to be found in junkshops and flea-markets which keen collectors may snap up for a song and carry home in triumph. But there are not many discoveries to be made without expert knowledge and a great deal of luck. With folk art, as with any other commodity, value is determined in the final analysis by supply and demand – and by what a person who has fallen in love with an object is prepared to pay for it.

The fact that nowadays so many people are in love with works of folk art, however, is certainly to be applauded for more than merely financial reasons.

Above and below: Christmas biscuit-moulds, northern Frisia

Page 245 a Carnival mask, Basle; *b* Sealskin mask, Iceland

Page 246 Masks: *a* Lötschental, Switzerland; *b* Tyrol; *c* St Gall, Switzerland; *d, f* Upper Bavaria; *e* 'Bran spout', Black Forest

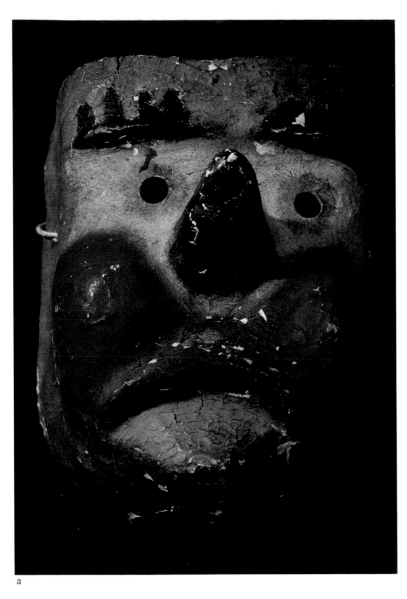

a

b

a b c

d e f

a

b

c

d

e

f

References to the plates and figures are given in the margin of the text, with the page number followed, where appropriate, by a letter; thus 176e refers to the illustration lettered e on page 176.

Captions give a description of the object, the artist's name, the place and the date of origin, so far as these facts are ascertainable.

Objects illustrated in this book are to be found in the museums and collections listed below, with references.

NORWAY

Vestlandske Kunstindustri Museum, Bergen: 179d
Drammens Museum, Drammen: 59b
Aarstad Collection, Egersund: 73b
Haugesunds Museum, Haugesund: 240d
Kunstindustrimuseet, Oslo: 54c, 167a, 179c
Norsk Folkemuseet Bygdöy, Oslo: 34c, 54d

SWEDEN

Nordiska Museet, Stockholm: 13, 14, 15, 16, 17, 36, 55b[f], 56h, 57d, 58a, 90a, c, e, g, 106, 131, 133b, 134 (2nd row. r.), 178a, 203, 223, 233

FINLAND

Seurasaaren Ulkomuseo, Helsinki: 10e, 22, 23, 30, 31, 84d, 107, 114b, 170, 171, 190, 195a, 198c, 200c, 222, 276b, d
Suomen Kansallismuseo, Helsinki: 46a

ICELAND

National Museum, Reykjavik: 59h, 185b, 195d, 268a, b, 276e

DENMARK

Museum Den Gamle By, Aarhus: 33b, d, 59a, 134 (3rd row, l.)
Nationalmuseum, Copenhagen: 35c, 54b, 58f, 92e, 101b, d, 114c, 176c, 280d
Haderslev Amts Museum, Haderslev: 46g, 59f, 68a, 90i, 126b, 146c, 147b
Koldinghus Museet, Kolding: 146i
Lolland-Falsters Stiftsmuseum, Maribo: 60d
Skive Museum, Skive: 38d
Tønder Museum, Tønder: 39c, 46d, 53c, 84a, 146b, 176e, 267a

SCOTLAND

National Museum of Antiquities of Scotland, Edinburgh: 166a
Alexander Fenton collection, Edinburgh: 56e, 84e, 101a, 127b

ENGLAND

Fitzwilliam Museum, Cambridge: 148a
Luton Museum, Luton: 126a(ii), 267b
Museum of English Rural Life, Reading: 12, 45a, 46h, 56d, f, g, 62, 63, 70, 71, 77, 78, 114e, 122, 123, 124, 127e, 130, 138, 139, 146g, 162, 163, 165c, 178b, c, 183, 191, 215a–d, 225, 228c, 277a, 280a
Averil Colby collection, Reading: 198b
Margaret Fuller collection, Reading: 142c, d, 143b, d
Castle Museum, York: 92d, f

IRELAND

National Museum of Ireland, Dublin: 68b, 255b, d, 274a, b

NETHERLANDS

Rijksmuseum voor Volkenkunde 'Het Nederlands Openluchtmuseum': 7, 9, 55c[g], 57b, 58e, 59d, 68c, 89a, 90h, 102a, 126a(l.), 134 (2nd row, l., bottom row, r.), 135 (2nd row, l. & r.), 146h, 161, 168b, 177a, 193, 217c, 241, 248, 266a–d, 273d, e
Westfries Museum, Hoorn: 34b
Nederlands Museum van Knipkunst: 150, 160
Marcel B. Keezer collection, Wassenaar: 134 (top row, centre), 264

GERMANY

Städtisches Museum, Flensburg: 26–7
Hansen Collection, Munich: 38c, 53b, 142a, 143a, c

Page 247 a Mask, Lucerne; *b* Flour spout, Sarre-Union, Alsace; *c* Carnival mask, Salzburg, eighteenth century; *d–f* Flour spout, Alsace

Page 248 Pipe-smoking Negro, woodcarving, Netherlands

252

a   b

a

b

c

d

e

f

g

h

i

j

a

b

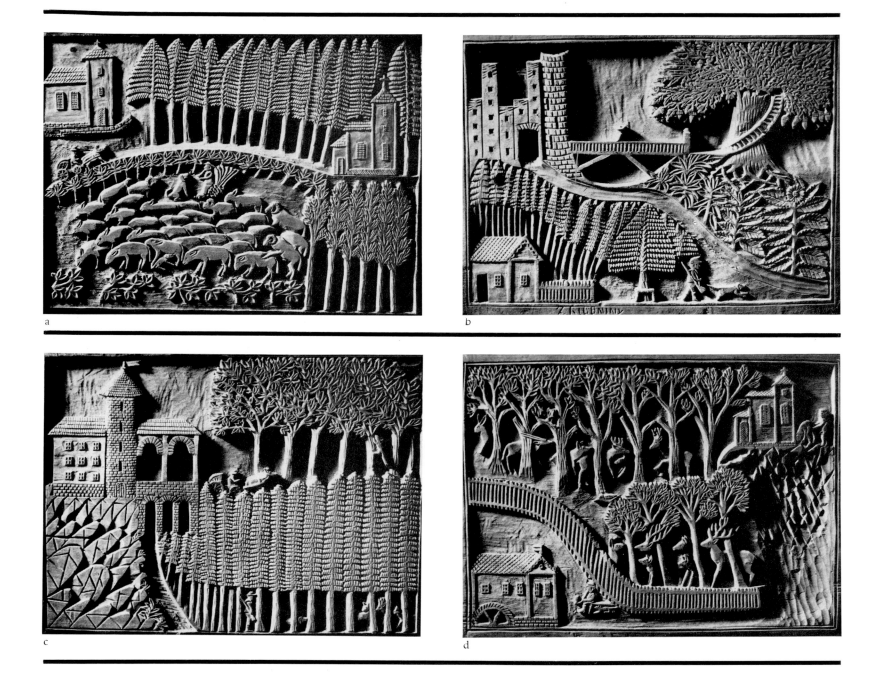

a

b

c

d

a

b

Alings, H.W.: *Amsterdamsche Gevelsteenen.* 1949

Alvarez, José Rogelio: *Chilte.* Guadalajara 1960

Alvarez, José Rogelio: *Vidrio soplado.* Guadalajara 1960

Andersen, Ellen: *Danske Bønders Klaededragt.* Copenhagen 1960

Andersen, Ellen: *Folkedragter i Danmark.* Copenhagen 1952

Aranzadi, T. de: 'Etnografía, filología y folklore sobre ruecas, husos y torcederas'. In: *Memorias de la Real Academia de Ciencias Artes y Letras,* vol. XXVII. Barcelona 1944

Argentina–Gran Manual de Folklore. Buenos Aires 1964

Arte Popular em Portugal, 3 vols. Lisbon 1960

Atwater, Mary M.: *Guatemala visited.* Big Sur 1964

Bakardžiev, G.: *Keramikata v Bulgaria.* Sofia 1956

Barber, Joel: *Wild Fowl Decoys.* New York 1934

Bátky, S. and Györffy, E.: *L'Art populaire hongrois.* Budapest 1928

Baud-Bovy, Daniel: *Art rustique en Suisse.* London 1924

Beitl, Richard (ed.): *Wörterbuch der deutschen Volkskunde.* Stuttgart 1955

Berliner, Rudolf: *Die Weihnachtskrippe.* Munich 1955

Bernet Kempers, A. J.: *Toen Marken nog 'het Eiland' was.* 1965

Black, Mary and Lipman, Jean: *American Folk Painting.* New York 1967

Blair, M.: *The Paisley Shawl.* Paisley 1904

Blöndal, S. and Sigtryggsson, S.: *Alt-Island im Bilde.* Jena 1930

Bolivia – *La Paz en su IV. Centenario 1548–1948.* La Paz 1948

Bossert, H. Th.: *Ornamente der Volkskunst,* 2 vols. Tübingen 1952/53

Bossert, H. Th.: *Volkskunst in Europa.* Berlin 1926

Božinov, Al., Vakarelski, Chr. and Drumev, D.: *Kovano željazo.* Sofia 1957

Bruun, Daniel: *Fortidsminder og Nutidshjem paa Island.* Copenhagen 1928

Budry, P. and Wyss, R. L.: *Les Plaisirs de la Table et de la Vaisselle ancienne en Suisse.* Zurich 1956

Cáceres Freyre, Julián: *Arte popular y artesanias tradicionales de la Argentina.* Buenos Aires 1964

Caro Baroja, J.: *Los pueblos de España.* Barcelona 1946

Carreras y Candi, F.: *Folklore y costumbres de España,* 3 vols. Barcelona 1931

Ciarrochi, Arnolde and Mori, Ermanno: *Italienische Votivbilder*

Christensen, Erwin O.: *The Index of American Design.* New York 1950

Christie, D. R.: 'Scottish Woollens over the Centuries'. In: *Texture,* vol. I, No. 3, 1953

Christinger, R. and Borgeaud, W.: *Mythologie de la Suisse ancienne.* Geneva 1963

Christison, D.: 'The Carvings and Inscriptions on the Kirkyard Monuments of the Scottish Lowlands'. In: *Proceedings of the Society of Antiquaries of Scotland.* Edinburgh 1902

Coluccio, Felix: *Diccionario Folklórico Argentino.* Buenos Aires 1964

Cortés Vázquez, L.: *La alfarería popular salmantina.* Salamanca 1953

Cortés Vázquez, L.: 'Las cucharas de mango corto salmantinas.' In: *Zephirus,* vol. XIV. Salamanca 1963

Cortés Vázquez, L.: *Las ovejas y la lana en Lumbrales. Pastoreo e industria primitiva en un pueblo salmantino.* Salamanca 1957

Creux, René: *Schilder vor dem Himmel.* Lausanne 1962

Davis, Mary L. and Pack, Greta: *Mexican Jewelry,* University of Texas Press 1960

Dereko, Aleksandar: *Narodno neimarstvo.* Belgrade 1939

Deutsche Vokskunst (series of regional monographs). Munich 1925ff., Weimar 1940ff., Marburg 1951

Döderlein, Wilhelm: *Alte Krippen.* Munich 1960

Drumev, D. and Vasilev, A.: *Rezbarskoto izkustvo v Balgaria.* Sofia 1955

Duchartre, Pierre-Louis: *Art populaire.* Paris 1931

Dunbar, J. G.: *The Historic Architecture of Scotland.* Edinburgh 1966

Dunbar, J. Telfer: *History of Highland Dress.* Edinburgh and London 1962

Eaton, Allen H.: *Handicrafts of New England.* New York 1949

Eldjárn, Kristján: *Alte isländische Kunst.* Munich 1957

Enriquez, M. D.: *El mueble español en los siglos XV, XVI y XVII.* Madrid, n. d.

Faleyeva, V. A.: *Russkoye narodnoye iskusstvo.* Leningrad 1959

Feddersen, Arthur: 'Islandsk Kunstindustri'. In: *Tidsskrift for kunstindustri.* Copenhagen 1887

Fél, Edit: *Hungarian Peasant Embroidery.* London 1961

Fél, Edit and Hofer, T.: *Husaren, Hirten, Heilige.* Budapest 1966

Fél, Edit, Hofer, T. and Csilléry, K.: *Ungarische Bauernkunst.* Budapest 1958

Finlay, I.: *Scottish Crafts.* London 1948

Finnbogason, G. and Jónsson, R.: 'Skurdlist'. In: *Idnsaga Islands I.* Reykjavik 1943

Fisher, Leonard Everett: *Colonial American Craftsmen,* 10 vols. New York 1967

Fleming, J. Arnold: *Scottish Pottery.* Glasgow 1923

Folklore Argentino, Humanior. Buenos Aires 1959

Freyer, Kurt: 'Zum Problem der Volkskunst'. In: *Monatshefte für Kunstwissenschaft,* 1916

Gebhard, Torsten: *Die volkstümliche Möbelmalerei in Altbayern mit besonderer Berücksichtigung des Tölzer Kistlerhandwerks.* Munich 1937

Giono, Jean: *Le Déserteur.* Lausanne 1966

González Iglesias, L.: *El bordado popular serrano.* Salamanca 1952

González Martí, M.: *Cerámica Española.* Barcelona 1933

Grabowski, Józef: *Sztuka ludowa.* Warsaw 1966

Grabowski, Józef: *Wycinanka ludowa.* Warsaw 1955

Grant, I. F.: *Highland Folk Ways.* London 1961

Grass, Nikolaus (ed.): *Weihnachtskrippen in Österreich.* Innsbruck 1965

Gudjónsson, Elsa E.: *Gamle islandske motiver til korssting.* Copenhagen 1965

Gudjónsson, Elsa E.: 'Traditional Icelandic Embroidery'. In: *Bulletin of the Needle and Bobbin Club,* 47. New York 1963

Gudjónsson, Elsa E.: 'Um skinnsaum'. In: *Arbók hins íslanzka fornleifafélags 1964.* Reykjavik 1964

Haan, Tjaard W. R. de: *Volkskunst der Lage Landen,* 3 vols. Amsterdam 1965

Haberlandt, Arthur: *Taschenwörterbuch der Volkskunde Österreichs,* 2 vols. Vienna 1953/59

Haberlandt, Michael: *Österreichische Volkskunst,* 2 vols. Vienna 1911

Hahm, Konrad: *Deutsche Volkskunst.* Berlin 1928

Hanhart, Rudolf: *Appenzeller Bauernmalerei.* Teufen 1959

Hansen, H. P.: *Jydepotter og Löb.* Copenhagen 1944

Hazelius, Artur: *Afbildningar af föremål i Nordiska Museet.* Stockholm 1890

Heine, N. G.: 'Manglebraet og Folkekunst'. In: *Fra Nationalmuseets Arbejdsmark.* Copenhagen 1946

Heinonen, Jorma and Vuoristo, Osmo: *Antiikkikirja.* Helsinki 1965

Hemert, Maria van: *De handwerken van het Eiland Marken.* 1960

Hermannsson, Halldór: *Icelandic Illuminated Manuscripts of the Middle Ages.* Copenhagen 1935

Hernandez, Francisco Javier: *El juguete popular en México.* Mexico 1950

Hesketh, C.: *Tartans.* London 1961

Hovden, Knut K.: *Gammel Rosemaling i Rogaland.* Stavanger 1938

Hoyos Saínz, L. de: *Manual de Folklore.* Madrid 1947

Irwin, J.: *Shawls.* London 1955

Jensen, Andreas: *Jydepotten.* Copenhagen 1924

Jensen, Chr. A.: *Snedkere og Billedsnidere i Danmark.* Copenhagen 1911

Jensen, Chr. A. and Rondahl, E.: *Stilarternes Historie.* Copenhagen 1912

Johannsen, Ebbe: 'Mindeblade'. In: *Den gamle By Årbog.* Århus 1961

Karlinger, H.: *Deutsche Volkskunst.* Berlin 1938

Keiser, Herbert Wolfgang: *Die deutsche Hinterglasmalerei.* Munich 1937

Keyser, P. de (ed.): *Ars Folklorica Belgica, Noorden Zuid-Nederlandse Volkskunst,* 2 vols. Antwerp 1949 and 1956

Kleyn, J. de: *Volksaardewerk in Nederland 1600–1900*

Knaipp, Friedrich: *Hinterglasbilder aus Bauern- und Bergmannsstuben des 18. und 19. Jahrhunderts.* Linz 1963

Kojič, Branislav: *Seoska arhitektura i futurizam.* Belgrade 1958

Krassowski, Wojciech: *Architektura drewniana w Polsce.* Warsaw 1961

Kresz, M.: 'The historical background and the character of Hungarian popular pottery'. In: *VIIth International Congress of Anthropological and Ethnological Sciences.* Moscow 1964

Kresz, Mária: *Ungarische Bauerntrachten 1820–1867.* Budapest 1957

Kriss-Rettenbeck, Lenz: *Bilder und Zeichen religiösen Volksglaubens.* Munich 1963

Kriss-Rettenbeck, Lenz: *Das Votivbild.* Munich 1961

262

Krüger, Fritz: *El Mobiliário Popular en los Paises romanicos.* Coimbra 1963

Kunz, Ludvík: *Ethnographica* (Yearbook of Moravskí Muzeum). Brno 1959–66

Laedrach, Walter: *Der Bernische Speicher.* Berne 1954

Larkin, Oliver W.: 'Art by the People'. In: *Art and Life in America.* New York 1960

Lennep, J. van: *Ferdinand Huyck.* 1840

Lennep, J. van and Gouw, J. ter: *De Uithangteekens.* 1868

Lennep, J. van and Gouw, J. ter: *Het boek der Opschriften.* 1869

Lichten, Frances: *Folk Art Motifs of Pennsylvania.* New York 1954

Lichten, Frances: *The Art of Rural Pennsylvania.* New York 1946

Lipman, Jean: *American Folk Art.* New York 1948

Lipman, Jean: *American Primitive Painting.* Oxford 1942

Lipp, Franz: *Linz und die österreichische Volkskunst.* Linz 1956

Lipp, Franz: *Oberösterreichische Bauernmöbel.* Linz 1964

Longfield, Ada K.: 'Some late 18th and early 19th Century Irish tombstones'. In: *Journal of the Royal Society of Antiquaries of Ireland.* 1947, 1948, 1954, 1955

Lorenzen, Ena: 'Til vaevespjaeldets historie'. In: *Den gamle By Årbog.* Århus 1948

Lucas, A. T.: 'Penal Crucifixes'. In: *County Louth Archaeological Journal.* 1955

Lucas, Jan: *Das Buch vom Wein.* Prague 1964

Madrid – Trabajos y Materiales del Museo del Pueblo Español

Makovetsky, I. V.: *Arkhitektura russkogo narodnogo zhilishcha.* Moscow 1962

Manga, János: 'Hirtenkunst in Transdanubien'. In: *Acta Ethnographica.* Budapest 1961

Manuelli, Vinicio: *Il mobile regionale italiano.*

Manugiewicz, Jan: *Polskie stroje ludowe.* Łodz n. d.

Marin de Paalen, Isabel: *Alfarería/Tonalá.* Guadalajara 1960

Marković, Zagorka: *Narodni muzički instrumenti Jugoslavije.* Belgrade 1957

Marković, Zagorka: 'Narodne tvorevine'. In: *Turisticka enciklopedija Jugoslavije.* Belgrade 1958

Mattos, Armando de: *Jugos e Cangas do Douro-Litoral.* Oporto 1942

Maxwell, S.: 'Craftsmen in Wood'. In: *Scotland's Magazine.* February 1959

Maxwell, S. and Hutchinson, R.: *Scottish Costume 1550–1850.* London 1958

Maynard, Araújo: *Folclore Nacional.* São Paulo 1964

Meinander, K. K.: 'Folkkonsten i Finland'. In: *Nordisk Kultur.* Stockholm 1931

Meyer-Heisig, Erich: *Deutsche Bauerntöpferei.* Munich 1955

Meyer-Heisig, Erich: *Deutsche Volkskunst.* Munich 1954

Meyer-Heisig, Erich: *Die deutsche Bauernstube.* Nuremberg 1952

Meyer-Heisig, Erich: *Weberei, Nadelwerk, Zeugdruck.* Munich 1956

Mills, George and Grove, Richard: *Himmlische Zuflucht, Santos aus New Mexico.* Munich 1964

Mokłowski, Kazimierz: *Sztuka ludowa w Polsce.* Lvov 1903

Molen, S. J. van der: *Fryske Klaeijnge.*

Montgomery, Charles F. (ed.): *America's Arts and Skills.* New York 1957

Morán Bardón, C.: 'Arte popular'. In: *Actas y Memorias de la Sociedad española de Antropología, Etnografía y Prehistoria.* Madrid 1928

Moser, Oskar: *Kärntner Bauernmöbel.* Klagenfurt 1949

Nekrasov, A. I.: *Russkoye narodnoye iskusstvo.* Moscow 1924

Nemec, Helmut: *Alpenländische Bauernkunst.* Vienna 1966

Olrik, Jørgen: 'Folkekunst i Danmark'. In: *Nordisk Kultur.* 1931

Olrik, Jørgen: 'Kaerestegaver'. In: *Dansk Udsyn.* 1930

Ortiz Echagüe, J.: *Tipos y trajes,* 9th edn. Bilbao 1953

Osborne, Lilly de Jongh: *Indian Crafts of Guatemala and El Salvador.* Oklahoma 1965

Ottenjann, Heinrich: *Alte deutsche Bauernmöbel.* Hanover 1954

Palotay, Gertrud: 'Die historische Schichtung der ungarischen Volksstickerei'. In: *Ungarische Jahrbücher.* Berlin 1938

Palotay, Gertrud: *Les Éléments turco-ottomans des broderies hongroises.* Budapest 1940

Paterson, T. G. F.: 'Brigid's Crosses in County Armagh'. In: *Ulster Journal of Archaeology.* 1945

Pease, Z. W.: *A Visit to the Museum of the Old Dartmouth Historical Society.* New Bedford 1947

Peesch, Reinhard: *Holzgerät in seinen Urformen.* Berlin 1966

Peteva, E.: 'Balgarski narodni nakiti'. In: *Izvestiya na Narodniya Etnografski Muzey.* Sofia 1926

Piwocki, Ksawery: *Drzeworyt ludowy w Polsce.* Warsaw 1934

Plicková, Ester: *Pozdišovské hrnčiarstvo*. Bratislava 1959

Portugália, 1–2. Oporto 1899/1908

Poulsen, Hanne: 'Folkekunst på land og i by'. In: *Dagligliv i Danmark I*. Copenhagen 1963

Poulsen, Hanne: 'Traditionsdominanter i dansk folkekunst'. In: *Arv og Eje*. 1966

Prosvirkina, S. K.: *Russkaya derevyannaya posuda*. Moscow 1957

Rabotnova, I. P.: *Russkoye narodnoye kruzhevo*. Moscow 1956

Rácz, István and Valonen, Niilo: *Suomen kansantaiteen aarteita*. Helsinki 1963

Reinfuss, Roman: *Garncarstwo ludowe*. Warsaw 1955

Reinfuss, Roman and Swiderski, Jan: *Sztuka ludowa w Polsce*. Warsaw 1960

Ritz, Josef Maria: *Alte bemalte Bauernmöbel*, 4. edn. ed. Gislind Ritz. Munich 1965

Ritz, Josef Maria (ed.): *Süddeutsche Volkskunst*. Munich 1938

Roussell, A.: *Norse Building Customs in the Scottish Isles*. Copenhagen 1934

Rubi, Christian: *Peinture Paysanne*. Neuchâtel 1948

Rumpf, Karl: *Eine deutsche Bauernkunst*. Marburg 1943

Russkoye dekorativnoye iskusstvo, 3 vols. Moscow 1963/65

Russkoye narodnoye iskusstvo. Leningrad 1959

Sacher, E.: *Die aus Grassoden und Holz gebauten Höfe und Kirchen in Island*. Würzburg 1938

Saltykov, A. B.: *Gzhel'skaya keramika*. Moscow 1949

Sauermann, Ernst: *Schleswigsche Beiderwand*. Frankfurt am Main 1909

Sauermann, Ernst: 'Die Volkskunst'. In: *Schleswig-Holsteinisches Jahrbuch*. 1928/29

Schlee, Ernst: *Schleswig-Holsteinische Volkskunst*. Flensburg 1964

Schmidt, Leopold: *Masken in Mitteleuropa*. Wien 1955

Schmidt, Leopold: *Volkskunst in Österreich*. Wien 1966

Schmolitzky, Otto: *Volkskunst in Thüringen vom 16. bis zum 19. Jahrhundert*, n. d.

Schoubye, Sigurd: *Folkekunst på Tønderegnen*. Tønder 1955

Schröder, Albert: *Bemalter Hausrat in Nieder- und Ostdeutschland*. Leipzig 1939

Schuh, Gotthard and Arnet, Edwin: *Tirggel*. Zurich/Leipzig 1941

Seweryn, Tadeusz: *Polskie malarstwo ludowe*. Cracow 1937

Sinclair, C.: *Thatched Houses of the Old Highlands*. Edinburgh 1953

Sinninghe, J. R. W.: *Over Volkskunst*. 1949

Sirelius, U. T.: *The Ryijy-Rugs of Finland*. Helsinki 1926

Šourek, Karel: *Folk Art in Pictures. Nature – Human Life – Work*. London n. d.

Sousa, Ernesto de: *Para o estudo da escultura portuguesa*. Oporto 1965

Spamer, Adolf: *Das kleine Andachtsbild vom 14. bis zum 20. Jahrhundert*. Munich 1930

Spamer, Adolf: *Hessische Volkskunst*. Jena 1939

Stelmachowska, Bozena: *Sztuka ludowa na Kaszubach*. Poznan 1937

Stránská, Drahomíra: *Lidové kroje v Československu*. Prague 1949

Subías Galter, J.: *El arte popular en España*. Barcelona 1948

Swain, M. H.: *The Flowerers*. London 1955

Terra Portuguesa, vols. 1–5. Lisbon 1916/24

Thordarson, Matthias: 'Tracht und Schmuck auf Island'. In: *Tracht und Schmuck im nordischen Raum*. Leipzig 1938

The Complete Book of American Country Antiques. New York 1967

Toschi, Paolo: *Saggi sull'arte popolare*, Rome 1944

Toschi, Paolo: *Arte popolare italiana*. Rome 1960

Toschi, Paolo: *Guida allo studio delle tradizioni popolari*. Turin 1962

Toschi, Paolo: *Stampe popolari italiane dal XV al XX secolo*. Milan 1964

Toschi, Paolo: *Conosci l'Italia il Folklore*. Milan 1967

Trésors de nos vieilles demeures. Lausanne 1930

Uebe, F. Rudolf: *Deutsche Bauernmöbel*. Berlin 1924

Uldall, Kai: *Gammel dansk Folkekunst*. Copenhagen 1945

Uldall, Kai: *Dansk Folkekunst*. Copenhagen 1963

Václavík, Antonín and Orel, Jaroslav: *Textile Folk Art*. London n. d.

Vakarelski, Christo: 'Prinos kam estetika na balgarsvija narod'. In: *Izvestiya*, Fine Arts Institute, Sofia 1958

Vakarelski, Christo: 'Oeufs de Pâque chez les Bulgares'. In: *Archives suisses des traditions populaires*, 2–3. 1957

Vakarelski, Christo: 'Plastikata po ebrednite hljabove u balgarite'. In: *Izvestiya*, Fine Arts Institute, Sofia 1941

Vakarelski, Christo and Petkov, G.: *Die bulgarischen Volkstrachten. Farbige Wandkarte*. Sofia 1941

Vienna-Veröffentlichungen des Österreichischen Museums für Volkskunde in Wien. 1952/67

Viski, Károly: *Volksbrauch der Ungarn*. Budapest 1932

Vishnevskaya, V. M.: *Russkaya narodnaya rez'ba i rospis' po derevu*. Moscow n. d.

Page 265 a Noah's Ark, painted clay, Amozoc, Mexico; *b* Crib (detail), Italy, eighteenth century

Page 266 a–d Details of shepherds' staffs, North Brabant

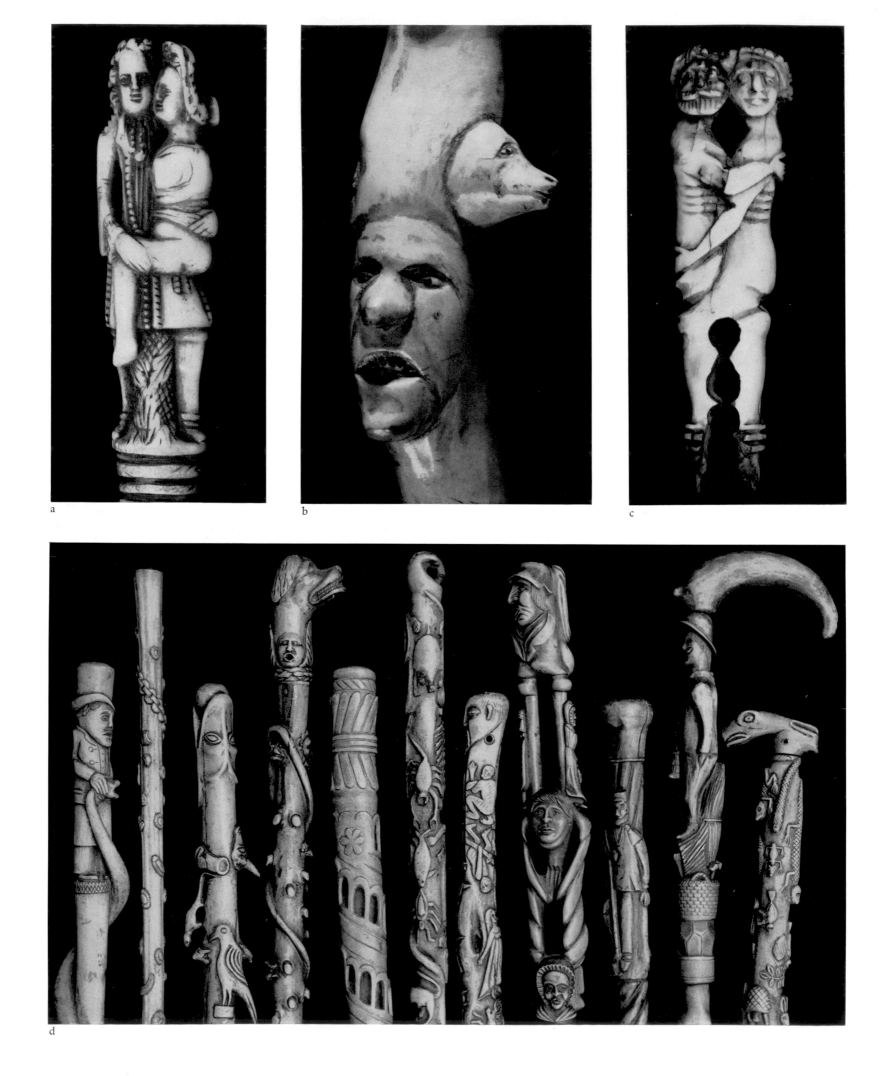

a

b

c

d

a

b

a   b

Vologodskaja i Jaroslavskaja narodnaja vyšivka. Moscow 1955

Voronov, V.: *Krest'yanskoye iskusstvo.* Moscow 1924

Vydra, Josef and Kunz, Ludvík: *Painting on Folk Ceramics.* London 1958

Vydra, Josef: *Ludová architektura na Slovensku.* Bratislava, n.d.

Vydra, Josef: *Die Hinterglasmalerei.* London 1957

Walzer, Albert: *Liebeskutsche, Reitersmann, Nikolaus und Kinderbringer.* Stuttgart 1963

Wyss, Robert L.: *Berner Bauernkeramik.* Berne 1966

Zderciuc, Boris, Petrescu, Paul, Banateanu, Tancred: *Die Volkskunst in Rumänien.* Bucharest 1964

Zilliacus, V.: *Bonde-Finland.* Stockholm 1949

Zuno, José G.: *Las Artes populares en Jalisco.* Guadalajara 1957

Page 267 a Painted wooden figure for tilting, Denmark, eighteenth century; *b* Painted wooden clown, St Albans, Hertfordshire, nineteenth century

Page 268 Carved cupboard doors, Iceland: *a* eighteenth century; *b* seventeenth century

Acknowledgments

European Folk Art: an introduction was written by Dr Robert Wildhaber, director of the Museum für Schweizerische Volkskunde in Basle, and the sections on individual countries by the following: *Norway* by Peter Anker, director of the Vestlandske Kunstindustrimuseum in Bergen, with remarks on textiles by Alf Böe, chief curator of the Kunstindustrimuseet in Oslo; *Sweden* by Albert Eskeröd, director of the Nordiska Museet in Stockholm; *Finland* by Toini-Inkeri Kaukonen, director of the Suomen Kansallismuseo in Helsinki; *Iceland* by Dr Kristján Eldjárn, director of the National Museum in Reykjavik; *Denmark* by Dr Sigurd Schoubye, director of the Tønder Museum; *Scotland* by Alexander Fenton, deputy director of the National Museum of Antiquities of Scotland in Edinburgh; *England* by Margaret Fuller, deputy director of the Museum of English Rural Life in Reading; *Ireland* by A. T. Lucas, director of the National Museum of Ireland; *Low Countries* by Dr Tjaard W. R. de Haan, editor of the publications of the Nederlands Volkskundig Genootschap in Wassenaar; *Germany* by Bernward Deneke, curator of the folk art section of the Germanisches Nationalmuseum in Nuremberg; *Austria* by Professor Dr Leopold Schmidt, director of the Österreichisches Museum für Volkskunde in Vienna; *Czechoslovakia* by Dr Ludvík Kunz, CSc., director of the Ethnographical Institute of the Moravian Museum in Brno; *Switzerland* by René Creux, Paudex; *France* by Pierre-Louis Duchartre, former principal inspector of ethnographical museums in France and vice-president of the Société d'Ethnographie de France in Paris; *Portugal* by Fernando Barbedo Galhano of the Centro de Estudos de Etnologia Peninsular in Lisbon; *Spain* by Professor Luis Cortés Vázquez of the University of Salamanca; *Italy* by Professor Dr Paolo Toschi, director of the Instituto di Storia delle Tradizioni popolari, University of Rome, and president of the Società die Etnografia Italiana; *Yugoslavia* by Zagorka Marković, director of the Etnografski Muzej in Belgrade; *Greece* by Popi Zoras, director of the Musée d'Art Populaire Grec in Athens; *Hungary* by Dr Edit Fél, director of the Néprajzi Múzeum in Budapest; *Bulgaria* by Professor Dr Christo Vakarelski, former director of the Musée National d'Ethnographie in Sofia; *Rumania* by Professor Dr Tancred Banateanu, director of the Muzeul de Arta Populara in Bucharest; *Poland* by Professor Dr Ksawery Piwocki, director of the Panstwowe Muzeum Etnograficzne in Warsaw; the *Soviet Union* by Dr Georg R. Schroubek of the Ethnographical Institute of the University of Munich; *North America* by Dr Richard S. Field, curator of folk painting in the National Gallery of Art in Washington, and the General Editor; *Latin America* by Gerd Dörner of Darmstadt and Mexico and Valentin Jacquet in Basle. The chapter *Folk art on the market* is by Marcel B. Keezer, art dealer and secretary of the Stichting Oude Kunst- en Antikbeurs in Delft.

In addition to the contributors, and the people, museums and collections named in the foreword and the note on the illustrations, the editor wishes to thank the following for information or for permission to photograph or reproduce illustrative material: Ralph C. Altman, director of the Museum and Laboratories of Ethnic Arts and Technology, Los Angeles; Mary C. Black, director of the Museum of Early American Folk Art, New York; Frederick J. Dockstadter, director of the Museum of the American Indian, New York; René Faille of Photographie Giraudon, Paris; Dr Gantner of the Schweizerisches Museum für Volkskunde, Basle; Professor Dr Max Heiss, director of the Stadtmuseum, Munich; Roger Henninger, curator of the Musée Alsacien, Strasbourg; Dr J. de Kleyn, custodian of the Nederlands Openluchtmuseum, Arnhem; Professor Demetrius Loukatos of the University of Ioannina; the Meridiane publishing house, Bucharest; the National Gallery of Art, Washington, D. C.; the Index of American Design, Washington; Mr Nemirov, press attaché of the Soviet Embassy in Bad Godesberg; Mr A. Poroshnyakov, editor-in-chief of the pictorial section of the Novosti press agency in Moscow; Blanche K. Reigle, director of the Pennsylvania Farm Museum of

270

Landis Valley, Lancaster, Pa.; Georges Henri Rivière, curator-in-chief of the Musée des Arts et Traditions Populaires, Paris; Frank H. Sommer, librarian of the Henry Francis du Pont Winterthur Museum, Winterthur, Del.; Professor Dr Tullio Tentori, director of the Museo Nazionale delle Arti e delle Tradizioni Popolari, Rome; Thaning & Appel, publishers, of Copenhagen; M. W. Thomas, Jr., deputy director and custodian-in-chief of the Farmer's Museum of the New York State Historical Association, Cooperstown, N. Y.; Dr Ernst Thiele, secretary-general of the Deutscher Kunstrat e. V., Cologne; Ernesto Veiga de Oliveira, director of the Centro de Estudos de Etnologia Peninsular, Lisbon; and Dr Rudolf Zöllner, custodian of the Städtisches Museum, Flensburg.

The following are to be thanked for photographs and other forms of reproduction (where this material has been taken from books, the title is given in parentheses and fuller details will be found in the Bibliography): Marianne Adelmann, Paris (28a, b, 66); Hördur Agústsson, Reykjavik (10f, 34d); Archiv für Kunst und Geschichte, Berlin (58d, 175a); Oliver Baker, New York (136a); Photo Barette, Beauvais (141b); Lutz Braun, Munich-Ismaning (38c); Karl Bürger, Oldenburg (83a, b); Centralna Agencja Fotograficzna, Warsaw (144, 207a, 254a, b); Luis Cortés Vazquez, Salamanca (38a, b, 53a, 65a–f, 89c, 92a–c, 113a, b, 121, 128, 177b, 187, 188a, 196c, 273c, 276c, e); René Creux, Paudex (109, 110, 111, 219a, 234a–e); Bogdan Czarnecki, Warsaw (55a, 135g, 207h, 192); Gerd Dörner, Darmstadt (40b, 126d, e, 127a, 147h, 197b, 207g, i, 214b, 230, 232, 260a, b, 265a); Etnografický Ustav, Brno (10a, 19b); Etnografski Muzej, Belgrade (19a, 59e, 91b, 174c, 176b, 195b, 198a, 235a, b, 255a, d, e); Alexander Fenton, Edinburgh (10d, 33a, 84e, 101a, e, 127b, 166a, 217a); M. Fourtin Châtel-Guyon (60a); Margaret Fuller, Reading (142c, d, 143b, d); G. Gestsson, Reykjavik (59h, 185b, 268a, b, 276f); Photo Giraudon, Paris (48a, 60c, e, 126c, 127f, 136c, d, f, 141a, 145b–d, 146f, 153b, d, f, h, 154d–f, 156a, b, 166c, 173c, 196a, b, 236, 256); Studio Girard, Abbéville (141e); J. Grabowski, Zakopane (206); Dr Tjaard W. R. de Haan, Wassenaar (79, 80, 81, 82); Hammerschmidt Foto, Aarhus (59a, 134g); Hans Jürgen Hansen, Gräfelfing, Munich (10c); The Henry Francis du Pont Winterthur Museum, Winterthur, Del. (28c, 220); Ivan Hevesy, Budapest (10b); Historia Photo, Bad Sachsa (42, 43); Knut K. Hovden (Gammel Rosemaling i Rogaland – 73b, 240d); The Index of American Design, Washington (46e, 203, 219b); Petr Jero, Brno (135e, h, l, 141d, 146a, 148c, 155d–f, 208b, c, 259a–d, 276a); Koldinghus Museet, Kolding (146i); Francis Lichten (Folk art motifs of Pennsylvania– end-papers, 240a, b); Jean Lipman (American folk art – 182, 192, 222), Walter Lüden, Wyk, Island of Föhr (33c, 34a, b, 36, 39a, b, d, 40a, 45a, b, 46b, 53b, 55b, c, 56a–h, 57a, d, 58a–c, 59d, e, 67a, b, 68a, c, d, 73c, 74a, b, 84a, g, 90a–j, 91a, c–f, 101c, f, 102a–d, 103, 104b, 114a, d, e, g, 115a–d, 116, 122, 124a–d, 125, 126a (l.), b, 133a–f, 134a–f, h–l, 135a–c, 136b, 142a, 143a, c, 145a, 146b–e, g, 147a–c, e, 154a–c, g–i, 155a–c, g–i, 165a–c, 168a–d, 173a, 176e, 177a, 178a, 180a–d, 186, 188b, 193, 194, 197a, c, 200a, 205, 207b, d–f, 208d, 213, 214a, c, d, 216a–c, 217b, c, 225, 226, 227, 228b, 233, 235c, 237a, b, 240c, 245a, b, 246a–c, e, 247a–f, 248, 253, 255f, 257, 265b, 267a, 273a, b, 277a–h, 278a–c, 279a–d, 280c); Meridiane, Bucharest (Die Volkskunst in Rumänien – 19c, 35b, 46c, 135j, k, 147g, i, 173b, 207c); Henryk Mogilnicki, Warsaw (195c, 208a); Musée Basque, Bayonne (60f); Musée d'Art Populaire Grec, Athens (173d, 179a, 218b, 258a, 275a, c); Musée de Cognac, Cognac (127c, 153e); Musée de l'Ain, Bourg-en-Bresse (35d); Musée Départemental de l'Oise, Beauvais (156c); Musée des Hautes-Alpes, Gap (84b); Musée du Berry, Bourges (148d, 156c); Musée du Vieux Nîmes (127d); Musée Historique, Lyon (141c); Musée National d'Ethnographie, Sofia (89c, 147f, 174d, 185a, 198d, 200b, 202, 280b); Musée Pyrénéen, Lourdes (114f); Museu de Etnologia do Ultramar, Lisbon (48b, 84f, 144a, c, 148b, 153a, g, i, 275b); Museum of English Rural Life, Reading (8, 92d, f, 123, 126a (r.), 127e, 138, 139, 146g, 178b, c, 183, 198b, 215a–d, 228c, 255j, 267b, 280a); Nationalmuseum, Copenhagen (54b, 92e, 101b, d, 176c, 280d); National Museum, Reykjavik (195d); National Museum of Ireland, Dublin (68b, 255b, d, g–i, 274a, b); Nederlands Museum van Knipkunst, Roden (150, 160); Nederlands Openluchtmuseum, Arnhem (9, 57b, 58e, 89a, 135d, f, 202, 266a–d, 273d, e); Néprajzi Múzeum, Budapest (46f, 57c, 59c, 73a, 84c, 135i, 147d, 166b, 176d, 280e); New York State Historical Association, Cooperstown, N. Y. (60b, 223, 238/39); Novosti press agency, Moscow (2); Pennsylvania Farm Museum of Landis Valley, Lancaster, Pa. (28d, e, f, 199, 243); Régis de Roten, Sion, Valais (59g); Hannes Rosenberg, Gräfelfing, Munich (246d, f); (Russkoye dekorativnoye iskusstvo – 167b, 176a, 218a, 258a); Dr Wolfgang Salchow, Cologne (54c, d, 59b, 167a, 179c, d); A. B. Saltykov (Izbrannye trudy – 167c, d); Schweizerische

Verkehrszentrale, Zurich (19d, 101g, 141f, 174b, 175b, 179b, 228a, 234f); Dr Sigurd Schoubye, Tønder (33b, d, 39c, 53c); *(Scottish Home and Country* – 50, 51, 158, 159); Stearn & Sons, Cambridge (148a); Suomen Kansallismuseo, Helsinki (10e, 22, 23, 30, 31, 35a, 46a, 84d, 107, 170, 171, 172, 190, 195a, 198c, 200c, 276b, d); Thaning & Appel, Copenhagen (35c, 38d, 58f, 60d); Foto Timm, Tønder (46d); Ullstein-Bilderdienst, Berlin (34c, 86, 87, 174a, 175c, d); *(Vologodskaya i Yaroslavskaya narodnaya vysivka* – 177c).

Page 273 a, b Wooden butter-pats, Sicily; *c* Horn spectacle case, Salamanca; *d, e* Horn snuff boxes, Limburg, 1822

Page 274 a Straw harvest knots (with the ears for women, without for men), Ireland; *b* St Bride's crosses of straw, Ireland

Page 275 a, c Distaffs, Greece; *b* Flax swingle handle, Minho, Portugal

Page 276 Woodcarving: *a* Ring, Czechoslovakia, 1774; *b, d* Distaffs, south-eastern Bothnia, Finland; *c* Flax swingle, Spain; *e* Spoon-box, Iceland, seventeenth century; *f* Spoon, Spain

a

b

c

GODISSOONEYDELYKGOED
INRI
DEPASSIENADAMENEVAN
d

DE12APOSTELLENVANIESUS
PEETERSCHEERSANNO16
DEGEBOORTELUCASANT2
e

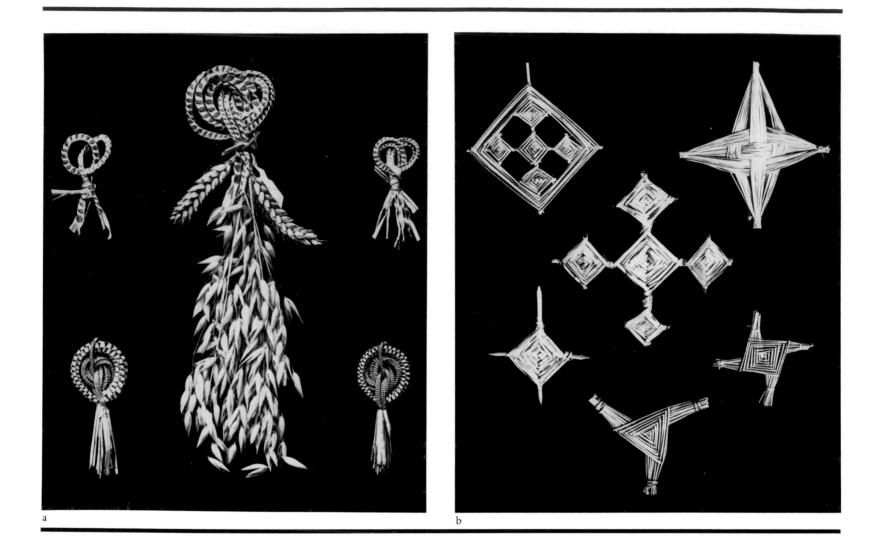

a

b

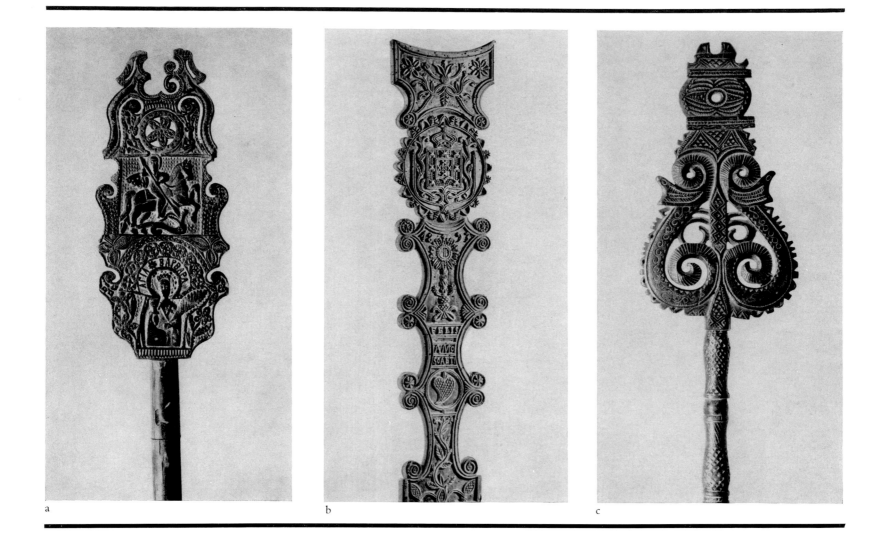

a

b

c

a

b

c

d

e

f

a   b   c   d

e   f   g   h

a

LUCERUR

b

c

a

b

c

a

b

c

d

e